ALSO BY ERIC FELTEN

How's Your Drink?: Cocktails, Culture,
and the Art of Drinking Well

LOYALTY

THE VEXING VIRTUE

Eric Felten

Simon & Schuster

New York   London   Toronto   Sydney

Simon & Schuster
1230 Avenue of the Americas
New York, NY 10020

First Simon & Schuster hardcover edition April 2011

SIMON & SCHUSTER and colophon are registered trademarks
of Simon & Schuster, Inc.

For information about special discounts for bulk purchases,
please contact Simon & Schuster Special Sales at
1-866-506-1949 or business@simonandschuster.com.

The Simon & Schuster Speakers Bureau can bring authors
to your live event. For more information or to book an event,
contact the Simon & Schuster Speakers Bureau at
1-866-248-3049 or visit our website at www.simonspeakers.com.

Designed by Nancy Singer

Manufactured in the United States of America

10   9   8   7   6   5   4   3   2   1

Library of Congress Cataloging-in-Publication Data
Felten, Eric, date.
  Loyalty : the vexing virtue / Eric Felten.
    p. cm.
Includes bibliographical references and index.
1. Loyalty. I. Title. II. Title: Vexing virtue.
BJ1533.L8F45 2011
179'.9—dc22   2010050292
ISBN 978-1-4391-7686-3
ISBN 978-1-4391-7688-7 (ebook)

for my own little platoon,

Priscilla, Greta, and Thaddeus

CONTENTS

LOYALTY

Introduction

"Be loyal." So says *Esquire* magazine, which included the advice in a recent list of practical virtues—"The 75 Skills Every Man Should Master." The items catalogued were, for the most part, glib and trivial—guys should know how to tie a bow tie, build a campfire, throw a football with a tight spiral. But there was one life-skill that stood out for being moralistic in nature: loyalty. The magazine pronounced it "the currency of selflessness, given without expectation and capable of the most stellar return."

It is no mistake that loyalty is to be found in a list of life lessons as old-school as the tying of bow ties. We're hardly the first generation to think that modern life has left no room for such a vintage virtue. *Whatever happened to loyalty?* It's a perennial question. In the late nineteenth century, Irish novelist and member of parliament Justin McCarthy wrote, "the old, devoted spirit of personal loyalty is dead and buried. It is gone! it is a memory! You may sing a poetic lament for it if you will . . ." He was convinced loyalty could "never be revived or restored."[1] A few hundred years before, Shakespeare had given us the picture of a faithful servant who would follow his master "to the last gasp, with truth and loyalty." The man was seen, even then, as an anachronism:

How well in thee appears
The constant service of the antique world
When service sweat for duty, not for mead!
Thou art not for the fashion of these times
Where none will sweat but for promotion.[2]

The complaint was the same in the thirteenth century, when French poet Rutebeuf huffed that the men of his day weren't like the stalwart heroes of old Roland's times. "Loyalty is dead and perished," he wrote in "La Complainte de Constantinople."[3] And when Roman playwright Terence, in the second century B.C., wanted to describe a character as loyal, he called him "a man of the ancient virtue." That led one cynical scholar of Latin maxims to observe that loyalty "is represented in all ages, as belonging solely to the elder times."[4]

Still, our modern, rootless times do seem to be a particularly inhospitable environment for loyalty. We come and go so relentlessly that our friendships can't but come and go too. What sort of loyalty is there in the age of Facebook, when friendship is a costless transaction, a business of flip reciprocity (*I'll go on your list of friends if you'll go on my list*)? Friendship held together by nothing more permanent than hyperlinks is hardly the stuff of selfless fidelity.

Loyalty is about reliability, and ours are unreliable times, when the bonds of friendship are as shaky as bonds backed by mortgage debt. How many "friends" did Bernard Madoff ruin with his Ponzi scheme? How much is the anxiety we feel these days a function of the disheartening suspicion that, in a real jam, there might not be anyone we can count on?

IF LOYALTY IS, and always has been, perceived as obsolete, why do we continue to praise it? Because loyalty is essential to the most basic things that make life livable. Without loyalty there can be no love. Without loyalty there can be no family. Without loyalty there can be no friendship. Without loyalty there can be no commitment to community or country. And without those things, there can be no society. As Robert Heinlein put it, wherever loyalty falls "into disrepute—get out of there fast! You may possibly save yourself, but it is too late to save that society. It is doomed."

By contrast, there is power and resilience in loyalty. When Bonnie Prince Charlie was on the run across Scotland after the failure of his Jacobite revolt, "He was obliged to trust his life to the fidelity of above fifty individuals," as Tobias Smollett tells it in his continuation of David Hume's *The History of England*. "Many of these were in the lowest paths of fortune. They knew that a price of thirty thousand pounds was set upon his head; and that, by betraying him, they should enjoy wealth and affluence: but they detested the thought of obtaining riches on such infamous terms, and ministered to his necessities with the utmost zeal and fidelity, even at the hazard of their own destruction." The prince escaped.

Hazarding destruction may be an extreme case of what loyalty entails, but only as a matter of degree. The measure of loyalty has always been the most acidic of tests, a matter of proving how much one will endure to remain true. The great biblical study of loyalty—the book of Job—is an exercise in just how much misfortune can be piled on a man before his fidelity fails. Job passes the test, praising God even when ruined and despairing, but the whole point is that the only true test of loyalty is fidelity in the face of ruin and despair. "Loyalty," G. K. Chesterton mused, "implies loyalty in misfortune." Or, as the philosopher Josiah Royce put it, it is an "obvious truth of human nature, that loyalty is never raised to its highest levels without such grief."[5]

We may hope we can count on our friends, but we can never know when the going is good. As Billie Holiday sang, money buys lots of friends; but when your money runs out, your friends go with it. Which is to say they were never really friends to begin with—a brutal realization coming, as it usually does, when one is most in need of some helpful friends.

Still, if we're lucky, we do find there are friends, family, lovers we can rely on—people we can trust. None of those relationships can exist without the trust that allows us to let down our defenses. A willingness to share at least some unguarded thoughts may not be the definition of friendship, but it is essential to anything worthy of the name. And if you don't trust an acquaintance enough to open up to her, you'll never become true friends. That sort of trust is even more important when you live with someone. Thomas Hobbes, in describing why life in the state of nature is "solitary, poor, nasty, brutish and short," explains that even in a developed society we lock our doors at night and keep our chests (the office safes of his day) locked even while we're awake. We have to protect ourselves. But the relationships that make life less nasty and brutish are those that allow us to unlock ourselves. We don't sleep comfortably next to someone we suspect may treat us the way a robber would. Trust is the key, and loyalty is the virtue of being trustworthy.

We celebrate loyalty even though we may sometimes despair of experiencing it. Perhaps its rarity just makes us value it all the more. By contrast, all too common is betrayal. There are little betrayals (the friend who repeats a minor secret told in confidence) and big betrayals (treason) and all manner of betrayals in between (from the husband who clears out the joint bank accounts before running off with his mistress, to the business deal done by buddies on a handshake, later undone for want of an enforceable contract). Betrayal is so common, in part, because of how easy it is for betrayal to undo loyalty. It would have taken but one person to sell out Bonnie Prince Charlie for him to have been captured. Perhaps loyalty appears scarce not because there is none to be found but because all it takes is one traitor to render the loyalty of forty-nine reliable men useless.

And though betrayal may be commonplace, no matter how often we experience betrayal, it never loses its sting.

For Dante, betrayal is the most despicable of vices. The *Inferno* takes us down through the levels of hell, each more excruciating and dire than the one before. After running a gantlet of mud, mire, scorching winds, blazing hellfire agonies, and rivers of blood, we arrive at the ninth circle, where the worst torments are to be found. That lowest level of hell is reserved for the lowest sort of sinners—the disloyal. Traitors to family, traitors to country, traitors to one's guests and friends, each worse than the last. And there, nearly at the bottom, encased entirely in ice, are those who, like Judas, betrayed their benefactors. Finally, at the very center of hell is Satan himself, three-headed and putting his razor-sharp teeth to work perpetually gnawing at the three poster boys of betrayal, Brutus, Cassius, and Judas.

As MUCH AS we may hate betrayal, as much as loyalty is the foundation of our relationships with friends and those we love, the virtue has a tragic flaw: Our loyalties are always getting hopelessly tangled and compromised. Even if we want to commit ourselves to being true, we can never escape the conflicting demands that our contradictory loyalties create. The loyalties we have to various people can come into conflict; the loyalties we have to family may clash with the loyalties we bear our friends; our personal loyalties may be at odds with our patriotic duties; and as Aristotle points out, what we owe our friends may be irreconcilably opposed to truth.

You can be loyal to a friend. You can be loyal to your family. You can be loyal to your country. You can be loyal to a principle or ideal. You can be loyal to God. But can you be loyal to all at the same time? Just try.

What do we do when loyalties collide? We try our best to reduce the conflicts, but there's no escaping them. If you have more than one friend, the possibility exists that those friends will come to be at odds. You'll have to be disloyal to one or the other. And then there are the clashes when commitment to a friend runs afoul of commitment to principle or the truth. What happens to loyal friendship if the qualities that inspire loyalty in the first place prove to be fugitive? What if a friend's conduct, so admirable in the past, suddenly violates an ideal that itself requires loyalty? Do we stand by even a treasured friend when, say, he starts cheating on his wife or taxes? Or what if our own principles and convictions change, making it hard to maintain the bond we once had with someone who has himself remained constant? The messy reality of life has always plagued moral judgments, and this is especially true when it comes to questions of loyalty.

The family has long been seen as the training ground for loyal living: The commitments we learn to keep at home build up the moral muscles we use in our commitments to friends, to community, to country, to the truth. And it's been argued that when family loyalties come into conflict with other imperatives, the family bond should prevail. French novelist and philosopher Albert Camus was born in Algeria, and in 1957 he was urged to praise the Algerians who were setting off bombs in cafés in their fight against French colonialism. He refused. Camus denounced terror because it "may any day strike down my mother or my family." His loyal commitment to his family demanded loyalty to the country that protected his family. And that core loyalty proved to be morally potent, saving Camus from endorsing what was then a fashionable moral abstraction justifying violence. "I believe in justice," Camus said, "but I will defend my mother before justice."

Is it any wonder that ruthless totalitarian ideologies see the family as a threat to their ambitions? The Nazis and the Soviets both sought to unravel family ties and establish the state as the only proper object of citizens' loyalty. Be very wary of any notion of "justice" that demands kicking your grandmother to the curb.

And yet, if loyalty to family excludes any and every other commitment, or a thoroughgoing disregard for justice, you end up with a dysfunctional, clannish society, the sort of Mafia culture that has plagued places such as Sicily.

Loyalty to family can also lead us into betraying the big obligations it's supposed to bolster. At the start of the Civil War, Robert E. Lee found himself trapped between commitment to country and fidelity to his family living in secessionist Virginia. He chose the latter: "With all my devotion to the Union and the feeling of loyalty and duty of an American citizen," he wrote to his sister, "I have not been able to make up my mind to raise my hand against my relatives, my children, my home."

There's no solving such questions with simple hierarchies of loyalties. We can't say that loyalty to principle always comes ahead of conflicting loyalties to people, nor the other way around. We can't say that family always comes before country, nor the other way around. We can't say that our obligations to friends trump all.

Perhaps the answer to these dire difficulties is to do without the relationships that entangle and frustrate us. No doubt, there's tremendous freedom in going one's way unencumbered by other people, their needs and expectations. This is the footloose ideal advocated by George Clooney's character in the movie *Up in the Air*, who argues against getting weighed down by carrying people on your back. One of loyalty's appeals is that it can act as a safety net or lifeboat. The loyal bonds of friends and family provide us with some insurance against the vagaries of fortune. And yet when we open ourselves to love and the bonds of friendship, we put ourselves at the most profound of risks. We tie our fates to others, which increases our odds of coming into contact with an unfortunate fate. And we put ourselves at moral risk, increasing the chances that we'll end up in a situation where we have to choose between betraying a commitment to a friend or a commitment to principle. It's a strange sort of risk mitigation that brings with it so many added risks. There are those—including purists as varied as Thomas à Kempis and Mahatma Gandhi—who have argued it is better to swear off friends altogether. That way there's no friendly inducement to wrongdoing, nor any disappointment at the feeble loyalty of false friends.

It should come as no surprise that their solution to the problems of loyalty—abjuring any and all friendship in this world—has never caught on.

EVEN IF OUR various loyal ties didn't get so terribly tangled, loyalty would still vex us. We tend to be a little suspicious of those who claim to put loyalty first. When we hear the phrase "political loyalists," do we think, *Those wonderful people who are true to their bonds and obligations of loyalty to their party and its candidates*? Or does the phrase smack of *Those low hacks who will do anything to win, who will break any rule, lie any lie, in service to their political masters*?

Just because loyalty is essential to strong relationships doesn't mean it's an unalloyed good. Tight social bonds—exemplified by the unwillingness to leave any fallen comrade behind—help the marines fight the good fight. But the U.S. military also knows that soldiers' loyalties to one another can lead them to cover up for a comrade who commits war crimes. Loyalty may be the most venerable of virtues, but clearly it can be a dangerous one too.

As Cold War polemicist Arthur Koestler put it, "No historian would deny that the part played by crimes committed for personal motives is very small compared to the vast populations slaughtered in unselfish loyalty to a jealous God, king, country or political system." Being unselfish, having a "self-transcending devotion," is the standard-issue stuff of morality. But it may not always be so desirable, especially when the object of devotion is a nasty one. Alas, "Man has always been prepared to die for good, bad, or completely harebrained causes."[6]

For many, this is the irredeemable downfall of loyalty: How can we say it is a virtue when it works just as effectively in the cause of vice? "The bare fact that some act is the loyal thing to do, or that some attitude is the loyal attitude to have, does not guarantee that there is any reason to do or have it," writes loyalty-averse philosopher Simon Keller. It is a mistake, he says, "to take loyalty seriously, or to listen to its demands, just because it is loyalty."[7] Adolf Hitler, after all, was a great advocate of loyalty, demanding that one and all swear oaths of allegiance to him. His personal army, the SS, wore the slogan "My Honor Is Loyalty" on their belt buckles. "We teach our SS men that there are many things which can be forgiven on this earth, no matter how evil they be," said Heinrich Himmler, "but one thing never: disloyalty to the Führer."[8] What did that loyalty entail? (Or perhaps more painfully on point, what *didn't* such debased loyalty entail?) For Himmler, the only real proof of fidelity was "the willing execution of orders . . . that others find immoral or distasteful."[9] How can loyalty be a fundamental virtue if the good associated with it depends on what or whom we are loyal to?

If the character of our loyalties is determined by whom

we give it to, we would be wise to choose our loyalties well. It is one of the great frustrations of making loyal commitments that we can't know ahead of time where those obligations may lead us. We have to choose a path, not knowing where it goes. Having devoted himself to Henry VIII, Cardinal Wolsey reached the pinnacle of power, only to find it all crumbling away when he was unable to secure the king an annulment. Accused of treason, Wolsey despaired. He was soon on his deathbed, where he said, "Had I but served my God as diligently as I have served my king, He would not have given me over in my grey hairs."

If it weren't bad enough that loyalties can lead us into morally suspect behavior, we tend to associate the trait with those who are rather less than clever. Think of George Orwell's *Animal Farm*, in which the paragon of loyalty is Boxer, a horse as hopelessly dim as he is brawny. He slaves for the pigs and ultimately gets the sort of reward for his fidelity that Ambrose Bierce's definition of the virtue, in *The Cynic's Word Book*, would predict—sold to the slaughterhouse, Boxer climbs right into the knacker's van in his dumb, docile way.

Russell Baker, in his introduction to the fiftieth-anniversary edition of *Animal Farm*, describes Boxer as "loyal but stupid." I suspect what he really meant to say was "loyal *and* stupid," as there is nothing to suggest that the horse's stupidity in any way stands in contrast to his loyalty—the two go hoof in hoof. Not only is Boxer both loyal and stupid, his stupidity bolsters his loyalty: He "seldom asked questions." (It wouldn't have taken much in the way of questioning to show how little loyalty was due to the farm's hoggish new rulers.) And it also worked the other way around—the old carthorse's stubborn fidelity bolsters his stupidity. Whenever something seems wrong, Boxer just repeats the loyalty oath "Napoleon is always right!" He spares himself the trouble of thinking troubling thoughts. And in so doing, he unwittingly contributes to the enslavement of his barnyard buddies.

The notion that loyalty is naïve attaches even when the loyal person is demonstrably brilliant. British logician and language theorist A. J. "Freddie" Ayer was one of the great minds of the twentieth century. Yet, for all his smarts, he had a penchant for loyal friendship that, however appealing it may have been to his pals, did nothing to burnish his intellectual reputation. "Freddie's unwavering loyalty to his friends is a childlike, pathetic, very endearing quality which always moves me a great deal," wrote his fellow Oxford don Isaiah Berlin to a friend in 1936. "The mixture of sophistication & simplicity is very odd & attractive." You can be a giant of logical positivism, but exhibit signs of loyalty and you get tagged as simpleminded.[10]

By contrast, nowadays we expect a genius to cast off loyalty, especially any lowly personal entanglement that might inhibit the free exercise of his calling. The great artist is supposed to have Gauguin's attitude toward marriage and family and friends—people to be betrayed at will if they threaten to impede, or even just inconvenience, the fulfillment of one's artistic vision. Critics don't chide Charlie Parker for being a lousy father, they celebrate him for it—the modern artist is expected to ruin himself and all those around him for the sake of his art. (And it is a very modern notion—no one ever told the überdomestic Johann Sebastian Bach that he needed to cast off care and concern for his many children in order to fulfill his potential as a composer.) But now blindness to pedestrian personal loyalties is taken to be the mark of the serious artist, musician, or writer. We've fallen into believing with Cyril Connolly that "there is no more somber enemy of good art than the pram in the hall."[11]

IF LOYALTY IS so dumb, so servile, such a lowly impediment to greatness, why do we praise it? Though loyalty is Boxer's undoing, he may be the only character in Orwell's fairy tale for whom we feel any admiration. For all the dangers that loyalty brings, for all the risks inherent in committing ourselves to others, we know that the alternative is bleak and inhuman. Life uncomplicated by other people's needs and expectations may have a certain appeal. There might even be a few hermits who can make it work. But for the rest of us, life is all about the many relationships we have—our varied and intertwined network of bonds with family, friends, and community.

None of those relationships is static, yet they demand of us a certain constancy. That core conflict causes a world of grief and frustration. Can it be resolved? Is there any way to shore up love, friendship, trust, and faith when the foundation for them is constantly shifting? Is there any way to escape the devastating inevitability of betraying and being betrayed?

Loyalty may be troublesome, but it is no less essential than it is impossible. Our challenge is to find how to stick with loyalty, however vexing the virtue may be. Perhaps by understanding the peculiar moral conflicts that loyalty creates, we can avoid the worst of the ethical wreckage and form reliable relationships. At this time of shaky institutions and shabby friendships, we need to rescue loyalty from contradictions and disuse and make it a functioning part of our lives once more.

If we're able to do that—and I hope that this book will help show the way—we may yet save loyalty from the dusty closet of antiquity and make it a virtue as practiced as it is praised.

1

The Power of Loyalty

"A steadfast soul shows that Fortune
has no power over it."
                                    —*Machiavelli*

End up in some dismal hellhole, and you'd better hope you've got a buddy at your side. For the survivors of the Bataan Death March loyalties made the difference between living and dying. Americans taken prisoner by the Japanese in the Philippines were packed into miasmic POW camps such as the wretched Cabanatuan compound. Crowded into squalid jungle huts, the men withered on starvation rations of stale rice; slaving in the blazing heat, they were beaten for sport; any offense that piqued the guards got one bound and beheaded. Chances of survival were a little better than fifty-fifty, and those who did make it were the ones who had a pal to lean on. Without someone to watch your back and buck you up, your chances were next to nil.

And yet there was at Cabanatuan a prominent counter-example, an army captain who was one of the most popular men in the camp, friends with everyone, but buddies with no one. A crack bridge player, he taught the game to anyone who wanted a distraction from the miserable tedium; he had a knack for telling mouthwatering tales of the hidden restaurants of San Francisco, transporting his fellow prisoners in delicious reveries of imagined food. He "made those days more endurable, for he was ever an optimist," recalled his fellow POW Frank Grady. "He had survived Bataan and had endured the Death March. He seemed to be the one man the Japanese couldn't vanquish."[1]

What made the captain remarkable was that he had managed to survive without any particularly close friend among his fellow prisoners. For most of the emaciated men, having a buddy was a matter of life and death. Scuffling to survive, the POWs didn't always play by Hoyle with one another, especially in the early chaotic days of their confinement. As Grady told it in his account of the Japanese prison camps, *Surviving the Day*, the men had to compete to stay alive: "This competitive attitude was expressed most often in the theft of food or valuables from a neighbor. But it also displayed itself in fiercely loyal partnerships between prisoners."[2] The man who had a buddy had a competitive advantage: the two of them together had a much better chance of hanging on to what measly scraps of food they could scrounge.

A loyal pair of buddies acted as a unit. The men in these partnerships provided each other something even more important than protection from the predations of fellow prisoners: They gave emotional support essential in an environment where going into a funk was lethal. The men were always sick, plagued with chronic dysentery, lethargic with beriberi, delirious with malaria, and spindly with malnutrition. But for all the manifest afflictions, if a man could somehow keep his spirits up, he could make it another day. Buddies "helped each other through dangerous emotional states," Grady wrote. Despair meant death. Only the determined lived; and only the loyal stayed determined.

Theirs was hardly a new predicament. During the Civil War, the best chance any Union soldier had of surviving the dreaded Confederate prison camp Andersonville was to have surrendered along with some loyal comrades. "If one was captured alone, put with strangers and became sick," wrote one Union prisoner of war, Lucius Barber, "it was ten chances to one he would die unattended by any human being."[3]

But then, how did the seemingly self-sufficient captain at Cabanatuan hold out and hold on so successfully? It turns out that his "strength came from his relationship with his wife, whom he adored. She was his 'buddy,' and no one could replace her."[4] She had been with him in the Philippines when Japan invaded and she had been taken to a women's prison camp. And then one day the Filipino underground got news to him that his wife had suffered a mental collapse and had been dragged off to a psych ward from which no one returned. The captain crumbled: "His independence worked well enough when his spirits were even," Grady wrote, "but when he faced an emotional crisis, he had no partner to buoy him up."[5] Two days later, he was semiconscious in the Zero Ward, the halfway hut where dying men waited for their turn with the burial detail. Grady and his buddy, Joe, tried to cheer him up, tried to boost his spirits with happy talk. But it was no use. The unvanquishable captain was dead in days.

Loyalty can be an essential lifeline. We often talk metaphorically about loyalty being a "bond" that ties us together. But metaphorical tethers don't bind us if we don't want to be bound. Life is full of Sirens singing, and as Odysseus found, it pays to be tied with something sturdier than good intentions. Mountaineers working as a team are literally tied to one another. It works as more than just a safety net: It changes how everyone thinks about the climb. You can make bolder, more daring efforts knowing you'll be caught if you fall. And at every step you are more attentive to the predicaments of your teammates, knowing they could drag you off the cliff with them. If good fences make for good neighbors, sturdy rope makes for sturdy friends on a mountainside.

A realization of that point must have gone through the minds of the climbers dangling from Pete Schoening's rope in a blizzard in August 1953. Eight Americans had been trying to scale the preposterously perilous Himalayan peak K2 when one of them, Art Gilkey, developed a blood clot in his leg. Unless they got him down the mountain, and quick, he was going to die. Saving the incapacitated climber meant terrible risks for the other men, who had to carry him in conditions that were treacherous for a skilled climber carrying nothing but his own pack. As they worked down the Abruzzi Ridge, one man, whose frostbitten fingers were too stiff to maintain his grip, slipped. He seemed to cartwheel down the luge-slick forty-five-degree slope, his gloves flying off his flailing hands, his shredded pack tearing loose, until in a second he was over the cliff and gone. That would have been the end for the unlucky climber but for the nylon rope that connected him to the men above—a rope that nearly killed them all. As the first man plummeted, he pulled another climber over with him. The weight of those two yanked a third, fourth, and fifth off the side of the mountain, sending them careening in a mad jumble down the icy slope to the precipice.

Up above, holding on to Gilkey, was Schoening. His end of the rope was tied to an ice axe jammed behind a boulder. As the others slid off the mountain, the nylon line started whipping past him. Schoening could have let the ice axe bear the violent yank that was coming when the rope went taut. It might even have held. Instead, in an instant he got under the rope, wrapping it over his shoulders and under his arms. He anchored his feet and, heaving up against the tightening rope, stopped their fall. Without letting go of Gilkey, Schoening bore the weight of all five men, the farthest of whom was 150 feet below. In a blinding snowstorm, he held fast as the battered men tangled far below came to their senses, realized they weren't dead after all, and scrambled up the line to safety.

Schoening's remarkable rescue is known among mountaineers as "The Belay." And the climber's art of "belaying" is a compelling example of loyalty made concrete.

Some forty-three years later, journalist Jon Krakauer was one of dozens of tourists paying to make a Himalayan climb, this one up Mount Everest. Not only weren't they a team, they barely knew one another. Each had paid $65,000 to attempt the summit, and each was focused on his or her personal quest. "I felt disconnected from the climbers around me—emotionally, spiritually, physically—to a degree I hadn't experienced on any previous expedition," Krakauer wrote of the night before they would begin their final climb to the top. "Although in a few hours we would leave camp as a group, we would ascend as individuals, linked to one another by neither rope nor any deep sense of loyalty."[6]

There have been many theories attempting to explain why eight people died on the mountain that next day—the clouds settling over the summit that, together with a fierce pelting snow, reduced visibility to a few feet; a freak weather pattern that caused the already paltry high-altitude oxygen level to drop; the climbers were amateurs, there not because they had earned a spot on an expedition, but because they had paid for the privilege. But any and all of those causes could have been overcome if the climbers had stuck together.

Loyalty is more than just a matter of working together, more than just the obvious observation that people can often achieve greater things by pooling their efforts. Loyalty is about being reliable. Sometimes that helps a group effort, but it can also empower individuals. Sure, we can do more when working together. But I can also accomplish more all by myself if I know I've got someone watching my back. Imagine deciding whether to walk a tightrope. You'd be wise not even to try it unless there's a net underneath. But with the net, you're willing to give it a go. If you cross to the other side without falling, you could say that the net didn't, in any direct way, help you walk the tightrope. And yet, though you may not have *used* the net, it was there if you needed it to save you, and that's what made it possible to try in the first place. The net is empowering. Loyalty is what makes us hold the net taut for our friends. Even if they never need us to catch them, our friends are empowered by the knowledge that we're there. That is, as long as we can be trusted to catch them as promised. If we can't be relied on to keep a tight grip on it, then the net is worse than useless. If people act on the expectation that a net will be there for them, they find out one way or another only when they've actually fallen. And so the net can build confidence only if we can have confidence in the men holding the net, which is why we lavish such praise on people who are reliable.

"When men climb on a great mountain together, the rope between them is more than a mere physical aid to the ascent," wrote Charles Houston, one of the men who had dangled at the end of Pete Schoening's line. The rope connecting climbers "is a symbol of men banded together in a common effort of will and strength," fighting "against their only true enemies: inertia, cowardice, greed, ignorance, and all weaknesses of the spirit."[7]

—

LOYALTY IS THE stuff that binds men together when their lives are in the balance. Which is why no one puts more stock in loyalty than men at war.

Armies have long understood that when it comes to steeling soldiers against the temptation to run away, loyalty is the ticket. But what sort of loyalty? It isn't primarily a matter of fidelity to king, country, or creed. It is the bonds of loyalty soldiers have to their comrades that forge an effective fighting force. Economists Dora Costa and Matthew Kahn, doing statistical analysis of what made for successful military units in the Civil War, compared the effect of group loyalty, ideology, and leadership and found that "Group loyalty was more than twice as important as ideology and six times as important as leadership."[8] A unit with a fine officer but in which the men had no commitment to one another was a bust. A platoon made up of pals from some small town could fight effectively, even if burdened with a lousy commander. Emancipatory fervor would help keep Union soldiers from fleeing, and love of Mississippi or Virginia might embolden rebs to heroics, but those big-picture ideological loyalties couldn't compare with the motivation that came from sticking with the man by your side.

The same held true in World War II, even though the war was one of the world's great ideological contests, with at least the Western contingent of the Allies fighting for freedom as opposed to the enslavement offered by fascism. Even the patriotic enthusiasms of the Good War turned out to be less compelling for men at arms than their loyalties to one another. According to Costa and Kahn, "during World War II group loyalty was almost three times as important as ideology and fourteen times as important as [the quality of] leadership" in accounting for the success, unit cohesion, and "combat motivation" of soldiers.

Elite army units in ancient Greece and Sparta were built around buddy loyalties. Teenagers would be paired with grizzled veterans, and it is a measure of what these relationships entailed that the grown man was known as an *erastes*, or "lover," and the boy an *eromenos*, or "beloved." In old Japan, samurai and their apprentices were also bound together by affections not sanctioned by the old "Don't Ask, Don't Tell."[9]

But for a time, modern armies downplayed the loyalties men in battle have for their comrades. Big-picture loyalties to country or king were emphasized, courage and glory were extolled, and the professionalism of the day put a premium on unthinking, unhesitating obedience to orders from one's superiors. And that worked well enough up through the Napoleonic Wars, when you didn't have to wonder if your fellow soldiers were with you. The men stood in ranks, shoulder to shoulder. But then a nineteenth-century French colonel, Charles Ardant du Picq, noticed that, as modern battles became less regimented and more chaotic, soldiers could no longer see their comrades for all the smoke and confusion. "Cohesion is no longer ensured by mutual observation," Ardant du Picq wrote. How then to overcome the bewildering and enervating sensation that one was fighting on one's own? Colonel Ardant du Picq made a forceful and influential case that the answer was loyalty—the emboldening confidence that, even if you couldn't see the men of your platoon, you knew they were there and wouldn't let you down. Soldier-to-soldier loyalty emerged as the key military virtue, a quality that in modern military terminology would be called a "force multiplier."

Ardant du Picq argued that without the confidence that came from having loyal men at your side, courage had its limits. "Four brave men who do not know each other will not dare to attack a lion," he wrote. "Four less brave, but knowing each other well, sure of their reliability and consequently of mutual aid, will attack resolutely." Confidence in one's fellow soldiers trumps fear, making a unit effective. The French colonel was convinced that the moral force, or morale, built on mutual loyalties was so empowering it would help an army overcome bigger and better-armed foes: "In battle, two moral forces, even more than two material forces, are in conflict," the colonel wrote. "The stronger conquers."[10]

Ardant du Picq's classic 1880 text, *Battle Studies*, was published posthumously. He was killed in 1870 in the Franco-Prussian War when the material force of the Prussian army—in the form of a well-aimed artillery shell—proved to be too much for the colonel's moral force. The power of loyalty has its limits. Alas, such was not the thinking of the French brass, who in the Great War were in thrall of an unnuanced interpretation of Ardant du Picq's philosophy. They thought that loyalty to one's comrades would make men willing to mount bayonet charges across no-man's-land, and that the sight of such a charge would send the enemy fleeing. It didn't work out that way. Empowering as loyalty may be, you can't count on it to keep you safe in the face of an enemy's superior fire-power.

The U.S. Marines have always been about loyalty—what is *Semper Fi*, after all, but a pledge of endless fidelity. And at the battlefield level, that is expressed most vividly in the commitment never to leave a fallen man behind, whether wounded or dead. So successful has that doctrine been for the marines that the army has adopted it as well. Loyalty is a core value of the army's "Warrior Ethos," and an essential part of the Soldier's Creed, which all recruits learn to recite. "I will never leave a fallen comrade," they pledge.

The army's emphasis on loyalty got started after World War I as the military tried to find a way to encourage initiative and creative thinking without undermining obedience to orders. Loyalty was seen as the solution, opening up room for soldiers to improvise a bit as long as it was understood that the goal was always to fulfill a loyal obligation to the intent of their orders.[11] Ever since World War II, when the army turned to psychologists and sociologists to analyze what would keep men fighting, the U.S. military has focused primarily on the loyalties men have to one another.

Army Air Force psychiatrists Roy Grinker and John Spiegel argued that the will to fight was rooted in "the intense loyalty" soldiers have to one another in small combat groups.

"The men are now fighting for each other and develop guilty feelings if they let each other down." They found that men fought more *for* each other than they did *against* the enemy.[12] Even more influential in military circles was the work of Morris Janowitz and Edward Shils, sociologists who concluded that for men in battle, fighting spirit was a matter of "group cohesion," and groups were held together by loyalty to comrades, not by ideology or patriotic fervor or any quest for glory.

A historian who rose to the rank of colonel during the war, S.L.A. Marshall, wrote that it is "one of the simplest truths of war that the thing which enables an infantry soldier to keep going with his weapons is the near presence or the presumed presence of a comrade."[13] As the grunts he studied proved, "Men do not fight for a cause but because they do not want to let their comrades down."[14]

In the first months of the 2003 invasion of Iraq, Americans fighting there bucked this conventional wisdom, with a high number of soldiers saying they were motivated to fight as payback for 9/11. But as the war dragged out into an ugly and endless guerrilla conflict—and as the argument that the war had anything to do with 9/11 became rather less compelling—troops fell back on that simplest of wartime truths. "We weren't fighting for anybody else but ourselves," said one American soldier in Iraq in 2005, "we were just fighting for each other."[15]

Stephen Ambrose, in his portrait of Airborne Rangers fighting in World War II, *Band of Brothers*, recounts how often the wounded men of Easy Company would connive to get out of hospital and back to the front. It wasn't because they were hopped up on anti-Hun propaganda and eager to kill Germans. Private Rod Strohl had been back recovering from a wound for months when he wheedled a one-day pass from his doctors. He hitched a ride to the field where the rest of the company was getting ready to board a plane from which they would jump behind enemy lines. His captain warned him that by leaving hospital he was "going to be AWOL." Strohl didn't care: "He wasn't going to let his buddies go into action without him."[16]

Then there was "Popeye" Wynn, who caught it in the backside on D-day, earning himself a respite on nice white sheets in Wales. He learned that if he were away from his unit for three months, once he was fit for duty he would be sent to whatever company needed a replacement. And so he got himself released from the hospital days ahead of the deadline so that he could rejoin Easy, heading out to fight in Holland. He had to stand the whole flight, "as he was too sore to sit."[17] Popeye had the right idea. Because, even as a battle-tested soldier, if he found himself a stranger in a new unit, his prospects for survival would have been grim. He would have been a "replacement," which meant going into combat without any buddies. It's not that one wouldn't get any help—but one couldn't count on it. The men of Easy Company, for example, never bothered to learn their replacements' names, "as they expected them to be gone shortly."[18] Gone, as in no longer alive.

"Men, I now know, do not fight for flag or country, for the Marine Corps or glory or any other abstraction. They fight for one another." That's how popular biographer William Manchester explained why he sneaked out of his hospital bed to join the buddies he described as "my family, my home," men who were still up on the front lines. Manchester had been wounded at Okinawa, and could have sat out the end of the war in safety, but that would have meant he wasn't there for his pals. "They had never let me down, and I couldn't do it to them."

There's a cynical case to make that such loyalty is just a snare, a delusion contrived and exploited by the powers-that-be to get men to sacrifice themselves. No doubt loyalty is to a military's advantage—it keeps men from running away. And what's in the army's interest isn't necessarily in the individual soldier's interest—staying on the battlefield isn't exactly a savvy strategy for someone who wishes to maximize his own chances of survival. Loyalty keeps you fighting, and that means loyalty can get you killed.

Then again, traditionally, desertion and cowardice can get you killed too, so perhaps relying on your mates isn't such a bad idea after all. If your officers are stupid enough to send you over the top in a suicidal dash at a machine gun, loyalty, powerful as it is, may not help you very much. But in most conflicts, your best chance to make it through is to have reliable people on either side of you. And that means you have to be reliable yourself. For loyalty is fundamentally reciprocal, and reliability is all about delivering on your part of the bargain when it matters, usually at a moment when there is no one or no way to force you to deliver. "This is the nature of war. By protecting others, you save yourself," says Kambei Shimada, the leader of the itinerant mercenaries in Akira Kurosawa's movie *Seven Samurai*. He's teaching a rabble of farmers how to defend themselves against a ruthless gang of bandits. Having weapons and knowing how to use them is all well and good, but unless every man is committed to giving his life for the others, every one of them is doomed: "If you think only of yourself, you'll only destroy yourself."

Or, as William Manchester put it: "Any man in combat who lacks comrades who will die for him, or for whom he is willing to die, is not a man at all. He is truly damned."

DOES THE MILITARY'S attachment to loyalty have anything to teach us? Or is it just a specialized combat tool, like a foldable shovel, without much in the way of civilian application? Political scientist Samuel Huntington thought it did. Writing in the mid-fifties, he looked at the random assemblage of buildings in the little town of Highland Falls, next to West Point, and compared them (unfavorably) to the "ordered serenity" of the United States Military Academy. He didn't much like the motley, "garish individualism" of the average citizens, living their discordant lives of "small-town commercialism." Theirs, he suggests, were small lives, undisciplined, unfulfilled, and lacking purpose. What a contrast Huntington found with the men of West Point, who enjoy the peace, serenity, and security that comes "when collective will supplants individual whim." You could say that, in these two worlds, Huntington saw a clash of civilizations.[19] He concluded that the military values—the first and foremost being loyalty—"are the ones America most needs today."[20]

Huntington's case for army-style loyalty may not exactly be the most compelling. He saw loyalty as an antidote to American individualism, a way to put "an emphasis upon the collective aspect of human affairs, since common loyalty is the basis of group existence."[21] However, I rather like some of my individual whims and I can't say I'm eager to give them up for the pleasure of submitting to some collective will. We don't have to embrace collectivism to enjoy the benefits of loyal relationships, big and small. We don't have to embrace selflessness for its own ascetic sake. The American tradition is neither to reject the good that comes from self-sacrifice nor to worship self-sacrifice as an end in and of itself. Eminently practical, we don't generally go in for any of the hair-shirt business so attractive to some moral traditions. And at the opposite extreme, for most of us, the passion for Ayn Rand's brand of self-satisfied libertarian egoism rarely extends beyond a puerile undergraduate infatuation with *The Fountainhead.* Ours has long been a modest but effective sort of moral code, one that Alexis de Tocqueville called "self-interest properly understood."

American moralists, Tocqueville noted, were unwilling to challenge the prevailing notion that it is good to be self-centered, and so they generally tried to show that "working for the happiness of all would be to the advantage of each citizen." Plenty of examples could be found where "individual self-interest happens to coincide and merge with the interest of all," and by highlighting those instances Americans have traditionally bolstered the belief "that man helps himself by serving others and that doing good serves his own interest."[22]

This might not be the most ennobling of moral theories, but Tocqueville thought it was, on balance, the most effective. Not a grand aesthetic of virtue focused on celebrating the beauty of a pure soul, but "enlightened self-love," is the best bet for inspiring average men to behave decently, Tocqueville argues.[23]

Often, the best way to achieve my own best interests is to pursue what's best for some group of which I'm a part. But even if I recognize that my overall well-being is best served by pursuing the common good, temptations to defect—to sell out the common good for immediate, personal gratification—are always hopping by. Jean-Jacques Rousseau tells of a group of men who go hunting deer. To get the big game, every man "must abide faithfully by his post."[24] But then along comes a rabbit. Any one of the men can bag the bunny without help from the others. Chasing the hare, though, means scotching the others' chance to take the stag. The overall benefit of taking the deer is far greater than the small, individual return on chasing the rabbit. But if the hunter who spots the bunny makes a strictly rational calculation, he'll break ranks—a rabbit in the hand being worth more than a fractional share of a speculative deer in the woods. But of course, if the men are always chasing after every hare that hops along, they never fell a stag, and never enjoy the bigger payday.

We need a way to guarantee that no one leaves his post. Unless we can credibly commit ourselves, our larger enterprises come unwound and our "self-interest properly understood" suffers. Loyalty is the tie that binds us together and holds us back when we'd like to chase after rabbits. By restraining us from pursuing some of our immediate, self-interested options, it can make bigger options possible.

Commitments that can't be counted on aren't commitments. And a world in which there aren't reliable commitments is a very inefficient and expensive one. To be loyal is to fulfill your part of what are usually informal social bargains. It's not unlike paying a credit card debt. With easy bankruptcy and other consumer protections that make one able to walk away from debt, it makes it harder to enforce the bargain. That means banks don't want to give credit unless you've proven yourself creditworthy—reliable. (And banks that don't pay attention to creditworthiness end up sinking in pools of toxic debt.) Loyalty works the same way. By proving yourself trustworthy and reliable, people can enter into reciprocal relationships with you without fear you'll stiff them when your turn to pay comes along. But if we can't expect people to live up to their obligations, we have to find ways to enforce our agreements. If a handshake isn't good enough to guarantee both parties to a deal will deliver, then they need an official contract. But legal contracts are costly, time-consuming, and often result in agreements that are inflexible. And of course, no matter how carefully constructed, contracts can still be broken, which means the time, expense, and uncertainty of litigation to enforce the terms—not to mention of the costs of the courts.

Enforceable contracts may be miracles of social organization, but they are awkward and inefficient. Honesty and reliability achieve the same things, but without all the expense and rigidity. Vigilance takes effort that could be put into more productive, creative endeavors. And so, in strict economic terms, being trustworthy is valuable. Hasidic Jews have traditionally had an advantage in the diamond trade by staffing their businesses with loyal family members, which means spending less time and money on preventing losses. Just think of how much money companies spend every year trying to keep their own employees from robbing them. The revenues of the Pinkerton types, with their stop-loss prevention plans, is testament to how little loyalty there is—and how valuable loyalty can be.

LOYALTY MIGHT BE valuable, but is it viable? The Prisoner's Dilemma, one of the most basic paradoxes employed by the peculiar study of psychology known as game theory, assumes that loyalty is too flimsy a reed to affect anyone's thinking or behavior. The paradox goes like this: Two conspirators have been captured by the police, but the cops have no hard evidence against them. The prisoners are separated, and encouraged to rat each other out. Here's the deal each is offered:

1) If you turn state's evidence and your pal doesn't, he gets ten years and you go free right away; 2) If you incriminate your pal and he also incriminates you, both of you get seven years in jail; 3) If you don't incriminate your pal but he incriminates you, you take the whole rap and do ten years' time; 4) If neither of you talks, both of you will be held for questioning for six months. The best deal for the pair is for both of them to keep their mouths shut—that is, their collective imprisonment would add up to just one year. But the strictly rational incentive is for each man to betray his buddy. Imagine you are one of the prisoners. Let's say you guess that your buddy is going to betray you: If you do the same, you get only seven years instead of ten. Let's say you guess that your buddy is no fink: It's still in your interest to fink on him—you get to walk away today instead of sitting in a cell for six months. Each man, acting strictly rationally, will talk. The paradox is that each acting strictly rationally ends up with both of them getting seven years when they could have both been out in six months.

For half a century, the Prisoner's Dilemma—with its perplexing demonstration of the bad outcomes rational behavior can produce—has been one of the most studied phenomena in social psychology. Strategists have played out the paradox in a string of computerized matchups, searching for a strategy that would succeed. It turns out that the most successful strategy ever mounted in these competitions was one based on giving loyalty a try. The winning player was the one who would refuse, in the first round, to betray his co-conspirator. But if he were betrayed himself, on the next turn, he would also betray.

If on that turn he wasn't betrayed, he would return to the loyal position for the next round. The interesting thing about the success of this "tit for tat" strategy was that it worked only when the player was willing to make loyalty his first move.[25]

Being loyal may work, but is it irrational? The school of rational-choice theory holds not only that people act on calculations of self-interest, but that they are right to do so, that calculating self-interest is the very definition of rationality. To buck the incentives built into the Prisoner's Dilemma is to behave irrationally, in this view. That's what makes the tit-for-tat strategy such an appealing conundrum for philosophers: *Hey, how crazy is it that the best strategy is not to think strategically?!*

But it turns out that people regularly act in ways that don't fit with the predictions of rational-choice theory. Perhaps that's because the average Joe is a bad strategist, either because he doesn't understand the nature of the game he's playing or because he can't do the math. Or maybe we should think twice before putting too much weight on the game theorists' notions of rationality. I was introduced to the Prisoner's Dilemma in a course on game theory at Harvard taught by one of the fathers of the field, the quirky, Nobel Prize–winning economist Thomas Schelling. I remember the class: Having drawn the matrix with its sets of payoffs on the chalkboard, Schelling asked what the right move was for either of the prisoners. There were a few stumbling stabs at it by the students quickest to put their hands up, but they didn't immediately grasp the basic calculation that whatever prisoner number 2 does, it is always the rational play for prisoner 1 to betray him, and vice versa.

The problem wasn't an inability to do the math, but rather that we students were bringing attitudes to the problem that didn't fit easily in the mathematical model being used. Most of us have an instinctive distaste for the notion of betraying a pal, and that makes the "rational" way to play the game unattractive. When we first try to play the Prisoner's Dilemma, there are more variables affecting our thinking than just how long one's stretch in the pokey is going to be. How will I be able to look myself in the mirror if I sell out my pal? What will he think of me? How will our friends treat me if they find out I ratted? These are all considerations outside of the simple matrix contrived for purposes of the dilemma. They may be emotional considerations, but they clearly affect how people behave in the real world, and even how people approach games that have specifically been constructed to get people to toss their emotional baggage overboard. As political scientist S. M. Amadae notes, "It turns out to be the case that people who have not been exposed to the logic of rational-choice theory do not readily [choose to betray one another in the Prisoner's Dilemma], even when paired with strangers."[26]

What does it mean that most people have to be taught the *rational* way to play the Prisoner's Dilemma? Is it that we're hopelessly muddled in our thinking? Or perhaps the theoretical model of calculating self-interest doesn't capture everything that goes into our deliberations. We could try to save the rational-choice model by calling various emotions "payoffs." For example, take a man who acts in a way that seems to be contrary to his self-interest. His willingness to make a selfless sacrifice earns him the respect of others. Perhaps he takes pleasure from being the object of respect, and so what appears to be a sacrifice is actually a self-interested effort by the man to maximize his preferred sort of pleasure. It's not a crazy idea. But it isn't a very good fit with our own experience.

When we act from loyalty we aren't making a calculation, we're stubbornly ignoring it. It is the paradox of the virtues that undoes the paradox of the Prisoner's Dilemma: In order to pursue our larger interests we have to learn how to ignore our immediate self-interest. And that means learning reflexive habits—virtues—that push us to behave in certain ways, even when those actions don't add up in any immediate calculation of rational self-interest. (Vices—reflexive habits that flummox our rational judgments—act in much the same way as virtues, then, but with the difference that they are habits that defeat our long-term self-interests rather than promoting them.)

A real-world version of the Prisoner's Dilemma plays out every day in precinct rooms across the country. Even when offered a sweet deal by the police, suspects aren't eager to flip. Partly this is because, in the real world, the matrix of self-interested calculation is complicated by rewards and punishments not included in the simple theoretical version of the Prisoner's Dilemma. Selling out a pal may spare you jail time, but may also cost you a beating or worse. Inner-city gangs have established a sort of public-service-announcement campaign to instruct the community on the wages of informing. "Snitches get stitches" is the slogan—and it's more than a slogan.

Even those who are not the target of gang intimidation

regularly resist police prodding to give up information that might incriminate their friends, their lovers, or their families. But it is friends, lovers, and family members who usually have the most damning evidence to offer about a suspect. Modern interrogation has been built on the premise that the only thing standing in the way of a nice quick bust are the misguided loyalties of the perp's pals. The Miranda mentality, with its Supreme Court–ordered emphasis on protecting the rights of the accused, doesn't let the cops use rubber hoses to overcome the force of those loyalties, and so psychological jujitsu has taken its place. The method is known as the Reid Technique, named after one of its inventors, John E. Reid, who developed the technique in the 1940s with colleagues from the Scientific Crime Detection Laboratory in Chicago. Anyone who has ever watched a TV cop show has a passing familiarity with its basics, which include browbeating suspects with relentless accusations, denying them any chance to deny guilt, and offering them, as their only respite, opportunities to make face-saving confessions. But those the police presume to be guilty aren't the only ones who face a barrage of accusations. Witnesses who refuse to cooperate, especially those suspected of trying to protect someone, must be broken too.

That can't be done as long as the potential witnesses are buttressed with loyalties. And so the "investigator should seek to break the bond of loyalty between the subject and the offender," counsels the primary textbook in the Reid Technique, *Criminal Interrogation and Confessions*. The first order of business is to get the person being interviewed alone—no friends, no family, no lawyers—so that there is no one around to give or demand loyal support. Then one gets down to the serious business of doing whatever it takes to smash the subject's loyalties.

One basic ploy is to convince the person being questioned that the "offender" has himself been disloyal, thus encouraging a little of the tit-for-tat endorsed by game theorists. If "a subject who is the mistress of the offender" is being interrogated, the Reid method suggests the police should tell her "that the offender was unfaithful to her and in love with another woman (whose true or fictitious name should be given)." If that doesn't work, the interrogator is to remember that "There is one consideration that a subject of this type is likely to place above all others: the protection of his own interest and welfare." And so the policeman is urged to accuse the person being interviewed of having committed the crime: "A witness or other prospective informant, thus faced with a false accusation, may be motivated to abandon his efforts to protect the offender."

Our first reaction to this technique may well be distaste with a method of questioning that is none too fussy about the finer points of truth-telling. (Many critics of the Reid Technique have argued that interrogators wielding lies are just as likely to cudgel out false confessions as true ones.) But it is a measure of the basic power of loyalty that police have to go to such unpleasant lengths to break it down.

Is loyalty—exploited as it is by criminal organizations—as hurtful as it is helpful? Can we think of it as a virtue at all?

The thug who is worried about what those in his gang think of him, who doesn't want to rat on his pals, is one who is exercising a capacity for loyalty. The object of his loyalty may not be admirable or socially beneficial. We may need to break up that loyalty to break up the gang. And yet whether we encounter them in novels or in the newspaper, we have a grudging admiration for the crooks who abide by some sort of personal code. Perhaps that's because criminals who have no loyalties are even scarier than those who are capable of organizing. They are the ones the psychological literature tags as psychopaths: "They cannot be relied on, they make unnecessary trouble" for their criminal cohorts, writes Robert Rieber. Though "they may be useful for carrying out specific acts of an unusually unseemly nature, there is no question of obtaining their long-term loyalty."[27] The criminal who is incapable of feeling loyalty goes in the most dangerous of diagnostic typologies, the "unprincipled psychopath."[28] And so maybe we embrace loyalty as a potent virtue even in a criminal context—it keeps the garden-variety crook from becoming an unfettered monster.

LOYALTY MAY BE stupid and it may be irrational, but its stubborn indifference to rational calculation is its very strength. But there is another way in which loyalty, by not being overburdened with rationality, is powerful. "Irrational" is one way to describe someone not behaving rationally, but another, more common tag for describing those who have abandoned the cool serenity of logic is "emotional." And when it comes to motivating action, the emotions have it all over reason.

Among modern moral philosophers, Immanuel Kant has perhaps been the most influential. He put forward an ethics grounded in the purest sort of reasoning, a "Categorical Imperative" that demands we act according to only those rules that can be applied as universal laws. There isn't much room for the emotions in this metaphysics of morality. Feeling something to be "right" isn't a moral judgment, according to the Kantian school, but just an expression "comparable to a cry of horror or of grief."[29] The problem for the Kantians, though, has always been the question of motivation. Even if pure, practical reason can arrive at a determination of what is right and what is wrong, how does that actually get anyone to do the right thing? Kant urges us to do our duty solely for the sake of doing our duty. It's an awfully austere notion, and one that isn't likely to inspire much practical action.

Such is the age-old conflict between reason and the emotions: Intellect informs us to behave in one way, while the passions push us to act in another way altogether. Not surprisingly, most intellectual accounts of this conflict favor the role of intellect, lamenting that emotion is a destructive force that bullies our higher, better selves. Reason is portrayed as the angel on one shoulder, counseling that which is right; passion is the guy with the horns and pitchfork. But of course, in that old comic shtick, it is the little devil that usually gets the better of the scuffle: He, after all, is urging the waverer to go with his desires, to do what his passions are already pushing him to do. Reason, locked in endless battle with desire, clearly has its work cut out for it. Loyalty, by contrast, not only gives us some sense of the right things to do, but moves us to action.

"The emotional character of loyalty," wrote philosopher Judith Shklar, "sets it apart from obligation."[30] We may recognize that we have obligations determined by various rules, and we may even have justified those rules through careful reasoning from foundational principles. But obligations, however strong the case for them might be, always have a way of feeling foreign. Obligation is always imposing its demands on us, endlessly barking, *You must do this, you must do that.* Loyalty, by contrast, is an emotional response; it wells up inside of us and carries us along. We don't argue our way into loyalty, we feel it.

Joseph Alexander Leighton, a philosopher with a religious bent writing nearly a century ago, argued that "feelings furnish the strongest and most enduring motives to action. They are the most lasting incitements to will."[31] Robert Frank, a modern economist studying, among other things, how people act when put in the Prisoner's Dilemma, arrived at the same conclusion: "Feelings and emotions, apparently, are the proximate causes of most behaviors."[32] Frank makes the case that the emotions, by overriding strict calculations of immediate self-interest, not only make it possible for us to act in ways that secure our broader, longer-term goals, but give us a good shove in that direction.

Loyalty may be the rope that keeps us from tumbling off the side of life's mountain, but this powerful and potent a life-saving tool has its risks. If we have even a small circle of friends and family, even the most modest of attachments to community and country, the lines attached to our waists proliferate. And with every rope we add, the odds get worse that we'll have to catch someone (or worse, that someone else's fall will pull us over the edge too). But that's just the price of insurance—as the benefits go up, so too do the costs. The real problem is that as we add more lines, the ropes we're counting on to break our fall can get easily fouled, snagging one another in the sort of impossible knots known to kids whose kites get crosswise. If we're going to enjoy the benefits of loyalty, we're going to have to learn to untangle the mess to which our multiple, muddled loyalties are prone. It may mean trying to belay with ropes looped in jumbles worthy of Celtic knotwork.

2

Loyalties at Loggerheads

Rummaging about the "wilderness of gorse, old trenches, [and] abandoned butts" of Berkhamsted Common, some twenty-five miles northwest of central London, a fourteen-year-old Graham Greene came across a rare find, a weedy shrub known as deadly nightshade. To his thinking, the poisonous plant was a godsend, a handy and permanent remedy for his deep unhappiness. Greene picked a bunch of leaves from the bush and proceeded to munch on them. He was disappointed to find that, instead of killing him, the leaves "had only a slightly narcotic effect." (Who knows whether he identified the plant correctly. After all, with greater arboreal expertise, Greene would have known that the leaves are not the most toxic part of the bush—had he eaten even just a few nightshade berries, he might have been out of his misery.)

When it came to suicide, Greene was as inept as he was

creative. On one occasion, he slipped into the "red Mephistophelean glare" of his mother's darkroom and guzzled a bottle of sodium thiosulfate, a photo-fixing chemical known as hypo, "under the false impression that it was poisonous." Another time, he emptied a bottle of hay-fever pills down his throat. No luck. He gobbled up a whole can of hair pomade. Nothing. He gulped a couple of dozen aspirins and then went for a swim in a deserted pool. Instead of sinking into insensate oblivion as he had hoped, Greene was left with a memory of "the curious sensation of swimming through cotton wool."[1]

He beat the odds playing repeated rounds of Russian roulette.

Why all the despair? Greene's trouble was school. Though he was free from the most obvious torments—"I wasn't beaten or bullied physically"—he felt like an outcast. Greene's father was the headmaster at Berkhamsted School and his older brother the "head boy," which left young Graham chafing under an obligation to his family that was at odds with the solidarity owed his dormitory chums: "I was in a hopeless position of divided loyalties. I was Quisling's son."[2] Greene would describe the school as a country under occupation and his classmates as the forces of resistance, "and yet I couldn't join them without betraying my father and my brother, and they regarded me like a collaborator in occupied territory."[3]

Caught as he was "between two fires" of enemy camps, no one trusted him. The "struggle of conflicting loyalties" left him confused, living a "strange, divided life,"[4] unable to forge bonds of true friendship with any of his fellow students. Greene described himself as being "in the situation of a leper,"[5] a plight distressing enough that he undertook all those hapless efforts at self-destruction to call some attention to it.

Loyalty may be empowering, may be ennobling, may be a fine source of moral motivation, but the virtue has a tragic tendency: Loyalties have a nasty habit of coming into conflict with one another. And for those caught between the irreconcilable demands of contrary obligations, the experience can be crushing. For Graham Greene, suicide seemed preferable to the excruciating "sense of inevitable betrayal"[6] that looms when loyalties are at odds. His might have been a typically adolescent overreaction, but who among us hasn't felt the angst of that sort of moral smashup?

We can try to pretend that, properly managed, our loyalties will mesh, nicely synchronized and self-reinforcing. About the time Greene was suffering his schoolboy agonies, an editorial printed in newspapers across the United States proclaimed, "The good American is loyal." The article urged that children be taught the full range of loyalty—to family, to school, to town, state, and country, and even to humanity itself. "If I try simply to be loyal to my family, I may be disloyal to my school," the editorialist wrote. "If I try simply to be loyal to my school, I may be disloyal to my town, my state and my country. If I try simply to be loyal to my town, state and country, I may be disloyal to humanity." But then the writer tries to wriggle out of the trap with one of the most basic moral Houdini gambits, the idea that fidelity to some overarching principle dissolves all dilemmas: "I will try above all things else to be loyal to humanity; then I shall surely be loyal to my country, my state and my town, to my school, and to my family." *Surely?* Hardly.

In a clumsy way, the newspaper moralist was echoing seventeenth-century metaphysical poet Henry Vaughan, who in his "Rules and Lessons" urged his readers "To God, thy countrie, and thy friend be true." Admirable advice, indeed. But of course, one's country may take a path at odds with what one believes God demands. And your friend could prove to be a heretic or a traitor. Can you be true to a friend who is false to your country? We may want to be true to God, countrie and friend all at the same time, but it may be impossible. Vaughan knew as much—as a young man, he had fought in the English Civil War, and nothing acquaints one faster with the agony of conflicting loyalties than getting caught up in a civil war. And so, a few lines into the poem, he gives his suggestion for how to navigate the contradictory demands of unruly obligations: "If priest and people change, keep thou thy ground."

It's a nice try. The assumption is that when we make our commitments and build our loyalties, everything is in harmony. Others change and thus throw that harmony out of whack. No doubt, that is sometimes the case. I might be pals with someone who proves to be a rotter. If my attachment to my friend was based on my admiration for his character and virtue, once he has abandoned those things himself, he has abandoned the basis for our friendship. I haven't been false to our friendship, he has—and he's done so by first being false to himself. If I don't follow along with a priest who veers off into apostasy, I haven't betrayed my faith, he has.

But friends don't have to change for our loyalties to be strained or broken. Let's say I have two great friends: I know Fred from a stint working on the West Coast; I met Joe at my kids' East Coast school. Finally, years down the line, when we're all in the same town, I get the chance to introduce these two friends of mine to each other. Disaster—the moment Fred walks into the room, Joe freezes. They are ancient enemies, old schoolmates still nursing mutual loathing from some bitter dispute involving a girl. Both stomp out, furious. Later, when I talk with them separately, each demands that I drop the other as a friend. This clash of loyalties isn't created because my friends have changed. In a way, the root of the conflict is that they haven't changed—each has been constant in his grudge. The problem is just that I didn't know, and had no way of knowing, when I became friends with each of the men, that they knew, let alone hated, each other.

Loyalties can come into conflict simply because of some measure of ignorance when we make our commitments. And since we can never enjoy the omniscience necessary to keep all our promises and loyalties conflict-free, we can never guarantee we won't be stuck having to betray one trust or another. As Judith Shklar says of the genus of virtues that includes loyalty, commitment, fidelity, and allegiance, "One thing ties all of these notions together: They all invite conflict; trouble is their middle name."[7]

—

We may value loyalty, and it may be a demonstrably powerful strategy for living, but the problem is how to decide who and what warrants our loyalties. And perhaps the biggest problem is figuring out how to decide which loyalties to honor when one's bonds come into conflict.

The novelist E. M. Forster suggested that loyalty to friends was a moral trump card: "If I had to choose between betraying my country and betraying my friends, I hope I should have the guts to betray my country." But these things depend, don't they? If your friend is a Jew hiding in the barn and your country is Nazi Germany, betraying your country is a good thing. But what if your good friend is a Timothy McVeigh or a Maj. Nidal Malik Hasan and you know what he's up to? Are we still quite so sure that refusing to betray a friend is always the right thing to do?

However we might decide to resolve a particular conflict, the tricky thing about loyalty is the very fact that it is a virtue rife with conflicts. The loyalty we bear to a friend may be at odds with the loyalty we owe to a brother or parent. The loyalty we bear to a spouse or lover may be irreconcilably opposed to the demands of loyalty to country. And even if I decide that, with Forster, what I owe to friends will come first, chances are it won't be long before I have to choose between two friends who have come into conflict, with no way to avoid disappointing one or the other. How many of us have seen our married friends get divorced and have had to choose which one of the couple retains our loyal friendship, and which gets shunted aside in the inevitable disputes?

Huck Finn nearly abandons his friend, the runaway slave Jim, because he is under the belief that by aiding Jim he has been stealing from a little old lady who had given him a home, a crime he's convinced God will punish him for. But loyalty to his friend wins out over loyalty to his guardian. And the way it wins out shows that Mark Twain understood the moral contradictions that loyalty can produce. Twain didn't explain away the conflict, as he might have, by saying that an unjust law such as slavery imposed no obligations. Instead, the very strength of Huck's bond to his friend is displayed by his willingness to risk the safety of his own soul: "All right then," Huck proclaims to himself, choosing to keep helping Jim, "I'll *go* to hell." Huck Finn has the sort of courage that E. M. Forster hoped for, and his decision is made all the more heroic because he hasn't dismissed the arguments to the contrary.

If asked to choose between betraying friend or country, no one could disagree with Forster or Finn more heartily than does Creon, king of Thebes, in Sophocles' grim tale of loyalties at loggerheads, *Antigone*. "Whoso greater than his country's cause / Esteems a friend," Creon proclaims, "I count him nothing worth." The king is confident there can be no conflict between loyalties to friend and country, because no enemy of the state can be deemed any sort of friend in the first place.

We moderns may be temperamentally inclined to find Forster's stand more appealing than Creon's—especially since the king of Thebes, with his relentless demands for blind obedience, ultimately proves to be the villain of the piece. But in a way, Creon is a very modern fellow, one who believes that what we might perceive to be moral conflicts aren't really conflicts at all. He presents the up-to-date notion that when moral claims clash, the stronger of the two obligations trumps the weaker. And as the play opens, Sophocles would have us think that Creon is on to something, presenting him as a not unreasonable sort.

Creon, cleaning up the wreckage of a bloody civil war, is eager to restore order by asserting the primacy of the state. The sons of Oedipus—Eteocles and Polyneices—have killed each other in a great battle for the throne of Thebes, with Polyneices leading a mercenary army against the city. As posthumous punishment for his treason, Creon wants Polyneices' body to rot in the field—"lying all ghastly where he fell / Till fowls o' the air and dogs have picked his bones."[8] Oedipus' daughter Antigone pleads to be allowed to bury her brother, but Creon refuses to accept that any loyal Theban can have any obligation toward Polyneices, not even the obligations of filial piety.

Creon has a compelling argument for why the claims of the state come first: We are all riding on the ship of state, Creon says, and "She only brings us safe: on board of her / Our friends we make—no friends, if she be lost."[9] Without the protection of our country, our lives are forfeit. And without life there can be no friendships. And so if friends come into conflict with the state, friendship has to lose out. It has a tidy logic. But Sophocles shows us that the dilemma doesn't go away. Instead, the tensions created by the moral dilemma fester. Creon's refusal to recognize the possibility of moral conflict merely makes those conflicts more agonizing and intense. First, Antigone is caught between her loyalty to the city and her duty to give her dead brother a burial, however rudimentary. She chooses to sprinkle Polyneices with dirt, earning herself a death sentence. That's when Creon's son gets his turn to be crushed by conflicting loyalties—his love for his fiancée, Antigone, smashes headlong into his obedience to his father, the king. It isn't until the stage is littered with suicides that Creon starts to suspect his brand of moral medicine is poison.

The Greeks were sticklers for the loyalties that make family and friendship flourish. Maybe it was this very emphasis on loyalty as a core virtue that gave them such a heightened understanding of the moral catastrophes that can come from trying to navigate conflicting obligations. Perhaps the most harrowing of these ethical disasters is the story of Agamemnon, commander of the great invasion force sailing for Troy. Except, as the playwright Aeschylus tells the tale, the fleet isn't doing much sailing: The boats are being blown against the rocky shore by a relentless, withering headwind. Trapped aboard ships battered by waves and wind, the vast army is wasting away in starvation and sickness. Looking for options, the general turns to his soothsayer, who offers a terrible prophecy: The only way to appease the gods and turn the wind in the general direction of Troy is for Agamemnon to make a sacrifice of his daughter, Iphigenia.

Now it is Agamemnon who is trapped: He has an obligation of loyalty to his daughter; he has an obligation to the men he commands; he has obligations to his country, embarked as they are on a momentous war. Which loyalty should he choose? Is there any right choice? Maybe not—which is why they called such dramas tragedies.

Agamemnon isn't in this fix because of any misdeed on his part. And yet he is on the moral hook. Any way he acts will entail a crime. Agamemnon is "a previously guiltless man, in a situation in which there is open to him no guilt-free course," writes philosopher Martha Nussbaum. She notes that such situations are "repellent to practical logic"—that is, we like to believe that the demands of morality are internally consistent. No system of ethics that embraces rudimentary logic, with its principle of noncontradiction, would require both that we do and not do the same thing. And yet, illogical as contradictory moral requirements may be, "they are also familiar from the experience of life."[10]

At first, Agamemnon recognizes the horrible jam he's in. "Hard is the fate not to obey; but hard is it if I must slay my child, the ornament of my house, polluting with streams of virgin blood a father's hands before the altar. Which of these is without its terrors?"[11] The chorus—the Greek theater's organ voice of right and wrong—is with Agamemnon so far, and might have stayed in his corner whatever he did, as long as he didn't fool himself into thinking that there was a good solution to his horrible plight. But that's just what the general does. Bowing "his neck to necessity's yoke," Agamemnon absolves himself of guilt—after all, he's only doing what is necessary, so how can he be blamed? And with his moral load lightened he slaughters his daughter without a tear, without any of the sense of terror that had first defined his deliberation. The chorus isn't happy with what it calls his "impious change of heart, unblessed and unholy."

Why should the chorus judge Agamemnon so harshly? Why should he be expected to weep and agonize about doing what he has to do? Because, as the chorus declares, the one enduring, universal law is that knowledge comes by suffering. Men learn discretion only by the "torturing recollection of woe."[12] This may seem a bit harsh, but it isn't crazy: Just because there is no choice but to violate one of two irreconcilable loyalties doesn't mean that there is no betrayal involved. Someone is being wronged and there's no making it right. Agamemnon just doesn't get it, a moral error that leads what's left of his family to turn their knives on one another.

The ancient Greeks blamed Olympus, lousy with gods, for the conflicting demands that plague our loyalties. Piety demanded honoring and obeying a multiplicity of quarrelsome deities who didn't bother to make their various commands consistent with one another. "It would seem that what is loved by the gods is also hated by them," Socrates says in his dialogue with Euthyphro. "What is agreeable to Zeus [is] disagreeable to Cronos or Uranus, and what is acceptable to Hephaestus [is] unacceptable to Herè, and there may be other gods who have similar differences of opinion."[13] For Socrates (and his amanuensis Plato) this was an indictment of the whole moral scheme. Plato strove to replace the old morality with a new system of ethics embracing logical consistency with the goal of shielding us from the ravages of tragic conflict caused by inconsistent loyalties.

But you don't have to buy into the fanciful theology of Athens to recognize that the myths tell us something about our awkward human condition. Right and wrong has to do with our interactions with others; because we are involved with so many others in the everyday course of our lives, the demands on us multiply and can't help but get jumbled. The Greek religious setup was a projection of messy human affairs—the gods imagined as one big dysfunctional family. As such, it did a pretty good job of capturing the essence of the irreconcilable loyalties that afflict us.

Which is why the old tragedies still speak to us, why (in answer to Hamlet's question) we weep for Hecuba. Those dramas demonstrate how loyalties collide, producing the most basic and perplexing of human dilemmas. What's a mother to do when the loyalty she owes her children can't be squared with the loyalty she owes her husband? What's a man to do when what he owes his family is at odds with what he owes his country? Or when any of those parochial ties runs afoul of the obligations to Truth and Humanity? "There is no escape for any one of us from these tragic collisions in human life," wrote Willard Sperry (who as dean of Harvard Divinity School for some three decades combined philosophical sophistication with pastoral practicality). "Each one of us has to endure the moral friction which arises when his loyalty to truth, to duty, to the absolute good, cuts across his devotion to family, friends, country, church." He concluded that loyalties, with their hopeless, crosswise habits, were responsible for "the deeper unhappiness and moral pathos of much of our human life."[14]

We can cross our fingers and hope for the best, but that isn't much of an endorsement of loyalty as a virtue. What kind of concept of morality leaves us at the mercy of luck? What kind of ethics allows that a good man determined to do the right thing can be blamed for committing a wrong he had no way of escaping? The worst irony is that loyalty, along with its conceptual brethren fidelity and allegiance, are all about remaining constant. And yet, if there is anything constant about loyalty, it is that the ground underpinning it is always shifting, tripping up even the most earnest devotees of the virtue.

WE VALUE THE virtue of constancy, the notion that a promise made will be a promise kept. But we don't expect to come across it very often. And no wonder there's so little confidence in loyalty: For a virtue meant to protect us from unforeseen circumstances, it is vulnerable to unforeseen circumstances. Ambrose Bierce, cynic that he was, wasn't far from wrong when he defined fidelity as "A virtue peculiar to those who are about to be betrayed."[15] And that's especially true if we allow that it isn't just people, but also events that can betray us and our intentions.

And yet, there is no doubt that we admire the loyal (perhaps for the same reason people put a high value on Honus

Wagner baseball cards—sheer scarcity of the good). We admire those willing to suffer to protect their friends, even those (particularly those?) who suffer to protect their friends who are in the wrong. How else to explain the feel-good finale of the movie *Scent of a Woman*? A young man named Charlie Simms is about to be expelled from a prestigious prep school because he won't give up the names of the boys he saw play a destructive prank on the headmaster. That is, until his friend Lt. Col. Frank Slade (played by Al Pacino) rises to his defense. "Be careful what kind of leaders you're producing here," the colonel bellows at the faculty. "I don't know if Charlie's silence here today is right or wrong. . . . But I can tell you this: He won't sell anybody out to buy his future. And that, my friends, is called integrity. That's called courage. Now that's the stuff leaders should be made of."

The speech is a triumph: The disciplinary committee absolves Charlie and the assembled students roar their approval. Watching the movie, we can't help but be swept along, condemning the sniveling snitches for their cowardice, roused by Pacino's full-throated call for loyalty as the basic currency of conscience. It's a measure of how powerful Pacino's climactic appeal to loyalty is that, for all its bombastic corn, the performance won him the Oscar for best actor.

But do we really want to embrace an ethic that puts personal relationships above every other consideration? A century ago, Josiah Royce tried to rescue loyalty as the core principle of morality. Among the objections he ran into was a complaint from the headmaster of a swanky private school who had had his fill of *Scent of a Woman*–style scenarios: "Loyalty hereabouts," the schoolmaster griped to Royce, "is a cloak to cover a multitude of sins." Instead of producing upstanding young men, loyalty was an excuse invoked to justify covering up for one's buddies. "What these youth need," the schoolmaster said, "is the sense that each individual has his own personal duty, and should develop his own conscience, and should not look to loyalty to excuse him from individual responsibility."[16]

Royce doesn't have much of a response to this objection: He just suggests that the schoolmaster isn't nearly as opposed to loyalty as it might sound. After all, Royce writes, the man had devoted his life to his students, thus exemplifying himself the sort of loyal commitment he questioned. But that's a fudge. It doesn't come close to resolving the conflict identified by the schoolmaster—that loyal obligations to one's friends can be at odds with one's obligations to truth, duty, or the law. This source of moral conflict continues to dog institutions that care about loyalty. And nowhere is this problem more acute than in the modern organization that relies most on loyalty—the military.

After finally exorcising the ghosts of Vietnam in the first Gulf War, the U.S. Army set about recommitting itself to the quaint notion that it should be in the business of winning wars. After decades of distractions, the army came up with a new "Warrior Ethos" to define what it is and means to be an American soldier. At its core are seven values: "loyalty, duty, respect, selfless service, honor, integrity, and personal courage." And though these values might often be in happy harmony, it doesn't take much imagination to see how easily these values can come into conflict. The army defines loyalty as bearing "true faith and allegiance to the U.S. Constitution, the Army, your unit and other Soldiers." But what happens if the soldiers in your unit aren't acting according to the demands of the U.S. Constitution? The army also says, "A loyal Soldier is one who supports the leadership and stands up for fellow Soldiers." But again, what happens when the leadership is making decisions that are detrimental to one's fellow soldiers? Relying on the concept of loyalty doesn't get you very far in sorting out what to do when different loyalties are at odds with one another.

The problem has been a constant one at the military academies, particularly since strict honor codes were put in place. Up until 1952, the Naval Academy used a normal military code of conduct, one that placed an emphasis on honorable behavior, but which also allowed room for midshipmen to be loyal to one another by not going out of their way to turn their barracks-mates in for breaking the rules. But then the academy instituted an honor code that demanded midshipmen "stand for that which is right." The Brigade Honor Program is straightforward: no stealing, no cheating, no lying. If someone in your unit is out after hours and you're asked about where he is, the honor code leaves no room for the loyal gesture of covering for him. Once upon a time, "midshipmen acted honorably by hindering officers from discovering classmates who had gone over the wall," but the honor code puts the goals of loyalty and honesty at "cross-purposes," according to Naval Academy graduate Todd Forney, "making it difficult for truly 'honorable' behavior."[17]

The problem is even more pronounced at West Point, where the honor code requires no lying, no cheating, no stealing, and *no tolerance for those who do.* How do you nurture the loyalty demanded by the Warrior Ethos when you've got an honor code that requires you turn in your fellow cadets?

That's certainly not the attitude toward loyalty that Al Pacino's colonel championed, and it seems that real-world cadets haven't always found it persuasive either. It was in the wake of a 1966 cheating scandal (in which forty-two students got the boot) that West Point toughened its honor code to make those who condone violations of the code as guilty as the offenders. It didn't take long for the "no tolerance" clause to be felt: in 1973 another twenty-one cadets were shown the door, many of them for turning a blind eye to others' cheating. A few years later the academy was roiled by an even bigger scandal, with scores of students accused of cheating on an electrical engineering paper, with many more in the dock for looking the other way. The commandant of cadets in those days, Brig. Gen. Walter F. Ulmer, Jr., allowed, "It's not natural for an 18-year-old to tell on his friends. It's something that has to be instilled."[18] But the resistance to ratting one another out wasn't just a matter of educating youngsters. It flowed from a fundamental conflict of loyalties—loyalty to the institution and its code versus loyalty to friends and comrades in arms. "Less than 10 percent of honor code violations are reported," wrote Richard U'Ren, an army psychiatrist based at West

Point in the early seventies. "The cadets' loyalty to each other is far stronger than their allegiance to the honor code."[19]

That strong sense of loyalty cadets have for one another is no accident; it is one of the main virtues taught at the academy. "West Point does everything in its power to develop a sense of cohesiveness among the cadets. They strive to develop a sense of loyalty," U'Ren said. "And then they ask these men to turn each other in on honor code violations. It really is a terrible bind for the cadets."[20]

After 152 cadets were sent packing in 1976, the army made changes in how the honor code is enforced, leaving more room for students to urge their code-violating friends to reform before being required to turn them in. But the conflict of loyalties—loyalties to friends versus loyalties to the academy, the army, and the Constitution—remains.

One way the army tries to resolve this tension is to maintain that loyalty to a liar, cheat, or thief is a degraded thing, not worth having (an argument that recalls King Creon's assertion that an enemy of the state can be no friend at all). Evan Offstein, a West Point grad who is now a professor of management, explains how the academy squares the circle: "Tolerating dishonorable acts of another never improves loyalty or cohesiveness," he writes. "In the end, loyalty based on dishonor will always erode."[21]

Journalist David Lipsky spent four years at West Point following the class of 2001. He found that, the honor code notwithstanding, the academy's emphasis on loyalty and unit cohesion "has a side effect: cadets rarely rat on each other."

Lipsky also discovered that the cadets had their own hierarchy of loyalties. If your pal's actions are a serious affront to the reputation, the *honor* of the academy, then "your loyalty is to the organization," one cadet told him. But if your pal has merely tripped over one of the many regulations that govern every aspect of the cadets' waking lives, that's a different matter altogether: "Are you gonna turn your brother in?" the young man asked. No way—and for reasons essential to the success of the entire enterprise: "You're supposed to stick together and help each other out, not screw each other over."[22]

Emphasizing a hierarchy of commitments is the other way that the military strives to resolve the problem of conflicting loyalties without undermining the idea itself. And as the cadet put it, there are times when the stakes are high enough that one's loyalty to the organization shoulders loyalty to friends aside. It's an approach that should work well in the army, with its hierarchical structure. When it comes to following orders, there may be contradictions, but there are no conflicts—it's just a matter of sorting out which order comes from higher on the correct chain of command. If the major tells you to stop and the colonel tells you to go, you go and that's that (unless the general weighs in). Unfortunately, that's not the way loyalties work.

Even if there is a superior, overriding loyalty, one's lesser loyalties don't cease to bind, or at least tug. The army is well aware of this, which is why the Cadet Leader Development System (which since the 1990s has been the core training manifesto at West Point) demands not only that cadets "Understand and demonstrate loyalty to the Constitution, the

Army, the unit, superiors, subordinates, comrades and self," but that they be able to "Explain the tension between loyalty to the Constitution, the Army, the unit, superiors, subordinates, comrades, and self." And finally, "Make rational decisions on how to resolve a conflict of loyalties."

What sort of decisions do soldiers make, in practice, when confronted with painful clashes between obligations to country, army, officers, and their fellow soldiers? The answer shouldn't come as a surprise. The army spent a lot of time and money on psychiatrists and sociologists during and after World War II, documenting what sort of loyalties matter in combat. The bonds that make for an effective fighting force, they found, are the ones the men share with their pals. That finding has defined how the modern military is organized and trained, with consequences—not all of them pretty—in the field.

The army still employs plenty of psychiatrists and sociologists, and one of their jobs now is to put together what are called MHAT reports. The Mental Health Advisory Team goes into the field and surveys how soldiers exposed to combat are thinking and feeling. The fifth of these MHAT reports was released in February 2008, and it stated as a given that "Soldiers' willingness to report unit members for unethical behaviors almost certainly runs counter to the strong sense of bonding that occurs among unit members during the deployment." In 2007 there was a high level of "unit cohesion"—higher than in 2006—and it turns out that the strengthening of soldiers' loyalties to one another was not an unalloyed good. Their greater commitment to one another meant they were less willing to report misdeeds. In 2006, only 37 percent of the troops asked said they "would report a unit member for the mistreatment of a noncombatant." In 2007, it was down to 34 percent. And what if someone in your squad killed an innocent noncombatant? In 2007, only 41 percent said they would report it, as opposed to 45 percent the year before.[23]

The army isn't exactly happy with these figures—no one wants another My Lai. The brass recognize that bad apples tempted to commit war crimes will be deterred if they "believe unethical behaviors will be reported by unit members." But when it comes to resolving this fundamental clash of loyalties—obligation to buddies versus moral obligation and duty to country—the military is stumped. The modern army is built on the proposition that an effective fighting force is one in which soldiers are loyal to the other men in their unit. High morale = unit cohesion = not ratting out your buddies. It is with an air of resignation that the MHAT-V study explains: Given that unit morale in Iraq and Afghanistan is high, "it is not particularly surprising that Soldiers continue to be reluctant to report ethical violations of unit members."[24]

YOU MIGHT THINK that rule number one in the official Code of Ethics for federal government employees would be "Uphold the Constitution, laws, and legal regulations of the United States." But no, that's rule number two. The first item in the code is one that pegs the source of most ethical problems—

the stubborn clash of incompatible obligations: "Put loyalty to the highest moral principles and to country above loyalty to persons, party, or Government department."[25]

The civil service enshrines the larger loyalties—those to moral principles and to country—as superior to what one owes to the folks we pal around the water cooler with. And frankly, subordinating personal loyalties should be an easier proposition at, say, the Department of Housing and Urban Development, where, unlike in the army, you don't generally have to rely on the guy in the next cubicle to keep you from getting blown up by an IED. But even where you don't have to count on loyal buddies to help you survive day to day, conflicting loyalties are troublesome enough to top the ethics chart.

How helpful is that government Code of Ethics? It does provide definitive guidance on the Forster question: If you have to choose between your friends or your country, country comes first. Which is all well and good, but not entirely unproblematic, in part because not even the government is willing to put country up there, unchallenged, at the top of the ethical hierarchy. Faithfulness to "the highest moral principles" shares the summit and, in fact, is mentioned first. That has a nice, high-minded ring to it. Who could object to making "moral principle" our lodestar? And yet, letting ethical abstractions overrule all other considerations of loyalty may be just as dangerous as giving one's commitments to friends pride of place. Once an appeal to the authority of one's own conscience is allowed as an excuse for violating an official trust or abandoning a personal commitment, what bad actor won't be able to find some puffed-up sophistry with which to explain away, or even celebrate, his betrayals? As sociologist Morton Grodzins put it, "the disloyal person in almost every circumstance will justify his action in terms of some larger ideal."[26]

Consider the moral character of the revolutionary, the type so eager to tear down his society, so untroubled at the prospect of selling out his friends and neighbors. Chances are, as historian and scholar of revolutions Crane Brinton put it, he is "not the embittered failure, not the envious upstart, not the bloodthirsty lunatic, but the idealist."[27]

British physicist Allan Nunn May was one of the traitors most responsible for the Soviet Union acquiring the Bomb. He handed the Russians not only nuclear secrets but even samples of enriched uranium. This he did neither for money, nor love, nor to help out a friend. Humanity was the object of May's loyalty, and he thought that leveling the nuclear playing field was the best way to serve his lofty principles. "The whole affair was extremely painful to me," May said in court, sprinkling his confession with equal parts self-pity and self-justification: "I only embarked on it because I felt this was a contribution I could make to the safety of mankind."

We don't trust those who proclaim themselves true to "mankind" or "principle" at the expense of loyalties to friends or country. And why should we? We know they aren't trustworthy. The instinct for self-preservation counsels us to steer clear of those who put grand abstractions ahead of their friends.

Brutus famously justified doing in his pal Caesar by making an appeal to lofty concerns of freedom and country. He planted a knife in his friend's back, "Not that I loved Caesar less, but that I loved Rome more." What sophomore English class is complete without studying the eulogies Shakespeare has Brutus and Marc Antony speak, one after the other, at the burial of Julius Caesar? Brutus, who helped with hacking Caesar to bits, sets out to justify himself. The nut of Brutus' apologia is that—though he was, and remains, Caesar's friend—he had to be true to a higher loyalty, an obligation that absolves him of any reproach. "As Caesar loved me, I weep for him; as he was fortunate, I rejoice at it; as he was valiant, I honor him: but," Brutus says, "as he was ambitious, I slew him." He may be a plodding speaker, but Brutus succeeds in winning over the crowd. As he closes, they are shouting for him to be crowned the new caesar, for statues to be raised in his honor.

Once Brutus leaves, Antony takes the pulpit and takes Brutus apart. It begins with that grim riff on what "an honorable man" Brutus is. It takes Antony only a few dozen lines of bitter irony to turn the crowd against the assassins: "Revenge!" they scream, "Burn! Fire! Kill! Slay! Let not a traitor live!" Antony's deft manipulation of the mob is usually parsed as a lesson in the power of rhetorical tropes: "The verse of Antony triumphs over the prose of Brutus" is the common conclusion.[28]

But maybe something else is going on: Perhaps Antony has such an easy time making mischief for Brutus for the same reason the old Greek chorus soured on Agamemnon. Brutus is too comfortable with what he's done. Having ascertained a superior loyalty to Rome, he's dismissed the demands of the competing loyalty he owed Caesar—even to the point of claiming that his friendship with the emperor was somehow undiminished. Given a chance to think it through, the crowd doesn't find Brutus' effort to argue away his fundamental conflict of loyalties any more persuasive or attractive than we do. Watch your back around idealists.

Which might also explain why Antigone is so much more sympathetic a character than either Agamemnon or Brutus. It isn't just that she is spared the ugly necessity of killing anyone other than herself. Antigone may talk about "piety," about how she is following the "Unwritten laws, eternal in the heavens," but she isn't driven by moral abstractions. The obligations she meets are those demanded by family ties, what she owes as a sister to a dead brother. Whether right or not, when small-scale loyalties to family or friends conflict with grand-scale loyalties to country or moral principle, we are inclined to be more forgiving of those who choose to honor the homely obligations of the home front.

YOU COULD SAY that life was easier (at least morally) for those living in aboriginal cultures, people who belonged to only one tribe at a time. There's less chance for conflict between family and country when they are essentially one and the same. The more complicated our lives become, the more loyalties we have, and the greater the risk of conflict among them. And we are nothing if not prolific in creating opportunities for loyalties to clash. "Man is both creator and creature of institutions; not of one, but of many," notes political theorist John H. Schaar. "And to speak of institutions is to speak of loyalties. As soon as variety is admitted the possibility of conflict appears. Nor is there any easy formula for resolving those conflicts."[29]

Well, there may not be an easy formula, but there's been no shortage of strategies proposed to limit the number of soul-battering loyalties let loose in the bumper-car pavilion at one time. One approach is to radically narrow our involvement in the world. Thomas à Kempis, a German monk living in late-medieval Holland, had a rather sensible suggestion for avoiding competing demands—have only one friend. And to make sure that you are never betrayed, be sure that one friend is Jesus: "The trust you place in men is a total loss," Thomas à Kempis writes in *The Imitation of Christ*. (The sentiment may be a bit harsh, but you can't say it's without empirical justification.) By contrast, the love of Jesus "is loyal and lasts."[30] And if your only friend is Jesus, Thomas à Kempis does not expect that you will ever have to choose between doing what is morally right and doing what your friend expects—they will be one and the same. It is a savvy and coherent strategy for avoiding the conflicts of loyalty that plague us, but it requires withdrawing to a monastic life of cloistered seclusion.

Athenian politician and military genius Aristides pursued a practical, secular version of the Thomas à Kempis approach. He avoided political friendships so that he wouldn't be pressured into mischief by buddies expecting favors. "Aristides walked the way of statesmanship by himself," Plutarch wrote, because "he saw that power derived from friends incited many to do wrong, and so was on his guard against it."[31] This earned him a reputation as fair and just, but his aloof impartiality also exposed him to certain problems: Suspicious of Aristides' all-too-virtuous reputation, the people of Athens voted to banish him from the city. He might not have been ostracized had he cultivated a phalanx of loyal friends to stand up for him.

Outside the hermit's retreat we can't help but have a multiplicity of relationships. And if those relationships are anything more than perfunctory, each will come with a set of expectations and obligations that, among other things, help define who we are. Philosopher and psychologist William James called each set of loyalties someone might have a "social self," concluding that a man "has as many different social selves as there are distinct *groups* of persons about whose opinion he cares."[32] Since each social self has its own defining attachments, chances are it won't be long before one of those selves is at the throat of another.

The problem is particularly acute for exiles and immigrants, whose identities are hyphenated, if not outright divided. If an Irish American pushes for U.S. policy that favors Ireland, in whose best interests is he acting? Armenian Americans would rather the United States not be too friendly with Turkey until Ankara makes a full accounting of the Armenian genocide. Cuban Americans look to Washington to keep the heat on the Castros. Indian Americans lobby against Pakistan; Pakistani Americans do the same for India.

Jewish Americans committed to a Jewish homeland in Palestine have often unfairly been accused of putting the interests of Israel ahead of those of the United States. Louis Brandeis, before he joined the Supreme Court, tackled the problem head-on: "Let no American imagine that Zionism is inconsistent with Patriotism," Brandeis declared. He was convinced that a surfeit of loyalties didn't have to trip us up. Instead, the various loyalties to family, friends, profession, lodge, college, city, and state could help build up our capacity for the patriotic loyalty we owe to the nation. "Multiple loyalties are objectionable only if they are inconsistent," Brandeis wrote, concluding, "There is no inconsistency between loyalty to America and loyalty to Jewry . . . Indeed, loyalty to America demands rather that each American Jew become a Zionist."[33]

That may well be true, but if so, it is a happy accident, and subject to change. Events can take happily coexisting loyalties and throw them into conflict. In the years before Archduke Ferdinand's unfortunate sojourn to Sarajevo, German Americans were able to maintain a relatively comfortable dual identity. Once the United States entered the European war, those loyalties were no longer compatible. German Americans found themselves accused of treasonous sympathies. Polemicist and Germanophile H. L. Mencken wrote to his friend Louis Untermeyer, "All men with names like yours and mine will be jailed before September, 1918."[34] Most rushed to proclaim their now-undivided loyalty to the United States, and even Mencken curbed his tongue. The fear of German-American treachery may well have been hysterical, but that outsized reaction simply highlights how tenuous is Brandeis's claim that divided loyalties can be kept in harmony.

Why not just get rid of conflicts altogether? From Plato to Immanuel Kant a long line of idealists has argued for a morality built on reason, for an ethics protected by the principle of noncontradiction, the fundamental law of logic that says you can't hold two contradictory things to be true at the same time. "As two opposite rules cannot be necessary at the same time," Kant writes, "if it is a duty to act according to one of them, it is then not only not a duty but inconsistent with duty to act according to the other."[35] By definition, Kant's system of morality is one in which contradiction and conflict are banished: Indeed, "a conflict of duties and obligations is inconceivable."[36] Which is all very nice and soothing, but even Kant acknowledges that the idea that moral conflict is impossible doesn't fit particularly well with our actual experience in the precincts of the real world. We certainly think that we sometimes have obligations that come into conflict. Kant deals with that conundrum by explaining that what we *think* is a competing moral claim is really just a pretender. Whenever there is a perceived conflict between two grounds of obligation, "then one of the grounds is not a duty." Problem solved.

There's no denying this solution has appeal. Think of Huck Finn's dilemma. It ceases to be a dilemma at all. As far as Kant would be concerned, Huck is simply mistaken in agonizing over his choice. All he has to do is determine which obligation binds him, and the other claim can be dismissed. We might think that Huck's problem dissolves once he recognizes that a law that enslaves men is unjust, and therefore can't be binding. Helping Jim escape is the only right thing to do, and it is Huck's duty to break the unjust law. That's the sort of solution we're comfortable with.

But at what cost? In order to eliminate conflict, Kant tells us to discard one of the demands, stripping it of any claim on us. One duty has to "wholly abolish" the other. This is a winner-take-all model of morality, and the metaphor philosophers have used in the last few decades (even though very few of their students know how to play bridge) is "trump." The stronger moral claim trumps the weaker one, leaving the weaker one with no claim on us at all. This strategy of dismissing all other considerations once "duty holds the field" leads to some bad ethical choices. Most notorious is Kant's claim that, should a murderer bent on mayhem come looking for a friend of yours who is at that moment hiding in your house, you can't lie to the murderer. Your obligation to tell the truth—*even to a crazed killer!*—trumps any obligation you have to protect your friend. And from Kant's point of view, you should feel no guilt in the matter even if your friend pays the price.[37] If this stern and unequivocal approach—with its echoes of Agamemnon's untroubled trip to the altar—is what it takes to spare us from the discomfort of conflicting loyalties, maybe we can live with the more unruly sort of morality.

Kant tries to resolve conflicting demands by saying there is only one right thing to do when duties appear to clash. French philosopher Jean-Paul Sartre takes the opposite tack, asserting that, when loyalties confound one another, anything you choose to do is the right thing. In the essay "Existentialism and Human-ism," he gives the example of a young man whose brother has been killed by the Nazis. The young man is eager for revenge; he wants to escape Paris for England, where he can join the Free French forces. But the young man's mother is dying of grief for the slain brother. The young man feels he is obliged to stay with his mother and care for her. He asks his teacher Sartre what he should do. "In coming to me, he knew what advice I should give him, and I had but one reply to make," the philosopher wrote. He told his student, "You are free, therefore choose—that is to say, invent. No rule of general morality can show you what you ought to do: no signs are vouchsafed in this world."

In cases of conflicting loyalties, the tragic view holds there is no right choice, making any choice the wrong one. By contrast, Sartre argues there is no wrong choice when loyal-ties collide, making any choice the right one. The choosing and then the acting are what count, not the particulars of the action chosen. It's a creative way to calm one's conscience but not much help in making serious decisions about how to live.

With such a frustrating set of moral options is it any wonder that Graham Greene finally arrived at another way of freeing himself from the tangle and crush of the conflicting loyalties that tormented him? He renounced loyalty altogether. In an in-troduction to the memoirs of British traitor Kim Philby, Greene pish-poshed the judgment "He betrayed his country" with the weary assertion of a man who has long suffered a divided life: "Who among us has not committed treason to something or someone more important than a country?" If loyalties can't help but come into conflict, then Greene would have us be done with the whole confounding business. He decried the worry and angst brought on by a sense of obligation as "brain worms, which creep into your mind so softly that you don't notice them but all the time they are gnawing away at the foundations." In a speech when accepting a literary prize, Greene celebrated what he proclaimed to be the liberating "Virtue of Disloyalty."

It's a clever bit of contrarianism, but no real way to live. Greene knew it as well as anyone. He has the "whisky priest" of *The Power and the Glory*—hunted by a ruthless anticlerical policeman—chastise villagers for protecting him. They have put themselves and their children in danger of reprisals out of loyalty to him, and he is exasperated with them: "It's *your* job—to give me up," he pleads with them. "What do you expect me to do? It's my job not to be caught." Greene combines here an exhortation to disloyalty and a display of doomed loyalty. The priest—in so many ways weak, pathetic, and ridiculous—is ennobled by his quixotic fidelity. Greene understood the treacherous quirks of loyalty, and though in his peevish moments he may have counseled being rid of it, in his art the power of loyalty comes through, giving life meaning and even offering redemption.

Disloyalty may sometimes be unavoidable, but embracing it as a virtue means trashing any hope of love, friendship, and community, the things that bring the most fundamental joys and satisfactions to our lives. The challenge—and clearly it is a daunting one—is to find a way to nurture these basic human needs, to protect them from the conflicts caused by our crosswise attachments.

3

The Ever Ready Accomplices

In the sweltering days after Hurricane Katrina clobbered New Orleans, Memorial Medical Center was swamped. The hospital, in a low-lying section of the city, had no power, no running water, and patients who were dying, among them eighty-two-year-old Vera LeBlanc. She had undergone colon-cancer surgery the week before, and had been too weak to be evacuated before the storm. After days of moldering heat she was weaker still. Doctors doing a rough-and-ready triage—sorting out the patients who could be saved from those for whom little could be done—put the dehydrated and fading LeBlanc with the hopeless cases. There she might have died, as did many of the other patients whose charts were marked with a "3" to denote their unlucky status at the bottom of the triage hierarchy. Some succumbed naturally; some were given a narcotic nudge by staff who didn't want to leave suffering

patients behind. Vera might have been among those eutha-
nized if it hadn't been for her son and daughter-in-law.

Mark and Sandra LeBlanc had left New Orleans ahead of
the hurricane, with assurances from the hospital that everything
would be fine. Once they learned that things were anything but
fine at Memorial, the LeBlancs hustled and cajoled until they
found three men with airboats willing to help them launch a rescue. They raced up to the hospital loading dock and went looking for Vera. When they found her—with the patients who had
been put at the end of the evacuation line—they went to move
her to the boat. But doctors told Mark and Sandra that, until the
patients ahead of Vera in the triage queue had been rescued, they
couldn't take her. "The hell we can't," Sandra shouted. They
pushed past the doctors and carried Vera to the waiting boats.[1]

Such are the bonds of family loyalty. Find yourself in real
danger and, if you're lucky enough to have anyone you can
count on, chances are it's someone bound to you by family
ties. City, state, and federal government agencies may do their
jobs in a crisis, but if I had to bet on where I could look for
help in the midst of a catastrophe—who would make my survival their dogged and utmost mission—family is it.

We may admire the children who come through for their
parents, but the lengths parents will go to for their children are
so great, and so natural, that we hardly give them a thought.
Indeed, we don't have to give them a thought—the impulse is
hard-wired.

In September 2009, in Swansea, Wales, Michelle Thomas
was fixing dinner for her four children when a gas leak was

sparked and the house burst into flames. Racing upstairs, Michelle managed to get her sons out the second-story windows before jumping herself to the lawn below. Frantically, she looked for her four-year-old daughter, Courtenay, who had been outside playing. Alas, the poor little girl had come inside unnoticed just before the explosion, and now she was banging on an upper window. Without hesitation, Michelle ran back into the house, disappearing into the inferno, where she perished along with her child.

Think about her sacrifice. Had a passing stranger seen the trapped girl and run into the burning house we would be flabbergasted at the extraordinary heroics. Even if a good friend from next door had attempted the rescue we would shake our heads in amazement. Michelle Thomas made no less of a sacrifice, but we aren't astonished by it. She flung herself into the holocaust because it was *her* child, and that's just what parents do. Such is the power of parents' loyalty that we almost take it for granted.

The extraordinary efforts family members make for one another can have much wider benefits. Even if they had done nothing more than to rescue Vera from Memorial Medical Center, the LeBlancs would have helped hospital officials by relieving them of the burden of caring for Vera. But of course, there was room in the boats for others too. Nor did they stop with the one trip: Once the LeBlancs had Vera safely in an ambulance on dry ground, they powered the boats back to Memorial, ferrying as many patients as they could throughout the day.

But disasters can also bring out the darker side of family loyalties. Many are the examples of emergency workers who, at the moment of public crisis, abandon their posts to look after the needs of their own families first. The evening of June 8, 1953, a devastating tornado plowed through the little community of Beecher, near Flint, Michigan. With winds over 300 miles per hour, the twister tore up the town, demolishing 340 houses. More than 800 people were injured and 116 died. But for all the wind-whipped carnage, there might have been fewer fatalities if everyone in the city's volunteer fire department had gone into action. Instead, the firemen went looking for their own families: "If their families were in danger, they saw to them first," investigators reported.[2]

That might sound reasonable enough—check on your family first, then grab your helmet and go. But in practice, it can be catastrophic. In another tornado-struck town a few years before, only one fireman showed up. And again, family loyalties were to blame. The lone firefighter recounted what happened:

> All the rest of the firemen had relatives that were hurt, and they stayed with them. Naturally they looked after them. If it hadn't been that my wife was all right, this town probably would have burned up. It's hard to say, but I kind of believe I would have been looking after my family, too.[3]

The man battled the fire alone until the National Guard arrived. He wasn't critical of his fellow firemen. "Naturally" is how he describes his comrades' ordering of priorities. He even admits that he would have done the same. The fireman's reaction is a measure of the respect we accord family loyalty—it holds a place so lofty in our hierarchy of virtues that we're willing to excuse dereliction of duty. It's also a matter of straightforward realism. Emergency planners have learned the hard way that when first responders are worried that their own families may be hurt or in danger, loyalties to their jobs and their communities lose out to family loyalty.

Even loyalties to friends can throw a wrench in rescue efforts. The Beecher firemen who checked on their own families first then turned to helping their friends and neighbors. They threw themselves into rescue efforts, valiantly fighting fires and digging out those buried under the rubble of their houses. But there was no teamwork, no coordination, no strategy, because the firemen responded to the call of their personal loyalties rather than meeting the demands of their official duties.

Instead of struggling to undo or overcome those tenacious bonds, disaster planners focus on finding ways to avoid the conflict in the first place. When "emergency managers, medical and emergency personnel, volunteers, and so on suffer conflicts of loyalty between the care of their immediate family and the imperative nature of their work," writes David Alexander in the textbook *Natural Disasters*, "the problem can be reduced by planning to take care of their next of kin."[4]

Such planning can help, but there's no planning for everything, which means the conflicts still turn up. Take the doctor at New Orleans's Memorial Medical Center who was most candid about getting stubbornly surviving patients to "go to

sleep and die"—Ewing Cook, a senior physician and adminis-
trator at the hospital. He prescribed to a faltering patient an increased dose of morphine he expected would kill her. "I gave
her medicine so I could get rid of her faster, get the nurses off
the floor. . . . There's no question I hastened her demise," he
told *The New York Times*. "To me, it was a no-brainer, and to
this day I don't feel bad about what I did."

Before he left the hospital, Dr. Cook says he told another
doctor how to administer drugs to the patients he thought were
doomed anyway. Why did Dr. Cook feel he had to share that
nasty business with a colleague? Perhaps because he couldn't
stick around himself. According to *The New York Times*'s exhaustive account of the nightmare at Memorial, dying patients
still filled the halls when Dr. Cook bugged out: He left "the
hospital by boat to rescue his son, who had been trapped at
his house" ever since the flood waters began to rise. You can't
help but wonder: If Dr. Cook hadn't felt the need to leave the
hospital so that he could go rescue his son, would he have
been quite so convinced that there was no choice but to expe-
dite the fate of Memorial's dying patients?[5]

So which is family loyalty: the foundation of all our other
loyalties, or a grubby sort of me-and-mine selfishness? Most
decidedly the former, according to Josiah Royce, the philosopher for whom loyalty was the essence of ethics. Not only did
he maintain that "The first natural opportunity for loyalty is
furnished by family ties," Royce was convinced that "fidelity
and family devotion are amongst the most precious opportuni-

ties and instances of loyalty," ties that give us our first taste of "the spiritual dignity which lies in being loyal."[6] The notion that family is a schoolroom where loyalty is taught—and tested—is not original to Royce. Go back a couple of millennia and you find the perfectly sensible conviction that those who are faithless with their families can't be counted on to keep faith with anyone or anything. St. Paul, tutoring his disciple Timothy in the basics of the apostle business, told him to watch out for ingrate children, the sort who can't be counted on to help their poor, widowed mothers: "if any provide not for his own, and specially for those of his own house, he hath denied the faith, and is worse than an infidel."[7]

Favoring one's own kith and kin may be natural, but not everyone is convinced that it's right: indeed, favoring family is the sort of thing that gets philosophers worked up about the evils of loyalty. The dominant strain of moral philosophy ever since Immanuel Kant penned *The Grounding of the Metaphysics of Morals* has been universalism—the idea that the only rules of ethics worth following are those that make no distinctions among people. What's right for Fred to do in a given situation must be the same thing that is right for anyone else. But loyalty is anything but universal: It's all about obligations that we have to particular people, flowing from the particular relationships we have to them. "Loyalty involves partiality," writes Simon Keller. "If you are loyal to your daughter, then you favor her over other children, just because she is your daughter." And though that might be perfectly normal, it doesn't cut it from the rather demanding perspective of universalist morality, which entails treating everyone according to the same standard. For Keller, loyalty is no virtue and there is no virtue in loyalty: "There is no conceptual reason to think that just because something counts as a loyalty, there is something good about it."[8]

Family loyalty falls under the heading of *particularism*, which for many modern ethicists is a dirty word. The modern universalists champion impartiality, and suspect there are no moral principles to support the notion that I should treat my own family better than I treat others. Universalist morality is all about Justice and, in the biggest and broadest sense, it is not unlike what we expect of justice in the narrower confines of a courtroom. What kind of justice is it if the judge is the father of the prosecutor or of the defendant? No sort of justice at all. We go to great lengths to keep even the slightest taint of favoritism out of trials. Before jurors are seated, judges make sure they aren't related to, or even acquainted with, any of the players in the drama to come. Judges and lawyers are expected to recuse themselves if they have any relationships that create conflicts of interest—which is to say any interest beyond that of impartial justice. We all recognize that in the courthouse, judgments influenced in any way by relationships of family or friendship are corrupt and dishonest. The advocates of universalist ethics want us to view the judgments we make in our everyday lives in the same way—that acting morally requires acting impartially. They argue that when we are influenced by any particular relationship, our moral judgments are as corrupt and dishonest as the lying testimony of a cop on the take.

Loyalty is not impartial. The same goes for its flip side, love. A saint of some sort might talk about loving everyone equally, but our own experiences of love generally involve emotions for particular individuals. And even if our love for some particular person is rooted in a moral good—say, an admiration for the loved one's kindness—that hardly means we extend the same sort of love to every individual who is equally kind. If that were true, universalist ethics could be a great boon to wandering husbands: "But darling, how could I not extend my love to that other woman given that she, like you, is generous, witty, charming, and kind? I couldn't treat her any differently than you without committing an offense against the demands of impartial morality . . ." Good luck with that.

Having loyalties to individuals means we treat people who are equally worthy differently. Not only that, we give all sorts of preference to people that may be *less* worthy. Though we might "admit that Mother Teresa was a more deserving person than our own mothers are," suggest philosophers John Sabini and Maury Silver, "who among us would have pitched our own mother out of the lifeboat to make room for Mother Teresa? Who among us would be that disloyal?"[9]

However natural family loyalty may be, take it to an extreme and you get some very ugly results. Mario Puzo captures an antisocial family-first attitude in *The Godfather*, describing Don Corleone's contempt for his son Michael joining the U.S. Marines. "Don Corleone had no desire, no intention, of letting his youngest son be killed in the service of a power foreign to himself," Puzo wrote. Shown a copy of *Life* magazine with a photo spread on Michael's heroics, the Godfather "grunted disdainfully and said, 'He performs those miracles for strangers.'"[10]

Puzo wasn't making that attitude up. In the 1950s, American sociologist Edward Banfield studied the persistent poverty of a little town in south-central Italy. He found that the people of Chiaromonte ranked family interest and family obligations not only above all others, but to the exclusion of all others. Banfield called their blinkered loyalties "amoral familism," and described it as "the inability of the villagers to act together for their common good, or indeed, for any good transcending the immediate, material interest of the nuclear family."[11] Italian anthropologist Carlo Tullio-Altan laments this familism and "its disastrous social consequences," blaming it as the root, not only of the country's endemic corruption, but of the national attitude of *I've got mine, you can go to hell.*[12]

That "mine" business has been a bother to egalitarian political thinkers as far back as we've had egalitarian political thinkers. Plato saw family loyalties as such a threat to his idealized Republic that he insisted on being rid of them altogether. "The greatest good for a city is what binds it together and makes it one," the philosopher wrote. The "group" has to be "like a single organism," and that means "no one distinguishes between what is his and what is someone else's." That's a bold enough notion when it comes to something as trivial as, say, property. But what chance is there that people will look at children communally, with none of that tacky

"Well, *my* little Jimmy" nonsense? Not much, so long as children are raised within families. Plato has a solution: "Children will be placed in a nursery and cared for by nurses. Parents and children will thus not know each other."[13] Oh, and yes, any children born outside of the official government breeding regime will be left on a hillside to die. (I'm beginning to suspect that, just maybe, Plato's idealized city-state might not have been a very nice place.)

Plato wasn't saying that the sort of loyalties one places in family are a bad thing, just that those loyalties should be developed on a larger scale: If you don't know who your father is, you have to treat every man of a certain age with the respect you would give your own dad. If any person of your generation could be your brother, Plato suggests, you can't help but have brotherly love for everyone. And so, even for those eager to get rid of family ties—in no small part because of the social rifts and infighting they can cause—family loyalties remain the gold standard by which all other loyalties are measured.

Do family loyalties always stand opposed to other commitments? The Anglo-American tradition has believed that the loyalties learned in the family provide us with training in how to be loyal to community and country. The most famous proponent of this view was eighteenth-century Irish philosopher-politician Edmund Burke. "To be attached to the subdivision, to love the little platoon we belong to in society, is the first principle (the germ as it were) of public affections," he wrote in *Reflections on the Revolution in France.* The love of the little platoon that is the family "is the first link in the series by which we proceed toward a love to our country and to mankind."[14] In the Burkean scheme of things, the family is where we learn to make sacrifices, where we learn to live up to our obligations. Instead of leading us to shut out the needs of community, family is what makes us capable of citizenship.

Get schooled in loyalty at home, and you may indeed learn to be loyal to your friends, to your community, to your country. But acquiring wider circles of attachment doesn't mean you lose your core commitments—loyalty to family isn't a seed that disappears as the larger plant comes to full flower. And so though family loyalty can support and promote loyalties to country and cause, it remains an allegiance potentially at odds with the big societal obligations. And for the exponents of authoritarian ideologies, family loyalty has been a problem even when it isn't in actual conflict with the demands of the Party. The mere existence of loyalties owed to something other than the state means that the commitment to the state is something less than total. And that just won't do: The god that failed is a very jealous god. Family ties represent a direct threat to the primacy of the state, which is why totalitarians of every stripe have tried to stamp out family along with all its parochial attachments. People gathered around the hearth are people who aren't out on the barricades. People trying to provide for their own families are people not putting the collective first. And people who find satisfaction and happiness in their little platoons are less likely to feel the need to go looking for meaning in the grand ideological endeavors peddled by propagandists.

Nazi Germany, for one, "suspected and attacked the family as a shelter against mass society." Writing just after World War II, sociologist Max Horkheimer explained that for the Nazis, family loyalties were "a virtual conspiracy against the totalitarian state."[15] And so Hitler's Germany set about disrupting and dismantling family life, primarily by trying to turn children against their parents. Members of the Hitler Youth were taught to treat the junior Nazi party as their real family. At school, teachers looking to encourage students to betray their folks assigned papers on such topics as "What does your family talk about at home?" Living with Hitler's littlest acolytes was dangerous for parents. Even committed Nazis might, in an unguarded moment, say something critical of the Reich, words that, if reported by eavesdropping *Kinder*, could mean a visit from the Gestapo. As Michael Burleigh tells it in *The Third Reich: A New History*, "Those with children began to envy the childless."[16]

The natural response to the sight of children bringing death and destruction to their parents is to recoil. And so when the Brits were waging a lonely fight against Germany in 1940–41, struggling to get help from the United States, they were sure to point out the Nazis' manipulation of children. Hitler was undertaking "the deliberate disintegration of the family," said the British ambassador to the United States, the earl of Halifax, on a 1941 speaking tour. "Children are taught that it is their duty to denounce their parents, and so at once the family atmosphere is polluted and befouled, and suspicions and hatred banish confidence and love."[17] In a way, it was an odd theme to emphasize: After all, why should it be any business of the United States how Germans raise their kids? Why would such a clearly *domestic* German issue matter to Americans still clinging to isolationist sentiment? I think it's a measure of just how visceral our reaction is when we witness family loyalty torn apart. It tells us something about our core commitment to the bonds of family that, in painting the picture of Hun atrocities, snitching on one's parents was considered a significant evil.

The Nazis were not the first to use children against their parents. Guillotining enemies of the state may have been a vivid symbol of relentless modern and efficient terror, but it was just one of the French Revolution's many innovations. One of the most chilling was the spectacle of children denouncing their parents, a practice encouraged by the likes of a *citoyen sans-culottes* named Chassant. Once a priest at the church of Saint-Germain-l'Auxerrois, he found a new vocation enforcing revolutionary purity. He taught children to spy at their homes in the hopes of catching their parents in the act of saying prayers or some other treasonous acts of Catholic fidelity. It was all a piece with the teachings of Robespierre's bloodthirsty acolyte Saint-Just, who declared that if "you wish a Republic" then you must be for "the destruction of everything which opposes it." If family gets in the way of *liberté* and *égalité*, well, too bad for Mom and Dad. And so much for your brother too, notwithstanding the call for *fraternité*. Owing a bond to a real, live brother tends to expose the political concept of *brotherhood* for the mere metaphor that it is.

As hideous as the orgy of beheadings was, the destruction of natural family ties was more shocking. Of all the prolific "seeds of depravity" that appalled John James McGregor in his 1816 *History of the French Revolution, and of the Wars Resulting From That Memorable Event*, none was more depraved than that "All the ties of relationship were burst asunder, and children were rewarded if they denounced their parents."[18] For John Adolphus—whose 1799 *Biographical Memoirs of the French Revolution* was one of the first serious histories of the Jacobin Reign of Terror—many were the events that made the heart "recoil." Topping his list was that "informing, treachery, calumny, and assassination were erected into virtues . . . the sentiments of nature were carefully extinguished, and fury, perfidy, and inhumanity lighted up in their stead." The absolute worst of the business, the proof that France had become a "corrupted country," Adolphus argued, was that "brothers accused their brothers, fathers their sons, and children their parents," and that they were applauded for it too.[19] In their reactions to the revolutionary practice of snitching on parents, Adolphus and McGregor both reflect our primal sense that family loyalty is a fundamental good, perhaps the most basic of human virtues.

The Russian Revolution picked up where the French Revolution left off, and did its best to build on its predecessor's most pernicious practices. Under Stalin, children who betrayed their parents weren't just encouraged and rewarded, they were canonized. Soviet tykes were urged to emulate little Pavlik Morozov, martyred, so the story went, by traitors to the state. The boy, a member of the Communist youth league called the Pioneers, became a hero by denouncing his father to the secret police on charges of corruption. When Daddy was executed the rest of the family was understandably upset; little Pavlik's grandparents, uncle, and cousin took him out in the woods and gave him his cocoa. They, in turn, were rounded up, lined up, and shot. This is the (mostly invented) tale the Soviets told in making Pavlik a hero of the revolution, and a model for all Russian children. There was a Pavlik museum, Pavlik biographies, a Pavlik play, and a Pavlik opera. In the 1950s the *Great Soviet Encyclopedia* was still plumping his legacy with an enthusiastic entry: Pavlik "spoke at the trial of his father and branded him a traitor," which made the boy "a model of fulfillment of duty and of devotion to the cause of the Communist party."

There was no shortage of teenagers willing to demonstrate their devotion to duty. A boy named Pronia Kolibin caught his peasant mother trying to hide away a little wheat that belonged to the collective farm. He denounced her as a "cruel saboteur," punching her ticket to the gulag; he got a trip to a vacation camp.

A Pioneer who didn't find someone, anyone, in his family worthy of denunciation wasn't trying hard enough—and frankly, might be suspected of lacking in revolutionary fervor.[20]

It's hard to have much of a family life when parents are terrified of their children, and that's just the way the Stalinists liked it. And Chairman Mao too—he realized that the traditional extended Chinese family was a source of social cohesion, a power base that would naturally contend with the Communist Party for primacy. And so he set about breaking it up. Children were indoctrinated to denounce their parents for any deviation from Party doctrine. As Wolfram Eberhard put it in his *History of China*, "The best formula for a revolution seems to involve turning youth against its elders, rather than turning one class against another."[21]

George Orwell thought such betrayal was characteristic of the totalitarian mind. In *Nineteen Eighty-Four*, the ominous O'Brien is at his most ominous when he takes a break from torturing Winston to deliver a soul-crushing speech. The topic: the inevitable omnipotence, the endless triumph, of the Party. It is the horror-show oration in which O'Brien presents the novel's most vivid imagery, a power-porn vision of what the state has in store for mankind: "If you want a picture of the future," he tells Winston, "imagine a boot stamping on a human face—for ever." It is one of the most monstrous moments in a monstrous tale.

It's worth remembering how O'Brien builds to his confident conclusion, what steps he sees as essential in extinguishing human hope. He begins his lecture by explaining:

> "We have cut the links between child and parent, and between man and man, and between man and woman. No one dares trust a wife or a child or a friend any longer. But in the future there will be no wives and no friends. Children will be taken from their mothers at birth, as one takes eggs from a hen. . . . There will

be no loyalty, except loyalty towards the Party. There will be no love, except the love of Big Brother."

Family loyalty may not always lead to the broader community virtues, but an absence of family loyalty is a pretty good precursor for murderous dystopia. When the great liberal philosopher-historian Isaiah Berlin took up the question of whether there were any moral absolutes applicable across all humanity, he suggested that if one couldn't go so far as to say there were universal values, at least we could generally agree on a few simple rules "without which societies could scarcely survive." To demonstrate the basic moral consensus, Berlin points to a few evils so obvious that none would try to defend them: slavery, Nazi gas chambers, and "the torture of human beings for the sake of pleasure or profit." Oh, and yes, Berlin notes one other indisputable society-destroying wrong: To the Middle Passage, the Holocaust, and sadistic cruelty, he adds "the duty of children to denounce their parents, which the French and Russian revolutions demanded."[22]

Most children put in the unenviable position of having to rat on their folks regret it deeply sooner or later. Later, as in the many Russian memoirists lamenting their collaboration in their parents' doom. Or sooner: There were enough "children emotionally torn by state demands to inform on their parents" in Nazi Germany that there was a diagnostic category for the affliction at the Third Reich's psychotherapy center, the Göring Institute.[23]

In countries free from such insanity, the law has long understood that society collapses if the termite teeth of disloyalty eat away at the foundations of family. Traditionally, spouses have not been required to testify against each other—an effort to avoid forcing wives and husbands to break their bonds of loyalty to each other. In the eighteenth century, English courts flirted with extending the same sort of protection to friends. "It is indeed hard in many cases to compel a friend to disclose a confidential conversation," found a judge in the 1792 case *Wilson v. Rastall*. "I should be glad if by law such evidence could be excluded. It is a subject of just indignation where persons are anxious to reveal what has been communicated to them in a confidential manner." The judge, Lord Kenyon, nonetheless realized that however unpleasant it was to see friends testify against friends, it couldn't be helped if there was to be any justice system worth a bean: "if a friend could not reveal what was imparted to him in confidence, what is to become of many cases?"

The same could be asked with regard to family. What would become of many cases if family members never had to testify against their kin? Prosecutors might despair of ever bringing charges. Because, though we may view the totalitarian perversion of family with contempt, our own legal system regularly demands that family members testify against one another. The needs of the family to protect its loving bonds of loyalty may be great, but the need for evidence, courts have ruled, is greater. In precinct interrogation rooms and before grand juries, family loyalties are regularly put to the test. Not only are witnesses pressed to betray their family bonds, but in a bit of legal jujitsu, the strength of their loyalties is used as leverage against them: If the target of an investigation is a father, nothing is likely to break him quicker than to make legal threats against his children.

Thomas Capano, scion of a prominent Delaware family, and once a politically connected Wilmington lawyer, is a big believer in the sanctity of family loyalty. He was also capable of murdering a mistress who had left him, stuffing her in a cooler and dumping her in the ocean. But that didn't mean he didn't have a highly developed sense of right and wrong. When it came to the tactics of prosecutors who tried to get evidence out of his daughters, Capano was roused to righteous rage.

During his trial for the murder of Anne Marie Fahey, Capano took the stand in an effort to explain the whole mess away as some sort of terrible accident. During cross-examination, prosecutor Colm Connolly asked why Capano hadn't been willing to sit down for an interview with the police—an interview that would have spared the defendant's daughters from being interrogated about their father's whereabouts on the date in question. Capano sputtered with outrage: "You heartless, gutless, soulless disgrace of a human being!"

Later convicted, Capano was given an opportunity to address the jury before sentencing. It was his chance to avoid the death penalty, and he used it to complain about how prosecutors had put the screws to his family.

Capano is an unfortunate poster boy for family loyalty, the embodiment of everything that can go wrong when the power of family loyalty is misused. Having killed poor Anne Marie, he needed help disposing of the body. Where could he turn? Whom could he trust? His brothers: Louis Capano owned a construction business with lots of Dumpsters to empty, convenient for getting rid of the blood-soaked couch where the girl died; Gerry Capano owned a powerboat, helpful for getting out to sea, where the body could be dumped. Both did their part, and at first kept their mouths shut.

To break down the family loyalties behind which Capano was barricaded, police and prosecutors had to turn the family's loyalties to their advantage. The cops suspected all along that it was boat-owning Gerry who had helped his brother get rid of Fahey's body. But Gerry clammed up nicely, and they got nowhere—that is, until the police found a pretext to search Gerry's house. They didn't find anything involving the Fahey case, but they did find some weapons, and a small amount of drugs. It was all the leverage they needed: Using the drugs and guns as evidence that Gerry might be an unfit parent, authorities started a probe that threatened to take his children away. And as far as family loyalties go, children trump brothers. Gerry caved and told prosecutors everything.

Faced with conspiracy charges backed by Gerry's testimony, Louis soon caved too. He presented himself as a victim of misguided notions of family duty: "Louis Capano in the past acted out of loyalty to his family," said his lawyer. "But more importantly, he acts now out of concern for doing the right thing." As much as we may value family loyalty, it and "the right thing" are not always the same thing.

The Capano case was no anomaly. To get family members to do the right thing, police regularly pressure them to do what seems to them a wrong—betray one another. Who is more likely to have information about an alleged perp's comings and goings than the people—often parents, siblings, or children—he lives with? Police use different tactics for different sorts of relations. Brothers may hold tough for a while, but mothers are often soft touches, credulous when the cops lay it on thick about how getting caught now will really be the best possible thing for their poor wayward sons. And if a mother decides to hold out, don't expect investigators to take it easy on her out of respect for her virtuous display of loyalty.

Consider the case of David Port, who, when he was seventeen, set out to rape postal carrier Debora Sue Schatz as she delivered the mail to his family's Houston house. When she tried to escape, he shot her. After driving some twenty miles with the body in the trunk, Port dumped the corpse in a bayou and went home. It didn't take police long to figure out where on her route Schatz's trail of delivered mail came to an abrupt end. Soon they had Port in custody and he was persuaded to confess. But prosecutors were concerned that the confession might be thrown out at trial, and they set about trying to shore up their case from every angle. Which is when Port's father and stepmother got their subpoenas to appear before the grand jury.

Bernard and Odette Port refused to testify. They claimed parent-child privilege. Though no such privilege was anywhere to be found in Texas or federal law, the Ports' lawyer argued that it was an ancient tenet of Jewish law, and thus protected by the Constitution's guarantee of freedom of religion. The judge didn't buy it. Bernard and Odette went to jail for contempt of court, and stayed there for months. David Port was convicted without any help from them.

The claim of familial privilege didn't succeed in the Ports' case, but it wasn't a wacky notion. Indeed, many people seem to think—and regularly act on the belief—that they can't be compelled to testify against their parents or children or siblings. It's a notion for which there has been some legal precedent. In the years just before the Ports found themselves in court, judges here and there had begun extending the spousal privilege to other members of the family. In 1978 a state court in New York ruled that parents didn't have to give grand jury testimony about private conversations in which their child admitted to guilt in a crime. "There is nothing more natural, more consistent with our concept of the parental role, than that a child may rely on his parents for help and advice," the court ruled. Fostering family loyalty was at the core of the decision: It is "critical to a child's emotional development that he know that he may explore his problems in an atmosphere of trust and understanding without fear that his confidences will later be revealed to others."[24]

The most robust precedent for such a privilege came in Nevada in 1983. The thirty-two-year-old son of a man accused of tax evasion refused to give testimony against his father. A district court decided he was in the right, and that there is "little doubt that the confidence and privacy inherent in the parent-child relationship must be protected and sedulously fostered by the courts." The court ruled the son couldn't be "compelled to be a witness and testify adversely against his father in any criminal proceeding." The privilege, the judges wrote, was necessary to protect "the institution of the family."[25]

Given our revulsion at the totalitarian habit of enlisting children against their parents, shouldn't the regard for family found in these rulings elicit huzzahs? Perhaps our instinct is, at the very least, to nod in agreement. But are we really eager to embrace a system of justice that protects family loyalties from the cops' investigative crowbars? Newspaper columnist Anna Quindlen is: "I would be fully prepared to lie under oath if I considered it to be the best thing for my kid," she writes, adding, "I would consider that a more moral position than telling the truth. And I am certain I am in the majority."[26] She may be right that hers is a majority view, but it doesn't mean it is the right one.

Instead of expanding the old common-law spousal privilege to include parent-child privileges, sibling privileges, and amorphous "family" privileges, the U.S. Supreme Court has moved in the opposite direction, limiting when wives or husbands can refuse to testify against each other, and eliminating the privilege altogether if a spouse is willing to testify. The court ruled in 1980 that the sweeping spousal privilege was a "sentimental relic."[27]

There are good reasons to resist the idea of family privilege. Tell brothers that they will never have to give evidence against one another and you encourage the felonious-minded to enlist their siblings in crime. This is no celebration of family loyalty, but an incitement to corrupt it. "The law should strew danger before every step which it could occur to a man to take in the path of criminality," argued the practically minded English philosopher Jeremy Bentham. What the law shouldn't be doing is giving anyone a "safe and unquestionable and ever ready accomplice for every imaginable crime."[28] Isn't it better for the cause of brotherly love not to ask one's brothers for help in tidying up after a grisly murder? Perhaps the law encourages family loyalty best by discouraging criminal conspiracies. The family that strays together isn't likely to stay together (well, unless they get assigned to the same cell block).

Bentham certainly thought so, to the point of caustic disdain for the spousal privilege itself: "Let us, therefore, grant to every man a licence to commit all sorts of wickedness, in the presence and with the assistance of his wife." He argued that though we should make "every man's house his castle," we shouldn't "convert that castle into a den of thieves."[29]

Even with the right sort of incentives in place, there will be parents, children, brothers, and sisters who find themselves having to make a hopeless choice between the good of the family and the more generalized good that Louis Capano's lawyer christened "the right thing." As much as we would like to say that family loyalty trumps other moral or legal obligations (anytime we can play a moral trump card, after all, we avoid the messy tangle of contradictory moral imperatives), not even family gets us to the point where we can be comfortable and confident that our loyalties are unimpeachable.

It was Ted Kaczynski's brother, David, who realized that

the Unabomber Manifesto published in *The New York Times* was the recognizable product of his sibling's deranged mind. After agonizing whether to "Do nothing and run the risk that Ted might kill again, or turn him in and accept the likelihood that he would be executed for his crimes,"[30] David finally sent an anonymous tip to the FBI.

Years later, locked away in a federal Supermax prison, Ted was still bitter at the betrayal, saying of his brother, "He is the lowest sort of scum, and the sooner he dies, the better." Asked by a reporter whether he would have turned David in if it had been the other way around, Kaczynski was emphatic: "I would have kept it to myself." He was adamant that family loyalty should override any other consideration. But, of course, Ted's a psychopath.

I think we can agree that David did the right thing, even though it was a betrayal of family loyalty. What's particularly interesting, though, is that David's initial effort to turn Ted in was an anonymous one. Even though he knew it was the right thing to do, he retained a lingering sense that what he was doing was unseemly.

Or perhaps even apocalyptic. When on the Mount of Olives, Jesus lists for his disciples the portents and signs that the world is coming to an end. He warms up with a litany of horrors—wars, earthquakes, famines. But that's just for starters. When the going gets really bad, "brother shall betray the brother to death, and the father the son; and children shall rise up against their parents, and shall cause them to be put to death."

And yet that basic wrong is sometimes right. Which brings us back to the great conundrum of loyalty: What use is it as a moral rule when we need to calibrate it against another moral rule to know what's what? Can there be any reason to think loyalty is a virtue at all? Yes, but only with the understanding that virtues taken to extremes lose their virtue. The virtue of family loyalty remains virtuous only within reasonable bounds. Those bounds may not always be clear, but that doesn't mean they're always obscure.

4

For Better or for Worse

In January 2010, Sandra Bullock found herself at the Golden Globe Awards, gathering a prize for best actress. After giving the standard litany of showbiz acknowledgments to colleagues, agents, publicists, and the like, she turned to thank her husband. It was a moving endorsement of loyalty, a testament to how the virtue can embolden and empower us. "To my husband: There's no surprise that my work got better when I met you," Bullock said, "because I never knew what it felt like for someone to have my back." It was a wise observation. Being able to count on loyal support lets us take bigger risks and gives us the confidence to make those risks pay off. Soon there was an even bigger payoff for Bullock, a "Best Actress" Academy Award. Again, she gave a teary nod to her remarkable good fortune in landing a man such as her husband (who was so moved that he too wept).

It was just a week later that Bullock had occasion to weep over her husband all over again, when it was revealed that while she was doing all that loyalty-empowered, love-enabled work he was off enjoying himself with a stripper/tattoo–artist who goes by the *nom de guerre* Bombshell.

It's a common-enough story, indeed commonplace. Which is why you could say that nothing has done more in our day to undermine the concept of loyalty than love. For it is in loving that the fragile manufacture that is our standard in loyalty is mercilessly exposed. The notion of making a commitment rarely comes up outside the precincts of the heart. But when it comes to romance, loyalty is not only demanded, it is on display. Unless we become citizens or join the military, occasions that both require the taking of oaths, marriage— with its ceremony built on vows—may be the main occasion that most of us ever make a public pronouncement of loyalty. "For better or for worse, richer or poorer, in sickness and in health"—the better, richer, and healthy parts we can assume are there merely by way of contrast. What really matters in the vow is the promise to stick around in illness and poverty—to the last gasp, you might say. This focus on fidelity in the face of misfortune is the very definition of loyalty.

Given the large number of marriages that go bust, we can't help but question just how reliable this loyalty business is. And unreliable loyalty is no sort of loyalty.

Love at least ought to mean never having to hire a private detective—or never having to go through your spouse's cell phone contacts in search of all his cookies, the unpleasant task that fell to Tiger Woods's wife. Like Sandra Bullock's husband, Woods couldn't even manage fidelity while the going was as good as it gets. Never mind better or worse or richer or poorer: Such men have been blessed with the best and richest of circumstances. And even that wasn't enough to be satisfied. You might say, well, they had more temptations than the average Joe, but still; as the temptations mounted, where were the bonds of loyalty that might have worked as a barrier? If loyalty is supposed to be the stuff to withstand the blasts of wretched fortune, what can we say of it if it can't hold fast even in times of pleasure and plenty? *Worthless* would be the first word that comes to mind.

And so it might be worth asking: What's with all the loyalty jazz when it comes to love anyway? Wasn't the sexual revolution supposed to free us from all those creaky old hangups regarding adultery? The very word—*adultery*—is mossy and cobwebbed, a relic of retrograde days (or rather, nights) when men thought women were their baby-making chattel. Yet opprobrium still attaches to married people who have sex with those not their spouses. Which is odd, because there is precious little left in the catalogue of sexual no-no's. We seem to have given up long ago on the idea that people should see the preacher before graduating from heavy petting to more intimate adventures. Goodness knows the back seats of Model A Fords saw plenty of action, but they were furtive couplings. Now it is perfectly normal for teens to have co-ed sleepovers. Sex has become such a commonplace activity, one so untethered from traditional notions of love and romance that it's just something you do with a pal when you're bored—as in the modern relationship category "friends with benefits."

Strangely, though sex has been decoupled from most of the moral niceties, cheating not only remains taboo, it has become more so.[1] "Despite increased permissiveness in attitudes in the United States toward *pre*marital sex," writes social psychologist Linda Rouse, "*extra*marital sex is clearly disapproved of by the majority, even among college students."[2] (I like that last observation, for if a sexual activity draws the opprobrium of that most libertine of demographics, *college students*, it has to be an outrage.)

Promiscuity no longer puts a ding in anyone's reputation. But add the injured wife to the equation and the randy man-about-town is transformed from a bold seeker of pleasure to a grubby, grabby cad. Had Tiger Woods not been married, his priapic adventures would have caused hardly a blush, would have presented no threat to his lucrative endorsements. Wilt Chamberlain boasted of bedding twenty thousand in his day, a claim that was seen as gross, perhaps even pathetic, tawdry but not cause for condemnation. Indeed, Chamberlain was confident that his moral compass was well calibrated: He didn't date married women. "I made a conscious effort to find out" if a woman had a husband, Chamberlain insisted. "Even as a single man, infidelity has no place in my life."[3] You could take that as a savvy survival strategy (out of twenty thousand outraged husbands, chances are more than a few would be good shots); or one could make the case that Wilt had a perceptive understanding of where the modern line of sexual respectability had been drawn.

It's a remarkable paradox—and one that would have perplexed modern moralists such as Bertrand Russell, who argued that an "attraction to one person" could easily "co-exist with a serious affection for another." He thought that the traditional disapproval of adultery was one of the more pernicious expressions of "conventional morals."[4] And yet here we are, the better part of a century later, liberated from such conventions to an extent that Russell would have been hard-pressed to imagine, and the old prejudice against adultery persists. If anything, it's become more doctrinaire and inflexible, a rebuke of the otherwise confident conceit that anything goes. In the nearly fifty years since the sixties swept the old order away, "the attitudes against adultery have gotten firmer," says David Popenoe, who founded the National Marriage Project at Rutgers University. Some 90 percent of Americans denounce infidelity as immoral.[5] I doubt you could build a consensus that robust in opposition to bestiality or necrophilia (or bestial necrophilia, for that matter).

What gives? If sex is no big deal, why all the gnashing of teeth and rending of garments over infidelity?

One possibility is that women, freed from patriarchal hypocrisies, no longer have to make excuses for wayward spouses and can finally express their anger and contempt for philandering. And though there may indeed be something to the notion that uncensored women's voices will naturally rail against horn-dog husbands, it doesn't come close to explaining the extraordinary modern consensus against stepping out. After all, a dominant trend in feminism over the last decade has been to celebrate women who embrace the sort of predatory attitude toward sexuality that, previously, had been associated with men. You would think that the *Sex and the City* feminists would be inclined to shrug off infidelity as a natural part of the pursuit of pleasure. And yet even women in the pleasure business express a yearning for exclusivity. Can there be any more odd example than the complaint by porn actress Joslyn James that Tiger Woods lied to her by not telling her he had other mistresses? "If I would have known everything that was going on," she said, "I would have done things differently."

If anything, the feminist project should have made male infidelity less of a threat to women, reducing as it did the masculine monopoly on wealth and power. Nineteenth-century philosopher Arthur Schopenhauer had imagined that withholding coitus was the only leverage the weaker sex had to acquire the worldly goods that men otherwise controlled. His was what you might call a "tender trap" theory of romance ethics: "All illicit intercourse is absolutely denied to the male so that every man is forced into marriage as into a kind of capitulation, and the whole female sex is provided for," Schopenhauer wrote. "Every girl who [engages in] illicit intercourse has betrayed the whole female sex."[6] Now that women are free to earn their own living, one would think that "illicit intercourse" would be less of a threat.

Perhaps adultery remains an affront because we are hardwired to demand exclusivity. As evolutionary psychologists Cindy Meston and David Buss argue, the children of women who lack committed mates don't fare as well as those with a providing father. Over the millennia, women who have chosen loyal partners have been more likely to have surviving descendants, and so the feminine preference for faithful, honest husbands came to be established in the gene pool. Darwinian theory also explains why men expect to have an exclusive contract on servicing their spouses: "Men in the past who were indifferent to their partners' having sex with other men are not our evolutionary ancestors."[7]

Or perhaps it's just a matter of avoiding problems related to sexual activity, most obviously disease. Where dread STDs are prevalent, spouses with wandering partners find themselves contracting infections that can cripple, render them sterile, even kill. Encouraging men to be faithful to their wives has been one of the strategies for AIDS prevention in Africa. In the United States, it's not uncommon these days for a wife who finds out her husband has been sleeping around to take battery of tests for venereal diseases—especially repeated blood tests for HIV.

The anxiety is understandable, and there's no arguing with such medical caution. And yet, by contrast, the unmarried indulging in casual couplings don't generally seem to be quite so worried about what they might catch from wading in the community Petri dish. Is it that the unattached underestimate their risks, or is it that sinned-against spouses seize on the microbial dangers as a justification for outrage? This much is sure: Take any possibility of disease out of the equation, and you still have tears and recriminations. The husband who says, "But honey, I had her get tested before I slept with her," isn't likely to get any credit.

No, the anger and pain people feel when a spouse strays isn't just a matter of practicalities—not just concern over chlamydia or worry that the family's wages might be garnished to pay love-child support. It is more fundamental, more visceral, "a devastating, destabilizing ordeal," as one recent sex therapy textbook put it: "the betrayed partner can experience PTSD [post-traumatic stress disorder] symptoms related to the trauma of the infidelity," including "emotions such as anxiety, lability, numbness, depression, aggression, jealousy, and loss of self-esteem."[8]

A less clinical description of this phenomenon can be found in John O'Hara's novel *Appointment in Samarra:* "I guess I've gone to pieces, because there's nothing left of me," says Caroline English, deep in the bewilderment of betrayal. Her husband, Julian, in a fit of drunken petulance, left her sitting in a nightclub as he took the club's floozy singer for a boozy romp in a car parked outside. The next morning, flustered and despairing, Caroline can't get herself out of bed. Julian has already left for the day, and so she practices telling him off, detailing the damage: "What you did," she tells her absent, errant husband, "what you did was take a knife and cut me open from my throat down to here, and then you opened the door and let in a blast of freezing cold air, right where you had cut me open."[9]

IN THE INCUBATORS of our modern notions of love and romance— the late-medieval courts of France and England—our current near-universal disdain for adultery would have seemed odd, and at odds with the true nature of love.

Roman poet Ovid was the reigning scholar of Venus. His instructions were treated as gospel in matters of the heart.[10] Ovid's racy book *The Art of Love* may have gotten him in trouble with Emperor Augustus in his own day, but centuries later it would make him a hero to the love-besotted courtly romantics who made him their "archpriest of transgression."[11]

The prime transgression, and one that Ovid had heartily recommended, was adultery (in no small part because he thought marriage and romance were incompatible).[12] And so for the courtly lovers Ovid inspired, adultery was the order of the day, an attitude helped along by killjoy ecclesiastical views of marriage. The medieval church denounced as adulterous all passionate desire—even for one's own wife.[13]

"Love cannot extend its rights over two married persons," was the received poetic wisdom of twelfth-century France, as captured contemporaneously by Andreas Capellanus. "Lovers grant one another all things mutually and freely, without being impelled by any motive of necessity, whereas husband and wife are held by their duty to submit their wills to each other and to refuse each other nothing."[14] For these courtly *philosophes de l'amour*, not only is marital fidelity unnecessary for love, it is an impediment.

Ah, but what a delicious impediment! Holding up adultery as the end-all, be-all of romance had a certain advantage. The problem with pursuing passionate desire is that satisfaction tends to blunt the heightened sense of excitement, deflating the lovers' imperative yearnings. Desire fulfilled is passion undone. But that great medieval bestseller, *The Romance of Tristan and Iseult*, offered a remedy: To maintain a constant, fever-pitched ardor, one's desire must remain endlessly, achingly unfulfilled. And that meant finding barriers to keep the eager lovers frustrated and apart. In the case of Tristan and Iseult, the primary impediment to their love is the inconvenient fact that Iseult is married to Tristan's uncle and liege. As Denis de Rougemont explains in *Love in the Western World*, the Tristan and Iseult myth promised that desire forever frustrated and thwarted would make for transcendent love, a "mystic passion to be *without end*."[15] Think of it like greyhound racing: For the sport to go on, the dogs must never actually catch the zooming robot rabbit. (Perhaps one reason romance is so flaccid in our day and age is that the mechanical rabbit doesn't move too fast—it rarely sprints past the third date, according to reports of modern convention.)[16]

For those medieval romantics who preferred their barriers concrete, there was the story of Pyramus and Thisbe, who enjoyed an honest-to-goodness wall that kept them apart. The stony barricade maintained the would-be lovers' passion at the desired fever pitch. When they finally arrange to meet in the forest—threatening to ruin the intensity of their romance with consummation—the poet has to contrive a catastrophe, a way of keeping them together by keeping them from getting together. Pyramus mistakenly thinks a lion has gobbled Thisbe, and in his inconsolable grief he falls on his sword. Thisbe finds Pyramus bleeding out in a fashion Quentin Tarantino would have admired; she does herself in too. For their love to last they must join each other in death. Theirs was a "chaste and stedfast love," Ovid wrote, and "death hath joyned [them] in one."[17]

This is not a vision of love that thinks very highly of the bonds of loyalty. And yet, interestingly, the goal of this sort of romance—what's presented as the great prize of life—is to find a steadfast and enduring love. It's just that there is so little faith in people's ability to maintain their devotion that the poets have to kill off the lovers before their affections have a chance to cool or fade. In the grand love stories, things almost never work out well. Perhaps it's the currency of drama. Which is more compelling, after all, the anodyne proposition "happily ever after," or the devotion demonstrated when doomed lovers die in each others' arms? Not only does the latter make for a more theatrical finale, it says something about how we regard love. Just try to imagine Romeo and Juliet retaining their status as romantic icons if they hadn't made such a muddle of the phony-death-potion business. Ponder the couple after a decade of wedded bliss: Romeo, taking out the garbage while he'd rather be watching SportsCenter; Juliet enduring her too-small kitchen, yelling for Romeo Jr. to set the table.

Denis de Rougemont calls this core problem "the passion-fidelity dilemma." It's a long-standing struggle, and we still haven't been able to decide whether passion and fidelity are compatible. We want love that lasts, but we also want passionate intensity, and we suspect that we will at some point have to choose which love is worth having, the epic but brief romance, or the companionship that goes the distance. Many facing this choice look at passion like ripe peaches—short-lived, but much to be preferred over fruit canned in cloying syrup. Love isn't shelf-stable. Where does that leave loyalty?

When Franz is wooing Sabina in Milan Kundera's *The Unbearable Lightness of Being*, he is confident that the constancy of his love will be the stuff that gets the girl. "Fidelity deserved pride of place among the virtues: fidelity gave a unity to lives that would otherwise splinter into thousands of split-second impressions," Kundera writes. And so Franz "assumed that Sabina would be charmed by his ability to be faithful, that it would win her over." Alas, Sabina was too romantic for anything quite so staid. She "was charmed more by betrayal than by fidelity." Forget that we are told from childhood that betrayal is heinous, it is also liberating—cast off your bonds and you're free to reinvent your life: "Betrayal means breaking ranks and going off into the unknown." And for Sabina this means that sleeping with another woman's husband is a much sexier possibility than chaining herself to someone solid.[18]

Eustacia Vye is very much of the Sabina school, which says love is a force that can't bear to be tied down, and that loyalty—a force that's in the tying-down business—is at odds with the experience of real passion. The (anti)heroine of Thomas Hardy's *The Return of the Native*, Vye is marked by a "celestial imperiousness, love, wrath, and fervour." You can imagine on what side of the passion/fidelity divide she falls. "Fidelity in love for fidelity's sake had less attraction for her than for most women: fidelity because of love's grip had much," Hardy writes. "A blaze of love, and extinction, was better than a lantern glimmer of the same which should last long years."[19] Vye was willing to be faithful, but not to a person. Her fidelity was to "love's grip," to passion. Her style of loyalty was decidedly in the courtly tradition, in which ever-so-ardent knights and ladies swore their primary romantic allegiance to love itself, as opposed to any particular object of love.

Needless to say, things don't work out too well for Eustacia, but that doesn't make her tale cautionary to those who are moved by the passion principle. It is the very possibility that things won't turn out well that gives them a thrill. The frisson of danger and the excitement of passion are, for them, linked sensations. Take psychotherapist and author Esther Perel. She laments that the domesticity so important to a flourishing family life is at odds with eroticism, because passion demands "unpredictability, spontaneity, and risk." She proclaims, "Eros is a force that doesn't like to be constrained. When it settles into repetition, habit, or rules, it touches its death. It then is transformed into boredom and sometimes, more powerfully, into repulsion."[20]

This breaking of the mind's chains is an image that appeals to moral aesthetes eager to free themselves from the stultifying weight of convention. They are bored by loyal love, which they think makes us little burghers of the heart—trustworthy, yes, but dull and uninspired.

"Those who are faithful know only the trivial side of love: it is the faithless who know love's tragedies."[21] So intones

Lord Henry Wotton in *The Picture of Dorian Gray*. Oscar Wilde doesn't present Lord Henry as a trustworthy guide to life, but one can't help but suspect that in Lord Henry Wilde found a mouthpiece for his own romanticism. (Wilde would admit only that Lord Henry is "what the world thinks me.") But whether Lord Henry is speaking Wilde's mind or not, he makes a compelling case—at least an elegantly insidious one—for the grand-passion principle. He celebrates as superior, aristocratic souls those who are in love with love; he denounces as shallow, insipid, and impoverished those who cling to one love in their lives. "What they call their loyalty, and their fidelity, I call either the lethargy of custom or their lack of imagination," Lord Henry sneers. "Faithfulness is to the emotional life what consistency is to the life of the intellect—simply a confession of failure."[22]

Come the "Me Decade" this aristocratic attitude was democratized. Tom Wolfe described (with no little disdain) the groovy lovers of the era who rejected the life "of a humdrum workadaddy, eternally faithful, except perhaps for a mean little skulking episode here." Instead, they embraced the prerogative of kings "to shuck overripe wives and take on fresh ones."[23] And in doing so they thought they were living large, with big, real emotions, not letting their romantic selves be strangled by crimped and crabbed restrictions.

So which is it? Is loyalty love's friend or its enemy? Does love bind things together or rip them apart? The advocates of passion celebrate Eros' tendency to smash the crockery. Real love, they argue, is unconstrained by stodgy, boring old notions of fidelity; real love proves its primacy by transgressing the petty boundaries of bourgeois morality; real love demonstrates itself by transcending inhibition and propriety. This is a view that aggrandizes the destructive tendencies of love and belittles loyalty as a wet security blanket. It is also a narrow, impoverished view, one with adolescent enthusiasm made possible by an adolescent understanding of what gives life satisfaction and meaning. As alluring as the passion principle may be, mistaking romance for love is one of the most common calamities known to humankind. And, as we'll see, the difference between the two is marked by loyalty.

THERE IS A tradition as old as the earliest Greek philosophers, ascribing to Love the power to hold the world together. For those early cosmologists Love wasn't just a human emotion, it was a force of nature—perhaps *the* force of nature—the counterbalance to chaos, the only thing capable of overcoming the entropic tendencies of the universe. For Empedocles, earth, water, air, and fire were the stuff that make up the world, and "these things never cease from continual shifting, at one time coming together, through Love, into one, at another each borne apart from the others through Strife."[24] A few thousand years later the poet Robert Frost would strike the same chord, describing love as "the one and only one / The element of elements / That all the universe cements."[25]

It's easy to understand how love was seen as a force akin to magnetism, drawing things together. We still describe romantic attraction as magnetic. And yet there's just as strong an argument to be made that love tears things apart. Hesiod describes Eros not only as "fairest among the deathless gods," but one who causes us to come undone. Love, in his telling, "unnerves the limbs, and overcomes the mind and wise counsels of all gods and all men."[26] Or, as eighteenth-century English poet William Blake put it, love is "Lawless, wing'd, and unconfin'd / And breaks all chains from every mind."[27] Wolfram von Eschenbach, writing in medieval Germany, arrived at the same conclusion in his epic poem *Parzival* (the Grail tale that provided the story for Wagner's opera *Parsifal*), describing love (and none too favorably) as the "destroyer of stout defenses."

As Sir Edmund Spenser told it, Cupid destroys more than just stout defenses. In *The Faerie Queene*, the god of love puts on quite a show, parading astride a ravenous lion attended by his helpers, Danger, Fear, Grief, Fury, and Cruelty. Shuffling along behind, like the routed captives in some Roman triumph, are Strife and Anger, Poverty and Infirmity. Inconstancy and Disloyalty are there too, in the shame-faced train of love's maladies, the last of which is "Death with infamie."[28] It's a shocking portrayal: We think of Cupid with his toy archery rig as cute and quaint. But we have to remember that when that imagery was formed, the bow and arrow were the state of the art in military hardware. Apollo, at one point, makes the mistake of chiding Cupid for playing with warriors'

weapons (and finds out it's a bad idea to tease such a dangerous pixie). So forget the dainty darts of love: To arm Cupid in
an equivalent modern context, we'd have to imagine the little
terrorist of the heart blasting away with an AK-47 or an RPG.

Come the late fourteenth century, the courtly romantics who
had embraced adultery with such ardent fervor were starting
to have second thoughts, an ambivalence expressed through
the fashion for poetic debates on the subject of love. *Les Cent
Ballades*, by Jean de Saint-Pierre, asked what made for the
best, most joyful love. And to test the case the poem presents
a debate between a great knight, Hutin de Vermeilles (who
makes the argument for loyalty) and a frisky young woman
called La Guignard (who makes the case for falsity). Hutin
claims that love is about more than just the "delectation of
the body" and that a man schooled in faithful love will be
one who can be relied upon in battle: Habits of fidelity applied across the board. La Guignard counters that loyalty is
for dullards, and promiscuity is for those who want to get the
most enjoyment out of life. In a sort of medieval version of a
blog with comments, the young guns of the French court set
about penning poetry of their own, detailing who they thought
had won the Hutin-Guignard debate, and why. Most embraced
loyalty (though there were a few cynics who thought the best
policy was to talk a good game of fidelity, all the better to
enjoy the fruits of falsity—and no doubt it pays for players
to praise loyalty, as it's hard to get very far with an ethic of
falsity if no one believes your oaths in the first place).

The debate continued among the poets of the era: Is love a passing fancy or a durable good? And the fashion became to pose the question in florid terms, with poets essaying whether the correct symbol of love is the short-lived flower or the long-lived leaf. This trendy question got going in earnest with a quartet of poems by Eustache Deschamps, a French contemporary of Chaucer, debating the comparative virtues of flowers and leaves. It wasn't hard to make a case for daisies and the like—flowers are beautiful and fragrant and they suggest, in the pleasure they give, passion and intimacy. But they are also quick to fade away and die. How odd, in a way, that we are in the habit of celebrating love with such perishable tokens. Do we mean to declare that our affections are as fleeting as roses, to be gathered while ye may? Or could we use a metaphor *d'amour* that suggests rather more staying power, something that eschews flash and show—perhaps, instead of the flower, some evergreen foliage? One of the four Deschamps poems made the case for the leaf as a symbol of perseverance and enduring love, but in the others he is a petal pusher, championing the flirty delights of the daisy.

But it wasn't the final word. The greatest elaboration of this debate can be seen in John Dryden's rendering of a fifteenth-century poem. Dryden's "The Flower and the Leaf" tells of two fairy courts that gambol in a verdant field on May Day. One group of ladies and knights wears garlands of flowers; and they pay homage to the bright new daisies. The other group has woodbine on their brows, crowns of leaves and chaplets of oak. Gathered in the shade and shelter of a spreading laurel, the leafy crowd "found retreat" and "shunn'd the scorching heat." But the followers of Flora soon find themselves wilting in the noonday sun. When a sudden storm appears, they're blasted by the rain and hail. The flower, and the sort of love it represents, is "A short-lived good, and an uncertain grace," Dryden writes. "This way and that the feeble stem is driven / Weak to sustain the storms and injuries of heaven." And what of the laurel-like love? "From winter winds it suffers no decay / For ever fresh and fair, and every month is May."

Our more modern poets have kept the debate alive. Cole Porter asked whether real love was made out of marble or out of clay, "a new Rolls [or just] a used Chevrolet." We still haven't decided what we think love is all about. We have our modern champions of the Order of the Flower. Arguably, when South Carolina governor Mark Sanford went "hiking the Appalachian Trail"—the fanciful cover story he contrived to camouflage his Buenos Aires getaway, where he met up with his Argentine mistress—he was embracing flower power. But the popular prejudice is for love that lasts. And, notwithstanding the odds, the popular prejudice is on the mark. Social psychologists Garth Fletcher and Jeffry Simpson have found that those who placed an emphasis on finding mates who exhibit loyalty "were involved in more satisfying and longer-term relationships" than those who chose their partners on the basis of "passion" or "resources," that is, good looks or money.[29]

For his part, Dryden was not immune to the tender charms of those flowery things "for pleasure made / [that] Shoot up with swift increase, and sudden are decay'd." But when asked "Whether the Leaf or Flower I would obey?" he says, "I chose the Leaf." Good for him. Wolfram made a similar choice, denouncing Cupid and his darts, dodging Lord Amor's spear, and steering clear of the searing torch of Venus. "The pangs you inflict are unknown to me," he wrote. "If I am to say I know true love, it can come to me only through fidelity."[30]

If WE BELIEVE, at some level, that faithful love is true love (and, after all, *true* is a word we use as a synonym for *faithful*), that might help explain why we get so bent out of shape about infidelity. But it doesn't explain why we've become less tolerant of fooling around than we were back when sexual ethics were a comparatively prim business. Maybe it is a matter not of virtue, but of vice—of jealousy. As the menagerie of sexual gremlins has been let loose, would it be a surprise if the green-eyed monster took the opportunity to do his worst? Goodness knows jealousy can be destructive. Edmund Spenser lamented the "more than hellish pain" caused by "gnawing envy," and the insidious worry about whether one is "lov'd alone." Jealousy is a "canker worm," he wrote, "which eats the heart and feeds upon the gall, turning all love's delight to misery."[31]

Jealousy is so devastating, writes English philosopher Roger Scruton—"one of the greatest of psychical catastrophes"—that it's best "we form the habit of fidelity," so that it can be avoided altogether.[32] And when jealousy isn't a psychical catastrophe, it just makes us plain ridiculous. Who gets played for bigger laughs on the stage than the farcical husbands with horns? The jealous man is played as a fool, in part, because excessive self-regard is foolish. François, duc de La Rochefoucauld, wrote, "Jealousy contains more of self-love than of love."[33]

For an extreme example of the reverberating damage done by betrayal, consider *The Thousand and One Nights*. King Shahryar comes home abruptly from a royal business trip to find his new bride canoodling with the palace staff. He has them all executed, but even this act of cathartic vengeance doesn't help Shahryar recover from this betrayal. He marries again and again, but has every bride killed (promptly in the morning after each wedding night). This way he ensures that he is not betrayed again. It is not until the last marriageable female in the kingdom—the clever Scheherazade—engages him in her wonderful serial storytelling that his bloodlust is blunted and he regains the capacity for trust, and thus for love.

Shahryar's jealousy—rooted in betrayal—led him to kill brides who never so much as hinted at infidelity (and how could they in their few hours of married life before the morning axe would fall?). This is jealousy at its worst, cropping up even when lovers are faithful, and it is such false suspicions that are to be avoided at all costs. "Jealousy sees things always with magnifying glasses which make little things large," Cervantes wrote: "of dwarfs giants, of suspicions truths." Othello's tragedy is that he gets his facts wrong about who is doing the betraying. Desdemona is not untrue to her vows, it is Iago, who pledges his fidelity to his captain as he plots his lord's demise.

Still, why do we get so riled by infidelity? Why, like Othello, would we "rather be a toad / And live upon the vapour of a dungeon" than have our lovers share themselves with someone else? Perhaps it is because adultery is a declaration that the relationship may at any moment be nullified. And uncertainty is a beast of a burden to bear.

That's the anxiety Frank Sinatra tapped into with his signature saloon song, "One for My Baby (and One More for the Road)." Sitting on a stool in front of the Count Basie Orchestra on the stage of the Sands hotel in Vegas, Frank would tell the audience he had a story for them about "a fella with problems," problems of a romantic variety. It wasn't a matter of unrequited love, or lost love, or aching passion, but of unfaithful love. "His broad flew the coop," Sinatra explained, "with another guy and all the bread." A lover who fools around is a lover who will leave you—and leave you stranded, or worse.

"A well-assorted marriage" is an ideal sort of friendship according to the pragmatic philosopher George Santayana, one in which, for all their differences, a "man and wife are bound together by a common dwelling, common friends, common affection for children, and what is of great importance, common financial interests. These bonds often suffice for substantial and lasting unanimity." Santayana said such calm and reasonable arrangements "may give a fair promise of happiness," and he might just be on to something—especially when it comes to the "common financial interests" part of his equation. After all, the cooperative endeavor is made so much easier by the shared bank account, but not if you have to worry that your partner might empty that account out.

Nor can you sleep easy if you think the person in bed with you might be interested in your demise. But that can be where infidelity leads. Think of John Edwards skulking about to meet his nutty New Age squeeze, Rielle Hunter, while his wife, Elizabeth, was struggling with the news that her breast cancer had spread into her bones. Just when she needed her husband to help her deal with the grim impertinence of death, Edwards was mooning over his pregnant mistress, and fantasizing about his wife's exit from the scene. Ah, the lavish wedding he and Hunter would have. A swanky rooftop in Manhattan overlooking the glittering city; the Dave Matthews Band playing *their* song; and all just as soon as old Elizabeth died. Who wants to share a bed with someone who wishes you were dead?

At its core, love is not about passion or desire so much as it is about trusting your life and your future to someone else. It is trust that binds us to the ones we love; without those bonds of loyalty the everyday furies of life fling us apart. And nothing breaks a relationship apart with quite so much crowbar leverage as a new lover looking to wedge his or her way in. An affair involves a third party who can't be expected to have the best interests of the preexisting relationship at heart, in no small part because the interloper will soon want things other than just sex, things even less consistent with the survival of the marriage. One may fantasize about finding a mistress who will make no emotional demands, have no expectations of commitment, but that isn't the way such things usually work. As John Updike put it, "The first breath of adultery is the freest; after it, constraints aping marriage develop."[34] Love— even just sex—has its own way of demanding a commitment beyond the immediate.

Perhaps it wouldn't be such a problem if the commitment to the marriage were guaranteed to trump any demands the newcomer might make. In arguing his case for the occasional extramarital romp, Bertrand Russell blamed the uptight American insistence on sexual fidelity on the weakness of "family feeling" in the States, "and the frequency of divorce." By contrast, in France "the family is strong, and parents very dutiful, in spite of an exceptional freedom in the matter of adultery."[35] He may well have been right—or at least his theory would help explain why attitudes against adultery have stiffened over the years. What with no-fault divorce, it's easier than ever to walk away from a marriage, especially if infidelity gives you a shove.

Even in mid-century France, Russell's supposed Disneyland of adultery, infidelity would break up marriages, in which cases public opinion was not with the illicit lovers. In Reims in November 1952 a packed courthouse heard the lurid details of how pistol-wielding Yvonne Chevallier placed five slugs in her wayward husband, Pierre. Monsieur Chevallier was a rising young politician who had just been named to the French cabinet, and in best French fashion—or perhaps even more so, in best politician fashion—he had a mistress. The husband came home one morning to get some fresh underwear, and his long-suffering, neglected wife might have just continued to look the other way. But perhaps feeling full of himself and his new stature, Pierre chose that moment to tell the unhappy Yvonne that he was leaving her to marry his fiery redheaded mistress. As Madame Chevallier would later tell the jury, her husband sneered that she should "go back to the barnyards" where she came from. Instead, she produced a gun and made herself a widow.

The jury acquitted her, and the courtroom burst into cheers.[36]

I suspect that the jurors, who might have been expected to give M. Chevallier's little fling a Gallic shrug, championed the avenging wife because the husband had broken the deal. He hadn't just slept around on his spouse, he was abandoning her. Our own growing intolerance for infidelity shares in that jury's sentiment. Now that marriages are rather more easily dissolved, infidelity isn't just an affront to a relationship, it is an existential threat. Since marriages are more easily ended than ever before, we are more wary than ever before of sexual infidelity, wary of the telltale sign a marriage will soon be over.

Maybe jealousy isn't such a vice after all. Perhaps it's a good thing that we aren't blasé about affairs, because it suggests we haven't fully divorced sex from love yet. For all its unattractiveness, we can't say that jealousy is illegitimate. After all, the God of the Old Testament is a jealous God. Or as more modern translations of the scripture read, "For I the Lord your God am an impassioned God," a variation made possible because the Hebrew word for passion and jealousy, *qanná*, is one and the same.[37] To be zealous in one's love entails being jealous. If you weren't distraught at the infidelity of a lover, you'd have to ask whether you were in love at all.

FOR ALL THE angst over infidelity, it would be a mistake to think of sex as the only realm in which lovers or spouses might betray one another. The traditional Christian marriage vows are instructive because they are rooted in an understanding of just how tricky forming a new union is. Create a new bond, especially one as all-encompassing as marriage, and it's almost guaranteed to run afoul of preexisting connections and commitments. How common is it for an old pal to feel that his newly married friend doesn't put the same effort in their friendship he once did? Even more troublesome, form a new family and it complicates the family ties you already had. Once you're married you can't have the same relationship with your parents that you had before. The mama's boy who always sides with her against his wife; the unhappy bride ever running home to Mother: These are stock comic characters for a reason. For starters, they are all too common types, and so jokes at their expense ring true. But perhaps more important, they illustrate a core problem with getting a marriage under way—the challenge of reordering the loyalties that have governed one's young lifetime.

It's a standard-issue conflict that marriage counselors have to confront: "Sometimes, spouses refuse to give their loyalty to their partners because they prefer to be loyal to the family of origin," write psychologists Terry Hargrave and Franz Pfitzer. They argue that giving in to parental demands for loyalty at the expense of one's spouse is particularly destructive of a marriage.[38] Not that it took modern psychotherapy to recognize the conflict: The standard church wedding script (rooted in Jesus' confrontation with the Pharisees over the nature of marriage) tackles head-on the question of where one's intergenerational loyalties belong, and proclaims that divided loyalties are no way to get a marriage started. A man will "leave his father and mother, and cleave* to his wife," Jesus says, "so then they are no more twain, but one flesh."[39] In the same Gospel chapter, Jesus restates the Old Testament commandment that one "Honor thy father and mother," but he does so only after explicitly limiting what honor demands of the married son or daughter. When Jesus declares, "What therefore God hath joined together, let not man put asunder," this antisundering injunction is meant to apply not only to home-wrecking hussies but also to pushy mothers-in-law.

Cleave is a tricky English word because it has two diametrically opposed meanings. The verb that gives the kitchen cleaver its name means to split or divide (not exactly what the old vows had in mind), whereas the archaic verb being used here means to stick together loyally and unwaveringly. There is no such confusion in the original New Testament Greek word, *proskollaomai*, which means to bind inseparably or to be joined through devotion. (Horst Balz, *Exegetical Dictionary of the New Testament*, vol. 3, p. 172.)

Then again, I suspect that these days the tug of apron strings may not be as much of a problem for newlyweds as they once were. In our highly mobile age, parents exercise somewhat less influence over their far-flung adult children than when young couples set up house down the street from their folks. If there is a clash of loyalties likely to cause heartburn among married moderns, it is the question of what happens to love when those great, insatiable competitors for affection—babies—get in the game.

One might say that this is a source of conflict as old as Oedipus, but that wouldn't be to look back nearly far enough in the mythic mists of the past. The most ancient of ancient Greeks pegged most of the rather dramatic unpleasantness that afflicted the gods to the threat that children posed to the primacy of their parents (and their parents' relationships with each other). Uranus (the sky) and Gaia (the earth) started filling out the world with young gods, and in the process conceived some rather bizarre bundles of joy, frightful creatures with too many arms or too few eyes. Uranus locked the monstrosities away. Gaia, doting mother that she was, wanted them set free and so she encouraged the most capable—and ruthless—of her brood to give her husband what for. She fashioned a sickle and handed it to her young son Cronos, who promptly castrated his father and usurped his celestial throne. All too intimately aware of the threat ambitious children can pose to their papas, Cronos set about devouring every one of his own issue, a strategy that worked until his sister/wife (it's hard to avoid incest at the dawn of time) hid one son away. That child, Zeus, would end up doing for his father what Cronos did for his. It's a measure of just how fundamental a threat children can seem to lovers' bonds that the Greek creation myth is built around successive generations of men violently, horrifically undone when their wives conspired with their sons.

In a modern context, children are seen as a different sort of threat to their parents' union—they "make the erotic connection more difficult to sustain," according to passion advocate Esther Perel. "Children are a blessing, a delight, a wonder. They're also a minor cataclysm," she writes in her book *Mating in Captivity*: "romance gets blasted by the realities of family life."[40]

Children may compete for love and affection, putting a strain on the bonds of love and affection that married couples have for each other. But it seems that most people think that's the way it should be. Why else would novelist Ayelet Waldman have achieved something approaching infamy for her 2005 *New York Times Magazine* article "Truly, Madly, Guiltily"? In it, she admitted that, unlike other young mothers, she was "incapable of placing her children at the center of her passionate universe." She begins by noting that the wives she knows who have young children aren't having any sex because the libido has given way to "all-consuming maternal desire." The commitment they have to their husbands has been tempered, if not displaced, by a new commitment to their children. As Waldman says of such a wife and mother, "Where once her husband was the center of her passionate universe, there is now a new sun in whose orbit she revolves."

Waldman, by contrast, wasn't about to let the kids cool the heat of her marriage to novelist Michael Chabon. She declared that the only infatuated devotion she had was for him. "If a good mother is one who loves her child more than anyone else in the world, I am not a good mother," Waldman wrote. "I am in fact a bad mother. I love my husband more than I love my children."

That statement caused a sensation—and got Waldman booed by the audience on *Oprah* (the closest thing we come to a choric condemnation in our modern media age). But at least credit Waldman for highlighting the potential for conflict when one has more than one object of loyal love. Much of the antagonism she provoked, I suspect, was because she had broached a topic so fraught that most of us would rather pretend that it doesn't exist. But no small part of the angry reaction came from *how* she chose to resolve the perceived conflict of loyalty. To illustrate her choice she indulges in a game of God Forbid. That is, she imagines if, God forbid, one or more of her children were to die, and then wonders how she would react: "If I were to lose one of my children, God forbid, even if I lost all my children, God forbid, I would still have him, my husband." The death of her husband, by contrast, she can't even imagine.

How might that ordering of affections and priorities play out in the real world of awful possibilities? Playing our own game of God Forbid, let's imagine Chabon is driving the kids one day, loses control of the car, and plunges into a river. All of this happens in front of Waldman, who has but seconds to decide whom to rescue from the sinking station wagon. If she chose Chabon mightn't the children be justified in granting Mom the "bad mother" title she embraces so facetiously? Don't imagine that such scenarios are contrived: In November 2009 a New Zealand man, standing in disbelief and horror on the shore of the Wanganui River, was confronted with that exact choice. He saved his wife; his teenage son drowned. The public reaction was illuminating of our attitudes—people were generally aghast that he chose as he did. Never mind that he tried, and failed, to free his submerged son before abandoning that effort in order to save his wife; there was a sense that his agonized choice wasn't just wrong but shameful.

Such, as we've seen, are the horrible jams that multiple loyalties can create for us. We're taught to look for win-win solutions to the dilemmas we face, but the grim reality of a world in which loyalty matters is that we may find ourselves in situations that are irrevocably lose-lose. Lucky is the parent who is never forced to make a Sophie's choice. In the case of the sinking car, I think that for most of us, saving a child would be the best of the horrible options. Such a choice—unlike the betrayal of infidelity—is consistent with commitment to the shared life of the marriage. The children, after all, are a joint endeavor. And only the most base of parents would choose to be the one saved. Save the child, and you are furthering the heartfelt final wish of your spouse.

Tricky enough are the everyday questions of how to manage conflicts between love for children and love for one's husband or wife. Recall the scene in *The Jazz Singer*, when little

Jakie Rabinowitz's father drags him home for a whupping. The boy has been shuffling and warbling on the stage of some juke joint, defiling, as his father sees it, the voice God gave him. As Cantor Rabinowitz takes off his belt, his wife pleads with him not to beat her son. Such family conflicts are hardly unique to the screen. Unlike the case of the sinking station wagon, the right answer (short of condoning the parental lash) is not to let husband and wife be divided and conquered. Most people in successful marriages seem to realize that sticking with one's spouse in a unified front is the only hope they have of keeping the rascals from taking over.

Still, for all the havoc children are capable of causing in their parents' loyalties, for the most part, they actually end up reinforcing those bonds. For all the stresses they cause, kids embody (quite literally) their parents' union and can help strengthen their commitment. Not that the presence of children is always—or even usually—enough to keep couples together, as the prevalence of lawyers specializing in custody arrangements will attest.

LOYALTY MAY BE key to keeping a marriage together, but what does loyalty in love demand of us? Is it just a simple matter of abjuring the temptation to stray? Perhaps that, plus an obligation to support and comfort a struggling or ill spouse—the in-sickness-and-in-health part of the vow isn't there for nothing. Or do we think that the bonds of love and marriage ought to be so strong that they will survive whatever is dished out, not just by fickle fortune, but even by one's beloved? Recall, in *Appointment in Samarra*, the miserable state in which Julian English leaves his poor wife. By the time he does finally get around to talking with her, he's managed to spend the day making a raging wreck of their lives by getting into drunken scuffles all over town. He won't tell her exactly what he's done (among other shameful things, he's beaten up a one-armed war hero), but desperate for some proof that he hasn't lost her, he demands she demonstrate her loyalty to him by taking his side in everything, regardless of his actions:

"This is a pretty good time for you to stick by me," Julian says.

"I can't stick by you if you don't tell me what for."

"Blind, without knowing, you could stick by me," he sputters. "That's what you'd do if you were a real wife, but, what the hell."[41]

That's certainly one definition of loyalty—a definition particularly appealing to those who've had trouble holding up their end of the romantic bargain. And it's not just the stuff of novels. As Mark Sanford mooned over his Argentine cutie, wallowing in the bittersweet agony of forbidden love, he turned for relationship advice to his trusted friend, confidante, and political ally—his wife. He seemed to think that the loyalty she owed him included accepting, and even facilitating, his connection with the woman he considered his "soul mate." Then again, how surprised could Jenny Sanford have been? When she married the future governor of South Carolina, he insisted on one curious change to the traditional litany of vows. He refused to swear that he would be faithful. If he thought that, by so altering the marriage agreement, he was carving out some officially sanctioned space for extracurricular canoodling, he didn't understand just how fundamental our expectation of fidelity in marriage is. And so he seemed to be surprised that, when he asked his wife for advice on how best to pitch woo to his mistress, she wasn't exactly supportive or understanding.

Graham Greene just might have endorsed Mark Sanford's peculiar view of what loyalty entails. Perhaps not surprising, given his own difficulties with the virtue, Greene seemed to think that the real test of loyalty in a relationship is a willingness to suck it up and accept betrayal. In the short story "May We Borrow Your Husband," a despairing newlywed thinks she would rather die than have her husband fool around (and who can blame her, it being her honeymoon, no less!). Greene's narrator, watching the little drama of seduction unfold, wishes he could set her straight and tell her not to care or despair, because "at the end of what is called 'the sexual life' the only love which has lasted is the love that has accepted everything, every disappointment, every failure and every betrayal." It's worth being a doormat, Greene writes, because it's the only realistic way to keep a couple together and "in the end there is no desire so deep as the simple desire for companionship."

Though there's no doubting that a little company in one's dotage is one of life's great prizes, I doubt that many of us are willing to accept "everything" in order to get it. Disappointments, yes; failures, sure; betrayals, I don't think so.

The point of love is not simply to possess the objects of our affections, but to be loved in return. We give love in no small part to get love, and it's not a very satisfying deal to give love and, in return, get a painfully honest appraisal of just what one's love was really worth. As novelist Leonard Michaels put it, "Adultery has less to do with romance and sex than with the discovery of how little we mean to each other."[42] Or, to recast his observation in a positive way, it is through fidelity that we demonstrate how much someone matters to us.

Even if you're willing to be belittled in exchange for some company in old age, chances are that ignoring the indiscretions of a faithless spouse isn't going to get you very far. Sociologists and psychologists have been piling up data showing that the folks engaging in extramarital affairs are generally those who don't expect their relationships to go the distance: Infidelity is "associated with less commitment to a future together."[43] An unfaithful marriage is an unhappy marriage, whether the infidelity begets the misery or vice versa. Either way, marriages so fundamentally fractured are likely, sooner or later, to come apart. Rare is the marital breakup that isn't preceded, and given a good shove, by extracurricular sex.

Take the author and NPR commentator Sandra Tsing Loh. In her 2008 memoir of motherhood, *Mother on Fire: A True Motherf%#$@ Story About Parenting!*, she laments that her "salt of the earth" spouse, Mike, is too even-keeled and practical to give her the steamy loving she craves. You can guess where that was heading. The next summer Ms. Loh began chronicling her divorce in the pages of *The Atlantic*, sharing with all and sundry that, after the thrill of a hot and heavy affair, she decided not to go to all the trouble—the "arduous home- and self-improvement project"—of falling back in love with her boring old spouse. "I would not be able to replace the romantic memory of my fellow transgressor with the more suitable image of my husband," she wrote.

Poor Mike. One would think that having a wife cat around would be enough of an assault on his manhood. But just to twist the blade she has to explain to anyone willing to pick up a magazine that his marriage failed because he couldn't cut it in the passion department. This is another, particularly brutal sort of betrayal that afflicts our confessional age. Ms. Loh is just one of a legion of scribblers eager to divulge the intimate details of their marriages. The hot new genre is the tell-all of sexual disappointment written by women having their Peggy Lee moment: "Is That All There Is?" Male writers are well behind this curve, retaining some vestigial hesitation to expose their wives in print. But give them time. Everyone these days seems to be at somewhat greater liberty to share private matters. Sometimes the indiscretions are small ones: DoubleX.com, a sister site to Slate, asked its contributors for their Christmas wish lists. First up was Rachael Larimore, who proclaimed, "All I want for Christmas is for my hubby to get a vasectomy. And he is!" I'm sure that having the details of his personal plumbing made public just made his day. Still, that's nothing compared to what gets aired in coffee klatches, where, according to writers such as Ms. Loh, the ladies get together to talk about how their husbands haven't touched them in years.

Julie Powell, the author of 2005's *Julie & Julia*, provides one of the most savage examples of the genre. Her 2009 book *Cleaving* is ostensibly about a year apprenticing with a butcher, but in large part is devoted to telling all about how she indulged in "rough and tumble" infidelity. The humiliation she heaps on her cuckolded husband is excruciating; he is spared no embarrassment. By contrast, the man with whom she has a kinky and obsessive affair is identified with only a "D." For him, she is discreet. One might conclude that Ms. Powell has a problem prioritizing her loyalties.

Sexual infidelity aside, how destructive of love is the now-commonplace practice of sharing the intimate details of one's relationships? An unequivocal rebuke to this habit comes from the romance novelist Barbara Taylor Bradford. She endorses loyalty as the stuff that "cements your relationship" and puts it "above all others." But interestingly, as she details the ways in which loyalty bolsters love, she doesn't focus on the question of sexual infidelity, but rather on the everyday acts of trustworthiness that make intimacy possible. *"Be loyal to your partner's secrets,"* she urges. No divulging pillow talk—or pillow behavior, for that matter. "There are no exceptions to this rule, not even your mother or your best friend."[44] It's not exactly the stuff of bodice-ripping passion, but it's probably the truest thing Bradford has ever written about love. Old-fashioned and homely as this notion of protecting secrets may be, I suspect that such basic lapses of loyalty have been responsible for withering more affection than most any other cause.

THOMAS SCHELLING ONCE wrote that murder is "the only crime worth solving in a detective story."[45] His point was that unless the stakes were that high, unless they were a matter of life and death, they didn't matter enough to give us a reason to slog through all the plot, procedure, and evidence. We can say something similar about love. Unless it is about a commitment that at least aspires to be ended only by death, a romance is a trivial thing.

Love that isn't inspired by the possibility of permanence is no sort of love at all. No one dreams of someday "hooking up." We aren't riveted by tales of lovers who are indifferent to the question of whether their relationship will last. The real benchmark of love isn't a matter of counting sighs (orgasmic or otherwise) but taking the measure of devotion. To say that someone is "afraid of commitment" is to say that he isn't, in any significant way, in love at all. When Meg Ryan's character in *When Harry Met Sally* finds out her old boyfriend is going to marry his secretary, she blubbers to Billy Crystal, "All this time I've been saying he didn't want to get married." After another sob and a gasp she gets to the heart of the matter: "The truth is he didn't want to get married to *me*. He didn't love *me*."

Where does that leave the giddy feeling of falling in love? It may be wonderful and exhilarating but, as it is just a feeling, it can never last. Not only can't it last, who would really want it to? "Who could bear to live in that excitement for even five years?" C. S. Lewis asked. "What would become of your work, your appetite, your sleep, your friendships?" Passion may be thrilling, but the idea of being in a constant state of emotional arousal is about as appealing as the prospect of one of those erections, warned about in the Viagra ads, that lasts more than four hours.

Which isn't to say for a second that love should be without passion, for that is the only emotion potent enough to set our shared lives in motion. It may be the quiet, steady sort of love on which "the engine of marriage is run," Lewis writes, but "being in love was the explosion that started it."[46] Or we could use a space-age metaphor. You need a massive booster engine to launch a rocket into space, but once there, a satellite can swoosh around Earth indefinitely, held in orbit by the planet's gravitational pull. In this analogy, passion provides the blastoff, and loyalty is the steady force that keeps us in each other's orbit.

The passionistas seem to think that a sprint is the only exhilarating race. But marathoners famously enjoy an endorphin surge that comes from steady, long-haul running. Is it possible that lasting love doesn't have to mean a dreary slog, but perhaps promises something like the runner's high—a sense of elation and well-being that kicks in when exhaustion seems imminent, when one had almost been ready to quit? And indeed, neuroscientists at UC Santa Barbara have found that about a third of people who have been long married get a rush of pleasure out of seeing their spouses—the same boost of brain chemicals that researchers find in the newly infatuated.

Still, those who think that love means blazing with mad desire are likely to be disappointed with married life. As Denis de Rougemont says of the limits of passion, "To try to base marriage on a form of love which is unstable by definition is really to benefit the State of Nevada."[47] If the hot flame of passion can't help but burn itself out sooner rather than later, why have marriage at all? Because the rewards of loyal, faithful love can't be had any other way. Not only are those rewards remarkable, we don't need anything quite so newfangled as neurobiology or evolutionary psychology to explain them. When Plutarch, the preeminent biographer of the classical world, took up the subject of love he described marriage as the beginning of a friendship that would communicate and impart "great and sacred mysteries." Sex is a lovely part of it, he said, productive not only of children but of a deeper sort of relationship between spouses. The "mutual love and fidelity which daily germinates from this," Plutarch wrote, meant that there was no error in calling "the conjunction of man and woman by the name of friendship." Which is an archaic way of saying there is an intimacy born of trust that is deeper and more satisfying than the hot-and-heavy of romance.

Not that enduring, companionate marriage is without its physical satisfactions: Chasing after passion may not do much to foster fidelity, but committed, faithful relationships leave plenty of room for romance. The sociologists of sex repeatedly find that boring old married couples have more fun in the sack than singles do.[48] Which is a very good thing, because as Plutarch is quick to point out, if the sacred mystery of companionate marriage is to be sustained, the coals can't be allowed to get too cold. He praises the great lawgiver Solon for having decreed that husbands and wives should get busy at least three times a month. This, not for the sake of pleasure per se, "but that, as cities renew their treaties one with another at such a time, so the alliance of matrimony might be renewed by this enjoyment, after the jars which may have arisen in the mean time."[49]

Solon seems to have been not just a statesman and poet but the Dr. Phil of Athens. (And it also seems that make-up sex has been around well over two thousand years.) Solon's advice is solid, practical, and eminently sensible, which is why it isn't likely to speak to the romantically minded. What a shame it would be if the dreamy acolytes of passion—those ardent followers of the Court of the Flower—were to disdain loyalty, to dismiss it as a glum preservative of stale relationships. And so it's worth pointing out that loyalty in love has its poetic champions, odesmiths who find fidelity to be the stuff of rhapsodies.

There is American poet Richard Watson Gilder, who declaimed, "Love is not a summer mood / Nor flying phantom of the brain." These are obviously not empirical observations about the normal course of human frailty, but they are sentiments dear to the balladeers' hearts. Keats wishes to be like the bright North Star, steadfast and unchangeable. And seventeenth-century English poet Abraham Cowley promises his love is as steady as a compass, no more likely to cease than "the needle its dear North forsake." But the best case is made by Shakespeare, in his Sonnet 116:

. . . love is not love
Which alters when it alteration finds,
Or bends with the remover to remove.

O no, it is an ever-fixèd mark,
That looks on tempests and is never shaken;
. . .
Love's not Time's fool, though rosy lips and cheeks
Within his bending sickle's compass come,
Love alters not with his brief hours and weeks,
But bears it out even to the edge of doom . . . [50]

That's loyalty in love. Yes, it may be as rare in the wilds of our hearts as sightings of the ivory-billed woodpecker. But there's no doubt it's sexy stuff. And without it, after all, love is not love.

5

The Thousandth Man

"There is nothing I would not do for those who are really my friends," says Isabella Thorpe in Jane Austen's novel *Northanger Abbey*. "I have no notion of loving people by halves." Hers is an uncompromising view of what loyalty demands in friendship, one that is meant to demonstrate that she—and women in general—are capable of the most solid bonds: "Men think us incapable of real friendship, you know, and I am determined to show them the difference."[1]

Isabella is hardly the paragon of loyalty she pretends. Once she gets engaged to be married, she starts flirting with other potential suitors in the hopes of finding a husband richer than the one she has on deck. She's quite willing to love people by halves—if her devotion to her fiancé is any measure. Austen had a pretty good idea just how difficult it is to love one's friends without any hesitation or scruple—it's a theme that runs through her novels—and I suspect she put this bold statement of what loyal friendship entails in the mouth of a flibbertigibbet on purpose.

Even so, Isabella was expressing what she thought was the correct thing (or at least the thing most flattering to her own vanity) about friendship and its obligations. Were it not for the unsubtle excess of her statement, we would be likely to agree with her. Because what is friendship if it doesn't entail a willingness to go beyond just what is pleasant and beneficial to oneself? That friendship is defined by loyalty—the willful, suffering sort of loyalty—is a constant theme from the ancients to our own day. But what exactly are we, or should we be, willing to suffer for our friends? Inconvenience? Sure. Hardship? If we must. Complicity in crime? Maybe not.

There's an expectation that we should go out of our way for our friends, especially when they're in need. We expect that they will do the same for us. And yet there are no exact terms for this bargain. A friend may expect us to stand by him when he has done something dishonorable or disreputable; we may find his offense a deal-breaker. But friends don't sign prenup-like agreements detailing what is entailed by the relationship; no one establishes explicit understandings, complete with morals clauses, delineating the margins of mutual commitment. It might help to set out the by-laws of a given friendship: *I will stand by you even if you disappoint me by sleeping around on your wife; all bets are off if you sleep around with my wife. I will stand by you if you are accused of embezzlement; all bets are off if you are convincingly convicted of trea-*

son. But try as we might to anticipate the difficult situations that will test our loyalty, the possibilities are beyond listing. And so we hope to rely on our friends' character, on their ability to know the right thing to do by us, whatever the situation. Which is one reason why friendships so often come to grief in difficult circumstances. My sense of the right thing to do by you in a crisis may fall short of what you believe you're owed, and even if I'm confident I'm right, you'll feel betrayed.

Even without disagreement over the proper bounds of obligation in friendship, loyalty is a shaky business. When it comes time for a friend to help a needy friend we aren't all that confident who can be counted on. But we do realize that whether one comes through in a pinch is the measure of friendship that matters. Loyalty may not be sufficient for a real friendship, but it is necessary. Perhaps most frustrating of all, whether we have that necessity is never known until the moment it is needed.

BILLIE HOLIDAY WAS hardly the first to complain that, though money attracts lots of friends, penury is a comparatively lonely business. Is there a language that doesn't have its own maxim to that effect? The English adage, which goes back at least to the seventeenth century, is a neatly cynical distich: "In time of prosperity friends will be plenty / In time of adversity not one amongst twenty." But it is a contemporary of Shakespeare's who puts it with the most bitter bluntness: "Every man will be thy friend / Whilst thou hast wherewith to spend," Richard Barnfield writes. "But if store of crowns be scant, / No man will supply thy want."

Of course, the plentiful friends in times of plenty aren't really friends at all. Ben Franklin is precise in making the distinction, writing, "A false friend and a shadow attend only when the sun shines."

There must have been a lot of false friends in the ancient world, because the theme of relationships tested in trying times and found wanting is standard fare in epigrammatic Greek and Latin. "Prosperity is not a just scale," goes a saying attributed to Plutarch; "adversity is the only balance to weigh friends." Cicero noted that the fickle whims of fortune provide the only reliable test of our friends' reliability, and he quoted the early Roman poet Ennius saying, "In doubtful times the genuine friend is known." Such observations are most often made out of a grim sense of abandonment. Banished from Rome for offending the emperor with his bawdy verse, Ovid ruminated on friendship and ruin. "All are the friends of the fortunate, but let but his fortune desert him, and the throng of friends vanishes instantly away," he lamented: "This I have now learned by sad experience." Ovid gives a metallurgical metaphor for true friendship: "By adversity it is tested, as gold by fire."

For all his sad experience, Ovid does not despair of finding gold in the flames. He was writing to a friend who had passed the test, one who was "the first to console me in my calamity," and who had dissuaded the exiled poet from doing himself in. I imagine it wasn't any particular argument or encouragement by this friend that kept Ovid from laying violent hands on himself. Rather, I suspect that what bucked him up was the mere fact of finding he had a real friend. This is such a restorative revelation that Ovid describes it as the only good to have come from his banishment: "If I had not experienced misfortune perhaps I should never have discovered your loyalty."[2]

It may not matter *what* help friends give us when we are in crisis so long as they are there for us. Take the ordeal of Ting-Yi Oei, an assistant principal in a Virginia school who in 2008 was falsely accused, arrested, and prosecuted on charges of child pornography. He had been given the task by the school's principal of investigating rumors that students were "sexting"—sending nude pictures of one another via cell phone. He quickly tracked down the student in question, a boy who had forwarded to all his friends a photo of a woman in her underwear. The boy admitted sending the picture, and e-mailed a copy to the assistant principal for the file.

There it might have ended, if the boy in question hadn't pulled down a girl's pants in class a few days later. Oei suspended him from school, which outraged the boy's mother. She called the cops, accusing the assistant principal of trafficking in kiddie porn for having collected a copy of that photo her son was forwarding all over. Preposterous as it was, Oei was cuffed, booked, and found his mug shot posted at the *Washington Post* website.

Oei described himself as being "crushed" by the friends who doubted him or kept their distance. But there were others, the friends who "kept me going," he would later write, the ones who "stuck with me, attending hearing after hearing" until a sensible judge dismissed all the charges against him.[3] These friends didn't do anything for him—they didn't go to the judge and plead on his behalf; Oei didn't need them to come up with cash for bail. No, they did nothing more than make it clear they were still his friends, that they believed in his innocence, and that he had not been abandoned. That was enough to save him from despair.

Could this be why we ultimately have friends? Not for casual chitchat, not to bulk up our Facebook listings, not for entertaining dinner parties, but to stand by us when accused of some heinous crime or otherwise brought low by fortune. Lucky are those who never have to find out what the real bonds of friendship are about. They are apt to be disappointed, as was the ancient Greek poet Theognis, who, on the losing end of a revolution, was bitter in his exile: "You will find few men who prove trustworthy comrades in difficult circumstances." Too true. But there are those who are luckier—like Ovid and Oei—who learn in a crisis that there actually are such things as friends, and that the value of such remarkable creatures is far beyond anything previously imagined. "A holy tie," Dryden calls friendship, not just tested in tough times, but "made more sacred by adversity."[4]

Euripides puts the question of whom one can count on at the core of his tragedy *Orestes*. When last we visited Agamemnon, he had just sacrificed his daughter, Iphigenia. Right or wrong—or both—the killing tips over the first of several deadly dominoes. Iphigenia's mother eventually avenges her, killing Agamemnon; in turn, Iphigenia's brother, Orestes, avenges his father by giving his mother what for. On trial for that killing, Orestes pins his hopes on his uncle to pull some strings and get him freed. But Uncle Menelaus takes a powder. And then, just when Orestes is about to despair, who should come to his aid but his pal Pylades, who says, "Your ruin would mean mine too, since friends share everything." The astonished and grateful Orestes declares, "This proves the proverb: 'Have comrades, not just kin!'" For Euripides, the "dearest of men" are those who are "trustworthy amid troubles," and they may well be friends rather than family (and given the dysfunction of Orestes' family, that may not come as much of a surprise). Who needs friends when the going is good, Orestes asks? Pylades not only comes through for him, he seems to relish the opportunity, the dangers be damned. "Where else shall I show myself a friend," Pylades asks, "if I do not defend you in dire misfortune."

When Euripides describes the dearest of men as being "trustworthy," the word he uses is *pistos*. The Greeks had no word for loyalty per se. The word they used to express what we would now think of as "loyalty" was *trustworthiness*. And there is reason to think it is a better word, one that captures more clearly and accurately what is needed in a friend. One might have many companions, and a much smaller circle of friends, but it is only the trustworthy friends who really count—and can be counted on.[5]

Many are the moralists who urge us to be reliable, to be the friends who can be counted on. "In adversity, do not shun those you sought in prosperity," writes the Latin poet Lucan.[6] Greek philosopher Epicurus, one of the ancient world's more staunch advocates for loyalty, said that calamities were the time to "face up to fortune" and prove one's worth, for the wise man "will not abandon a friend."

But even in those olden days, there wasn't much confidence in the reliability of friends. The Orestes-Pylades bond made for such riveting stagecraft, not because it was an accurate representation of everyday life, but because it was a dramatic expression of a rarefied goal. Playwrights have reworked Euripides' tale for centuries, including Roman poet Marcus Pacuvius, who set up the story with a payoff like that in the movie *Spartacus*, when man after man stands to say, "*I* am Spartacus." In the Pacuvius play, Orestes and Pylades have been brought before a king, who passes a sentence of death on Orestes but who doesn't know which of the two men actually is Orestes. Pylades steps forward and declares, "I am Orestes." Then Orestes does the same, and then back and forth again. "What shouts recently rang through the entire theater," Cicero wrote, describing the play's denouement. "The people in the audience rose to their feet and cheered this incident in fiction." But then Cicero asks, "What, think we, would they have done had it occurred in real life?" He doubts any of us would actually be able to live up to such an ideal no matter how loudly we cheer it. The audience "approved in another as well done that which they could not do themselves."[7]

Rare is the friendship that is put to such an ultimate test. For most of us, being a trustworthy friend involves smaller stuff. But big or small, the key is reciprocity. The Greek who helped a friend did so confident—or at least expecting—that he would be helped in turn.[8] Of all the things that go into friendship—pleasure in each other's company, shared interests, admiration of the other's character, like-mindedness—reciprocity is essential, now no less than in the ancient world. And reciprocity counts even in simple, straightforward matters such as gifts. A journalist friend of mine is pals with a very rich man who likes to go to Vegas (where he nibbles away at the edges of his wealth). Back from a trip to Sin City, my friend was waiting with his son for a bus and regaled him with how the rich man had lost $200,000 on one hand of poker. "But Dad, that's like four BMWs. Why doesn't he just give you a car?"

"If I were as rich as he is, he might give me a car, and of course I might give him one too. But the rich don't give expensive presents to those who aren't rich." It's hard enough to maintain a close relationship across a chasm of wealth (as Renaissance poet Petrarch put it, "Disparity of fortune is the bane of friendship") but it's pretty close to impossible if the rich half of the equation gets in the habit of giving gifts that cannot be matched. Reciprocity in gift-giving is one of the habits that builds trust between friends. It shows that neither half of a friendship is there to pile up goodies.

We may not be so far removed from the ancient world, in which the basic currency of friendship was the favor. Ours is an age of promiscuous friendships. Where once a few close friends were the difference between a flourishing life and a barren one, we now embrace a vision of friendship that is casual, wide-cast, and built around the exchange of trifling benefits. Reid Hoffman founded the LinkedIn networking website. According to *BusinessWeek*, "Hoffman looks at friendship as a marketplace in which we trade favors." The multitude of one's contacts go by the name of "friends" in social networking, and that's just fine with Hoffman, who says, "I think of them as light alliances."[9]

Real friendships are sturdier alliances than the LinkedIn sort. When we "network" we generally aren't using up any of our social capital; instead, we're growing it, expanding the circle of people we know and with whom we can make mutually beneficial contact. But the wider our network gets, the less our gaggle of acquaintances can be described as friends. Real friendship entails not just contact but a range of obligations, an implicit guarantee that we will come through for our pals whenever their moment of crisis may come. It also means favoring the interests of your friends—taking a stake in their interests. How many people's divergent desires can we embrace before we're no longer embracing anyone's particular interests? We've seen how, when we make multiple commitments, they're prone to fall into conflict. Grow your circle of friends too wide and shallow and you grow the risk of ending up with contrary and confounding obligations.

IF FRIENDSHIP IS just a matter of happy chat and shared entertainments, there isn't much to hold friendships together when they really matter. Loyalty alone may not be enough to define what it is to be a friend, but without it, what sort of friendship do you have? If we're looking for Orestes-Pylades-style loyalty, we're likely to be disappointed. But the fact that we can't count on a maximum sort of loyalty doesn't mean that there isn't a basic, baseline loyalty without which friendship can't function. Joseph Epstein writes in *Friendship: An Exposé* that a basic reliability is at the core of any real relationship: "Considering the obligations owed to genuine friends, at a minimum I should say that loyalty, or at least the absence of betrayal, is among them."

Betrayal is a broad concept, encompassing everything from an active handing over of a friend to his enemies to a mere failure to do everything a friend might want one to do in some situation. In short, betrayal is the opposite of loyalty. And if we want to get a sense of just how much we value loyalty, consider how much we loathe its antithesis. Is there anything that cuts us deeper than betrayal? Its wounds are like the prick of a pyracantha thorn—the puncture is painful enough, but the thorn's poison leaves us sore.

Take the praises Juvenal sang of a simple dinner in a simple, honest house. An invitation to dine is extended, with instructions about how best to enjoy the evening: "Cast care aside, shelve all your business worries," the great satirist wrote. Don't worry about money for a while, and if your wife stays out all night and shows up the "next morning with clothes suspiciously creased and spotted with damp," and "red in the face and ears," just forget about it. Put out of your mind the things that drive you crazy—the maintenance of your house, the endless hassles of having servants (including their lazy, clumsy habit of breaking your best dishes). But most important, advises Juvenal, "forget, above all, the ingratitude of friends."[10] After that litany of miseries, what is it that is given pride of place as the most miserable of miseries? The ingratitude of friends—and that's just a mild form of betrayal.

Novelist Henry Fielding wasn't far wrong when he wrote, "one of the greatest afflictions which, I think, can befall a man, [is] the unkindness of a friend."[11] We've all felt that sting, starting as children when we discover the brutal truth that our pals are fickle in their affections. Pity the girls of junior high—that awful age when this week's bosom buddy is next week's catty bane; that age when one is dying to share heartfelt confidences, only to find them dishearteningly betrayed all over campus. Adolescence is a gantlet in which we are battered and pummeled to build up the calluses needed to survive as adults. If childhood is, one can hope, a time of learning to trust, adolescence is a time of learning to be betrayed. If we're lucky, we learn to distinguish between true friends and false.

And yet, horrible as it is, betrayal is hardly rare. "Who has not been betrayed or betrayed someone?" Judith Shklar asked. "Betrayal is so common that its scope can scarcely be imagined." She marveled that something so ordinary, so frequent, so commonplace as betrayal never loses its horrible sting. Instead of being dulled to the experience of betrayal, we still find it "sharp and intense: we all hate being betrayed."[12]

We hate being betrayed because it is a testament to our

vulnerability, our inability to make life secure. We hate betrayal not only because it leaves us open to injury, but because it blindsides us. "An open foe may prove a curse," Ben Franklin aphorized, "but a pretended friend is worse."[13] A common metaphor in Colonial America for the danger of false friends was a biblical one—the Old Testament warns that if you make a staff out of a reed and try to lean on it, the reed won't just snap and leave you to fall, the jagged, broken point will pierce your hand.[14] By contrast, real friendship is a lifeboat, which is how popular nineteenth-century English poet Eliza Cook describes those we can count on: "As we prove the life-boat, so we often prove a friend." It is a gallant bark, she says, that is ignored until it is needed and then "proves a friend, when friends are wanted most."[15] But how disheartening if one discovers the lifeboats are made of rotten timbers, and how ruinous if one discovers it only as the women and children are lining up to board them.

We will find ourselves being betrayed time and again throughout our lives. It's a fundamentally human experience. Which is why Jesus had to be betrayed by Judas. As Jesus himself pointed out, day after day he had been teaching in the temple; the soldiers could have put the cuffs on him anytime; no one needed Judas to locate or identify him. But what could hammer home the humanity of Jesus more clearly than for him to be betrayed. He suffered pain; he was subjected to temptation: but his human odyssey wouldn't have been complete without that last particular, bitter indignity—betrayal.

Betrayal takes many shapes. There are the abandonments—the friends whose fortunes are entwined with our own and who casually discard us the moment they start to get ahead. There are the breaches of confidence—the friends who speak out of school, revealing damaging secrets with which they had been entrusted. There are the rip-offs—the friends with whom a business deal is made on a handshake who then take advantage of the fact that there is no enforceable contract.

And then there is the touchy subject of borrowing money, the crucible in which relationships so often melt that Rudyard Kipling argued a mark of the rarest sort of friendship was immunity to the destructive properties of debt: "You can use his purse with no more talk / Than he uses yours for his spendings, / And laugh and meet in your daily walk / As though there had been no lendings." I suspect that most of us find more empirically grounded the sly observation of Mark Twain, a writer much less prone to grandiloquent notions than Kipling: "The holy passion of Friendship is of so sweet and steady and loyal and enduring a nature that it will last through a whole lifetime," Twain observed, "if not asked to lend money."[16]

If being betrayed is painful, so too can be the experience of betraying a friend. Psychiatrist Aaron Lazare, in his book *On Apology*, recounts how a patient named Manuel brought himself to apologize to an old friend he had failed. To free himself from the guilt, he wrote a letter to his childhood chum, confessing his shame for not standing by him when he had the chance. Manuel had come along one day when they were kids to find his pal being viciously taunted by the neighborhood bullies. The other boys were ragging him with the classic *you-*

throw-like-a-girl taunt. Manuel stepped up and . . . he faltered: He joined, not his friend, but the ring of tormentors. In his letter of apology, Manuel described what happened:

> I did not stand by you. My vocal cords were paralyzed. I was struggling with the task of choosing between my two allegiances. I backed away from you and rejoined the other kids. My insides were churning and I remained there in the street forever.[17]

By apologizing, Manuel found some measure of relief and release from "that scene [which] has revisited me at various times over the years." He had been haunted for more than half a century by the simple knowledge of his own cowardice, by the shame of having failed when his loyalty was tested. Betrayal isn't just devastating to the betrayed.

Betrayal is a blight that makes us hard and brittle, small and mean in our dealings with others. For the ancient Greeks, nobility required a certain "openness" (*to euethes*), a mindset at odds with suspicious skepticism. Betrayal bludgeons us into abandoning generosity and openness, forcing us to protect ourselves by questioning everyone's motives. We learn to be distrustful. As Martha Nussbaum writes, "It is the experience of betrayal that slowly erodes the foundation of the virtues." How exhilarating and empowering to be the someone for whom someone else will go "to the last gasp." How spiritually debilitating to learn that you are someone for whom your so-called pals won't even be inconvenienced.

Who would know that sting of friendship betrayed better than Job? Stripped of all his worldly goods, he remains, at first, in remarkably good spirits—*hey, God gives, God takes, no problem!* And in any case, if things get dire enough he'll always be able to count on his friends, so how bad can it be? But in his hour of great need, when he does finally turn to his old friends for the loving kindness and help expected of true friends—*hesed* is the word in biblical Hebrew, a word that means both "love" and "loyalty"—his friends turn him down. That is when Job finally succumbs to despair. Because if his friends aren't loyal to him in misfortune, they were never loyal to begin with. And if his friends aren't loyal, then they don't love him. The most grievous blow to Job is this realization, born of betrayal, that he is friendless, unloved.

As DESTRUCTIVE AS it may have been to Job to find his friends closing their doors in his face, let's look at it from their point of view for a moment. They thought that his epic suffering was a divine indictment, proof positive that their friend had offended God. To take Job's side, they thought, would be to take sides against God, something they weren't willing to do. Were they looking for an out—were their claims to piety just a convenient excuse? Perhaps. But that sort of predicament is a very real one. The moral demand not to abandon a friend in need can crash headlong into other moral demands, depending on the nature of our friends' needs. It's just the sort of conundrum that we've found gives loyalty a bad name. Take Pylades, whom we've seen praised as faithful and true. But how does he earn that title? Yes, he stands by his friend when Orestes is accused of murder. But he's also an accomplice, so reliable a comrade that he lends a hand when Orestes needs help killing his mother in the first place.

Philosophy professors Jeanette Kennett and Dean Cocking have written about how friendship can put us in moral danger, and they illustrate the problem with an old joke: "A friend will help you move house, a good friend will help you move a body."[18]

Put that way, the perils of being a pal are clear. Though couldn't we just reject that definition of friendship and say instead that we will be reliable and trustworthy in helping our friends up to, but not beyond, the point at which we are asked to do something wrong? Indeed, we might say that anyone who asks us to do something wrong is no friend at all, thus relieving us of any obligations we might have to that person. It's a tidy argument, but one that is a bad fit with our sense of what friendship entails. After all, what use is having a friend who will embrace you only when you are eminently and unimpeachably embraceable? "The proper office of a friend is to side with you when you are in the wrong," Mark Twain asserted, noting, "Nearly everybody will side with you when you are in the right." Spot on. But how far should we be willing to go for our friends, how much moral peril should we risk? We might venture that, as a general principle, moving bodies is a moral fudge too far. If the limitless loyalty of friends tempts one to indulge in crime, then maybe such loyalties are best avoided.

Perhaps the preferable measure of loyalty in friendship is a willingness to accept our friends' misdemeanors. In an 1821 letter, Sir Walter Scott urged Lord Melville to be sympathetic to some young and indiscreet political operatives who had gotten themselves in a legal jam, accused of slander for writing some intemperate partisan tracts. Scott didn't argue that the men were innocent, but that they should be able to count on their allies nonetheless: "I like a highland friend who will stand by me not only when I am in the right, but when I am a *little* in the wrong."[19] Note the word *little*, the emphasis on which is Scott's own. It's not an exact moral gauge, but it is a sensible one. Aristotle gives a similar standard, but weighted even more toward sticking with friends even when they sin. He says not to renounce your old friends except when they exhibit an "excess of wickedness."

In practice this doesn't give us any useful tool for deciding one way or another, but maybe there's no better way to do it than to draw on a sense of what a "little" wrong is and what an "excess of wickedness" looks like. We discover a friend is cheating on his taxes. We might or might not try to discourage him from that bad behavior, but is there anyone who could be called a friend who would drop a dime to the IRS? The old pal with an inconvenient corpse on his hands is another matter altogether. If a given friendship entails accessorizing murder, that's a good time to make it an ex-friendship. Or, to put it all in one example, let's say an old friend whom we love dearly is being blackmailed. His career, marriage, and reputation hang in the balance. It's no stretch to suggest that friendship would demand not divulging the embarrassing information being used by the blackmailer. But what about dealing with the blackmailer? Suppose we know dirt on *him*. Would we be willing to engage in a little counterblackmail ourselves? Or suppose we don't have any dirt on him. Would we be willing to see to it he could never be a threat to our friend—or anyone else—again? We can ask what we would be willing to do, but it will depend on any number of slippery variables. Few of us would go so far as to put a shiv in our friend's foe. But we have to admit that we find such hard-bitten codes of come-what-may loyalty attractive (which is why we enjoy Humphrey Bogart movies so much).

What does this rough-and-ready standard tell us about resolving E. M. Forster's dilemma of whether to betray a friend or one's country? If we discover our friend is a budding Philby (the British intelligence officer who betrayed his country as a Soviet spy), do we treat his espionage like tax evasion or like murder? Since complicity in treason may well mean betraying all our other friends—no one knows how many of Philby's colleagues lost their lives due to his treason—the weight of loyal friendship isn't going to be on the spy's side.

How much nicer it would be to have clear-cut moral rules, unambiguous and universally applicable. This is a fundamental attraction of the type of morality championed by Plato and Kant, which may be strict and uncompromising, but is invulnerable to problematic circumstances and confounding contingencies. Sure-footed and self-assured as that sort of morality may be, confident in its categorical imperatives—never tell a lie!—it doesn't capture everything we recognize as good and valuable in our lives. It doesn't leave room for anything as messy as friendship. When we commit to friendship there's no escaping the possibility that we will be roped into wrongs, big or small. We may decide that a particular wrong is too much to ask, outside the bounds of friendship's bonds. But if we want to make ourselves entirely safe from corruption, if we want to protect ourselves from the inevitable clash between loyalty to moral principle and loyalty to friends, then friendship has to go. Because as Kennett and Cocking put it, it's "hard to imagine that there would be anyone left with whom we could be friends if we were so rigid as to rule out from friendship anyone who might make a mistake, get into trouble, and ask for help."[20]

Even those who are sticklers for the rule of law can find themselves making certain accommodations for the demands of loyal friendship. There is the policeman in O. Henry's story "After Twenty Years" who shows up on a dark, drizzly night to keep an appointment he made with his best friend. The two men had agreed, on the eve of striking out to make their fortunes two decades before, to meet on that given date. But as Jimmy the policeman approaches his long-lost pal, he recognizes him as a wanted man. He doesn't arrest him—he sends another man to do it, and sends a note with him. "When you struck the match to light your cigar I saw it was the face of the man wanted in Chicago," writes the patrolman to his old buddy. "Somehow I couldn't do it myself, so I went around and got a plain clothes man to do the job." Caught between loyalty to friend and loyalty to duty, Jimmy chose duty. But we understand his sheepish unwillingness to do the handcuffing himself—his is the act of a man who knows the moral jam he's in and doesn't try, Agamemnon-like, to pretend it away.

These are the sort of conflicts that led Mahatma Gandhi to warn against close friendships, to denounce them as a threat to moral purity. "I am of opinion that all exclusive intimacies are to be avoided," he wrote. Pals are more likely to lead us into error and wrongdoing than to inspire virtue in us. Echoing Thomas à Kempis's ascetic advice, Gandhi concluded, "he who would be friends with God must remain alone."[21]

How did Gandhi arrive at such an austere view of human relationships? It came from what he described as the first great shock of his life—and one that changed the course of it—the experience of getting caught between loyalties to family and friends. Gandhi's brother was accused of misusing a public office; Gandhi, then a newly minted lawyer, had an acquaintance from England who was the British officer who would be judging the case. "It is not proper for you, a brother, to shirk your duty, when you can clearly put in a good word about me to an officer you know," Gandhi's brother insisted. And so, feeling glum and guilty, Gandhi went to plead his brother's case to the man.

The officer was infuriated at the breach of propriety and gave the young lawyer the bum's rush. Humiliated and insulted, Gandhi made a pledge to himself: "Never again shall

I place myself in such a false position, never again shall I try to exploit friendship in this way." And years later, he was able to say, "since then I have never been guilty of a breach of that determination."[22]

The fascinating thing about the incident is that Gandhi, though he knew he was in the wrong, felt insulted nonetheless by the officer's refusal to give him special consideration. Why the outrage at being denied a shameful request? Because Gandhi thought that it was the mark, if not the definition, of friendship that it entails doing the wrong thing if that's what a friend asks. Gandhi had fancied that he had English friends. But when he tried to exploit one such friendship, he was refused. He assumed that the officer wouldn't have refused a friend, and concluded that the officer was no friend at all. In his embarrassment and pique Gandhi further concluded that he couldn't trust any of the English to be true friends.

So painful was Gandhi's realization that his friend wasn't a friend at all that he devoted himself to an ethical regime that would spare him from having to put his relationships to that sort of test again: He renounced the idea of close friendships altogether, abjuring them as leading, one way or another, to underhanded business. He endeavored to be friendly with everyone and intimate friends with no one.

George Orwell thought that was a monumental cop-out. It is "unquestionably true," Orwell allowed, that "through loyalty to a friend one can be led into wrongdoing." But accepting that risk is simply and inescapably what it costs to enjoy the good of friendship. We've already seen that loyalty is most clearly proved by one's willingness to suffer adversity for a friend's sake. Orwell extends this understanding to include moral adversity, arguing we should be willing to suffer some moral damage on behalf of our true friends just as we should be willing to suffer other sorts of loss if that's what it takes to help them. The way Orwell sees it, Gandhi isn't achieving a difficult and admirable virtue by renouncing friendship, he's just taking the easy path, saving himself the discomfort of trying to untangle the messy knots loyalty ties. "The essence of being human is that one does not seek perfection, that one is sometimes willing to commit sins for the sake of loyalty." Because otherwise we are left with a world in which people form no close bonds—a profoundly inhuman sort of dystopia. We have to be prepared, Orwell wrote, "to be defeated and broken up by life, which is the inevitable price of fastening one's love upon other human individuals."[23]

In the *Nicomachean Ethics*, Aristotle takes up the question of whether there is one Universal Good, as the Platonists held. Aristotle's endeavor is to show that ethics is how we live in the world, not how well we match up to an otherworldly (Platonic) ideal of how we should live. An advocate of the importance of friendship, Aristotle recognizes that there is a disloyalty inherent in his rejection of the teachings of his mentor: "Such an inquiry is not a pleasant task in view of our friendship for the authors of the doctrine of ideas," he writes. "But we venture to think that this is the right course, and that in the interests of truth we ought to sacrifice even what is nearest to us, especially as we call ourselves philosophers. Both are dear to us, but it is a sacred duty to give the preference to the truth." You can try to argue away the conflict here—perhaps by saying, well, Plato taught Aristotle to love the truth, and so Aristotle is honoring his friend by hewing to the most important of his teachings. But that's not the way Aristotle sees it: For him it is a matter of choosing, and he chooses truth.

Does this give us a hard-and-fast rule to follow—when obligations to truth and to friends collide, truth trumps? Hardly, because the test of loyalty doesn't just entail suffering *materially* for our friends, nor even just suffering *morally* for our friends, it entails taking an *intellectual* hit as well.

Like the assistant principal falsely accused of collecting child pornography on his computer, we would hope that our friends would give us the benefit of the doubt. We don't want our friends to be impartial judges of our behavior, we want friends who will assume the best of us, who will be committed prima facie to the proposition that we are in the right. For Kipling this was the very definition of loyal friendship: "His wrong's your wrong, and his right's your right / In season or out of season," he wrote. "Stand up and back it in all men's sight— / With *that* for your only reason!" The loyal friend doesn't look for exculpatory evidence to justify standing by a buddy accused. All he needs to know is what's right for his friend, and that becomes what's right for him.

It's hard not to find that stance attractive, but for many

critics of loyalty, it is a deal-breaker. What are we doing when we assume the best of a friend, even in the face of evidence that might persuade a disinterested bystander to arrive at a contrary conclusion? Making judgments on grounds other than reason and the facts. And in modern intellectual circles, this is denounced as "bad epistemic conduct." As philosopher Sarah Stroud puts it, "Friendship places demands not just on our feelings or our motivations, but on our *beliefs* and our methods of forming beliefs."[24] In other words, loyalty in friendship not only demands that we feel inclined to help our friends even when they're in the wrong, but that we feel inclined not to *think* they are in the wrong.

Suspending disbelief is a standard loyal practice, not just in friendship but in love and family and all the other realms of our lives. I remember, my junior year in high school back in Phoenix, playing baseball one hot and dusty afternoon. I was at second base and, alas, I can't say that I was the best fielder on the school's team (the first-string second baseman had torn up his knee a game or two before and I had been shifted in from the rather less-than-glorious right-field spot, where I would have been more safely sequestered). A ground ball was hit my way, skittering along the turf; I crouched to scoop it up; the ball scudded right past my glove, between my legs, and dribbled into the outfield. Not exactly an Eddie Collins moment. After the game I got in the car with my dad, who had been in the bleachers. "Shame about that grounder," he said. "It really took a strange bounce." Would my father have seen the ball as quite so tricky to field if someone else's son had flubbed the catch? I doubt it. My dad wasn't just trying to make me feel better—his loyalty to me made him perceive the play differently.

We find that part of what makes loyalty a powerful virtue is its ability to supplant rational decision-making. We might get a bigger payoff from betraying an ally, but loyalty is there to skew the immediate rational calculation, thus defeating the Prisoner's Dilemma. Now we find another sort of irrationality coming in to play. When we make judgments based on our commitments and relationships instead of basing our beliefs on an unbiased consideration of the evidence, sweet reason isn't exactly in the driver's seat. Stroud doesn't think that's all so bad—indeed, she suggests that the tug of loyalty provides us a valuable way of knowing, a type of knowledge that doesn't fit in the standard methodology of logic.

What if we find ourselves refusing to believe something that's obviously true because we simply will not believe something bad about a friend? There have been plenty of moral and mental absolutists who think that this is the damning downfall of loyalty. Who can claim to be true, they ask, if he has no commitment to the truth? Can we really call a character trait a virtue if, in practice, it corrupts and degrades our ability to make accurate judgments? Thomas Paine didn't think so.

"It is necessary to the happiness of man, that he be mentally faithful to himself," Paine proclaimed. "Infidelity does not consist in believing or in disbelieving; it consists in professing to believe what he does not believe." Always the revolutionary, he was arguing that priests bring themselves to believe theological doctrines that they don't actually buy, and fool themselves into thinking they are being faithful. They think they are being loyal to their faith, and end up being disloyal to the truth. "It is impossible to calculate the moral mischief . . . that mental lying has produced in society." Goodness knows there are many clerics who suffer doubts (Mother Teresa is but the most famous recent example), but there are probably far more who are sincere in their convictions than Paine would have credited. It is in the context of friendship, not religion, that mental faithfulness to oneself is most commonly compromised. Indeed, a willingness to indulge in some measure of "mental lying"—Paine's tidy phrase for believing something one knows to be false—seems to be a prerequisite for loyal friendship. If so, what can we say about loyalists who deny painful truths about their pals? "When a man has so far corrupted and prostituted the chastity of his mind, as to subscribe his . . . belief to things he does not believe," Paine complains, "he has prepared himself for the commission of every other crime."[25]

Our modern philosophers are less excitable. Professor Simon Keller writes, "There is always a loss, always something to regret, in a failure to follow epistemic norms." But that loss, those regrets, may be an acceptable price to pay for the benefits of friendship, he allows, "so long as the lapses in epistemic responsibility required for the sake of friendship are not too egregious."[26]

Keller gives an example: Imagine that you play in an amateur basketball league and that your blunder blows the league championship for your team. Your loyal friends will be "disinclined to think that you made a fool of yourself on the court, or that you were the weak link that caused them to lose."[27] Maybe—in which case they would be skewing their take on the game in the same way my father explained away my fielding errors. But they wouldn't need to go so far— their loyalty might not be quite so much about suspending disbelief as Keller thinks. After all, I suspect that if I miss the game-winning free throw, my teammates aren't going to dupe themselves into thinking I played well. No, they would fully realize I cost them the championship. But if they're my friends, they wouldn't hold it against me in the least. The game, the championship, would mean less to them than our friendship.

Think of Hollywood's paean to faithful friendship, *It's a Wonderful Life*. George Bailey's friends hear that he is in trouble and they come running. It isn't that they know the bank-fraud charges against him are false—though they probably do believe that he is innocent, because they know him to be a good man (after all, it is his virtue and selfless generosity that has earned him so many pals). No, they don't give a damn what the charges are. Their friend is in trouble and that's all they need to know. They simply don't need to make any judgment at all about the accusation to know what they are going to do. When George's wife, Mary, put out the word that George was in a terrible fix, his friends "scattered all over town collecting money." And soon they are at the Bailey house, cheerfully piling the money high on a table. As

Mary says, weeping with gratitude and amazement, "They didn't ask any questions—just said, 'If George is in trouble, count me in.'" Now, that's the sort of friendship that moves us. That's the sort of loyalty we christen with sentimental tears.

This sort of friendship is irrational in the sense that there is no desire for reasons. Elizabeth Bennet chides Mr. Darcy in *Pride and Prejudice* for being unwilling to do what a friend asks without being offered a proof of its propriety. She asserts one should be readily, easily persuaded by friends. But Mr. Darcy claims that it is no compliment to a friend "to yield without conviction." That doesn't persuade Elizabeth, who argues, "A regard for the requester would often make one yield readily to a request, without waiting for arguments to reason one into it."[28]

Loyal friendship can also lead us to tell lies. Fibbing fidelity is captured by songwriter Frank Loesser, who composed a mid-century tune called "That's Loyalty" for the boisterous Betty Hutton. She sings of how her boyfriend is always criticizing her; her clothes; her dancing; her makeup. But for all the grief *he* gives her, his sense of loyalty demands that everyone *else* treat her like royalty. *He* can tell her he doesn't like her hat, but just let anyone *else* try it, and he'll give them a proper thrashing, all while loudly proclaiming her hat to be the prettiest in town.

Publilius Syrus, author of Latin mottos (and a popular lyricist in his own day), put the same sentiment succinctly: "Admonish your friends in private; praise them in public."

That advice is every bit as sound today as when it was first written. But it means that, to the list of faults loyalty in friendship demands of us, we have to add dishonesty.

We can denounce dishonesty as a corruption of our relationships, or we can take it as a measure of just how much we care. In Kingsley Amis's novel *The Russian Girl*, Richard Vaisey is a professor of Russian literature who has fallen in love with a young Russian poetess. The problem is that her poems aren't any good: the presentation of her work at a reading makes him weep from its "cheapness, shallowness, dullness, vulgarity, [and the] number of sequences of words in which there was no vestige of poetic talent or feeling for literature." She was a golden goddess whose "words were made of lead." Vaisey can't bring himself to tell her, can't crush her hopes. When she asks him straight out what he thinks, he stumbles through the best lie-without-actually-lying he can contrive: "Before it was over I was in floods of tears. Not much poetry makes me cry."

He keeps up the fiction until she finally frees him: "When you told me that you thought those poems were good, I knew within a few seconds that you were lying," she confesses. "But that lie told me how much you loved me, and it means I'll always love you."[29]

JUST HOW PROBLEMATIC is loyalty? It demands that we be partial to our friends, where we commonly think that morality demands impartiality, a willingness to treat all people equally. Loyalty calls on us to break the rules, perhaps even the law, colluding with our friends when they are a "little" in the wrong (and maybe even more than just a little). Loyalty asks us to insult our own intelligence, to willfully believe things we know to be false. Loyalty encourages us to lie.

And yet, for all the transgressions that come standard with loyalty, we are outraged when we find our friends have not done what loyalty requires. What does that sense of outrage tell us? We could dismiss it as an indictment of our own corruption. We could conclude that, if that's what being loyal means, then loyalty is no virtue, it's just a vice—and a sneaky one at that. Or we could embrace that sense of outrage as a validation of the importance of loyalty in our lives: For all the moral peril loyalty entails, we still admire the loyal, we still hope our friends prove loyal, we still strive to be loyal ourselves. That's a remarkable endorsement of a vexatious virtue.

We wrestle with the conundrum that something that claims to be a virtue can lead us to act immorally, and end up concluding that friendship is a sort of good that we value not because it improves our moral standing, but because it is desirable in and of itself. And as with many desirable things, loyal friendship is rare. Rudyard Kipling riffs on Ecclesiastes 7:28, writing, "One man in a thousand, Solomon says / Will stick more close than a brother." Forget the fickle and phony 999, it is "the Thousandth Man will stand your friend / With the whole round world agin you." For all the faults, all the epistemological error and moral peril that loyalty brings, who wouldn't want the Thousandth Man for his friend? As Kipling says, "it's worth while seeking him half your days." But more important, who wouldn't want to be the Thousandth Man himself?

6

Bonding and Branding

In a modern world in which loyalty rarely registers other than as a moldy relic, there has been one civilian realm where the virtue has been a hot topic—business. The management bookshelf groans under the weight of such titles as *Loyalty Rules*, *The Loyalty Effect*, *Why Loyalty Matters*, *Lessons in Loyalty*, and *The Customer Loyalty Solution*. Loyalty even gets shoehorned into titles such as *Getting Naked: A Business Fable About Shedding the Three Fears That Sabotage Client Loyalty*. For the last twenty years, the corporate world has thrown itself at "loyalty marketing," an approach built on the observation that it costs far less to keep a current customer happy than it does to go out and rustle up new customers from scratch.

Corporate loyalty campaigns, launched in earnest by management guru Fred Reichheld in the late eighties, have had a particular sort of appeal to business. Companies have been promised that by embracing virtue they can improve profits. Reichheld calls it "doing business by golden-rule principles," and who can argue against that? Who wouldn't want to make money free from the taint of grubby self-interest? Reichheld gives it an almost messianic spin: "Mutual benefit and mutual accountability can be made flesh in a business institution."[1] But as nice as it may be to embrace trust and reliability as tools for taming the excesses of modern capitalism, our emphasis on the business world as a locus of loyalty has been misplaced. And by relying on bonds of loyalty when simpler, more direct business principles apply, we may be creating problems not only for companies, but for loyalty as well. Could it be that instead of elevating mammon, loyalty only gets dragged down and degraded?

THE MOST VISIBLE sort of loyalty marketing has been pioneered by frequent-flyer programs, rewards systems known in business circles as "loyalty programs." The idea is to give benefits to the customers who stick with you, a gesture of reciprocity. But does it really represent anything that can properly be called loyalty? Real loyalty shows itself in adversity, when one remains steadfast even when the benefits of the bond have been stripped away. Loyalty programs don't promise or foster anything of the sort. Frequent flyers wouldn't think of sticking with a carrier who announced that it was canceling the miles that customers had built up in their accounts. As it is, there are many flyers who feel ripped off by airlines' efforts to minimize how many free flights they give away, efforts that include raising the number of miles needed for a gratis ticket, limiting the number of such tickets available, and blacking out blocks of desirable dates to fly.[2]

Writer Joanne Kaufman recently detailed her frustrations with loyalty programs as the terms of her various frequent-buyer cards kept being revisited and revised. Having built up a bunch of points on her Duane Reade drugstore card, the program (and the promised rewards) evaporated as part of the store's sale to Walgreen's. When she took a handful of receipts to her local pizzeria to collect on the restaurant's buy-ten-get-one-free offer, she was told, "We changed things last month. Now you need fifteen." She complained of feeling like a marathoner who gets to what she thinks is the end of the race only to be told the tape is now at the twenty-seven-mile mark. "My loyalty," she declared, "was betrayed."[3]

Fostering customer "loyalty" may have been a business mantra for two decades, but how much do we really run into anything that we can describe as loyalty in the realm of commerce? For all the corporate happy talk of developing loyal customers, loyalty is almost always punished. Consider your credit card. If you have had the same credit card for twenty years—a remarkable expression of product loyalty—you are likely paying one of the highest interest rates around.

I found this out firsthand. I've never lavished time and attention on getting the best possible credit card interest rate.

I'm not one of the "butterflies," as the loyalty marketing literature calls them, who flit from one attractive introductory offer
to another. I'd rather get my credit card in place and not have
to think about it for a while. I make payments on time and
I roll over some balance here and there (which is where the
bank really makes its nut). In other words, I'm just the sort of
customer that the loyalty-focused businesses of today should
be making the most of. And, in a way, they do make the most
of that sort of customer—by taking them for all they're worth.
After getting the umpteenth attractive pitch from competing
credit issuers, the sort promising six months interest free and
then a low interest rate, I finally got around to calling my bank
to ask them to give me—the twenty-year loyal customer—the
same consideration that a bank I had never given any business was willing to extend. The response from the customer
service rep was priceless: "You need to talk to the cancellation
office."

"What do you mean?" I asked.

"I don't have that sort of deal in my computer to offer you.
The only people with those offers are the people in cancella-
tion. You need to tell them you're going to cancel your card.
Then they can match whatever deal you've been offered."

The helpful and unintentionally revealing customer rep
transferred me to cancellations, and soon the card I had been
paying double-digit interest on had been temporarily reset to
0 percent. I've learned to call the bank up every six months
to threaten bolting to the competition; I now pay a minuscule
fraction of the interest I used to pay.

"I SUPPOSE THAT in the days when your fishmonger knew your name and what sort of cod you liked on a Friday, 'brand loyalty' made sense," writes petrolhead Jeremy Clarkson, one of the car-guy hosts of the BBC show *Top Gear.* "Now [that] we live in a world of supermarkets and corporations, it is the most ridiculous thing on all of God's green earth."[4] And yet he readily admits that he sticks unthinkingly to particular brands, whether Levi's, or Alfa Romeos, or a Swiss firm that makes timepieces. "I am an Omega man," he says, declaring his fidelity to the make of watch his parents gave him the day he went off to school. He continued to buy Omegas over the years, even as they slipped into a dowdy dotage, "boring to behold" and "plainly designed by someone who had a black-and-white telly." And never mind that Omega isn't even a company of its own anymore, but rather, just part of the Swatch conglomerate.

Clarkson defines himself in part by the products to which he is loyal. And this is perhaps the most compelling reason to have a brand loyalty. There is something to the notion that choosing a brand and sticking to it is a way to define oneself. Loyalty has always been a matter of identity; betray your clan or country, and you are cast out. To be disloyal is to destroy the bonds of family and friendship that do so much to define who we are as people. When Peter goes into denial, he doesn't just abandon Jesus; he has to abandon himself, denying his identity. Could we say that a similar, secular sort of identity is lost when we discard our former buying habits? As *Esquire* magazine put it, touting the advantages of loyal customer conduct, the products you buy tell "a lot about who you are and where you came from."

But being loyal to a company or a brand may not be a particularly wise move. Once the company figures out that you're personally invested in buying the brand to express who you are, it's likely to find any number of ways to take advantage of you. Savvy marketers are always on the lookout for basic human needs to exploit. Our endless quest to identify ourselves through our purchases is one of the marketers' favorite leverage points.

And what kinds of identities do we adopt when we rely on brands to express who we are? What is the Polo Ralph Lauren brand but a contrivance that allows a middle-class kid from flyover country to identify himself with a WASPy East Coast elite to which he has no ties? Brands are more often than not vehicles of false identity. But even where one has an honest-to-goodness connection with a brand, a product rooted in one's own experience or in the town one grew up, the brand identity may be no more honest.

Take the strategy of the Pabst Brewing Company, which—its name notwithstanding—doesn't brew beer. The company realized that in old industrial cities around the country, there were beer drinkers loyal to their local breweries—rust belt icons such as National Bohemian and Blatz. The brands were being pushed out of business by the big national players, leaving the loyal local drinkers bereft. Pabst has bought up the brands, and keeps them alive—sort of. Pabst, you see, doesn't keep the local breweries brewing. The company hasn't even kept its own breweries working. They've all been shuttered. Instead, Pabst has the beer behemoth MillerCoors brew all its brands; the familiar local labels get slapped on beers no longer rooted in those local communities. Sentimental Brooklynites might favor Schaefer, but that beer is no more a part of the city than the Dodgers.

Those beer drinkers do represent the great appeal of brand loyalty, at least from the corporate point of view. Acquire a customer at an early enough age, and you can make your product an essential part of his identity. You get a customer for life, one of those desirable sorts who will keep buying the goods even when they aren't particularly good. At least, that's the story marketers like to tell themselves. I suspect that there aren't as many customers willing to indulge in loyal behavior as business would like to believe. And it is a mistake that has remarkable consequences. The notion that one can establish loyal customers for life is responsible for one of the most durably wrongheaded of business practices—the conceit that youngsters are the most desirable audience for commercial messages.

GIVEN THE MARKUPS on big-ticket items sold to wealthy adults, you'd think that TV shows with affluent older demographics would command the priciest ad slots. You'd think wrong.

Advertisers want to be where the boys are. They are willing to pay a steep premium to show their wares to people in the "all-important," "coveted," "highly desirable"—choose your adjective—18-to-34 age group. Advertisers regularly pay more than twice as much to air commercials on shows that deliver the youth market. The question is: Why? You'd think they would follow Willie Sutton's motto and go where the money is. And when it comes to selling stuff—especially expensive stuff—the money is in the pockets of consumers over forty-five.

And yet companies blindly chase the young. It can be a costly marketing mistake. Take Mitsubishi Motors' ill-fated efforts to woo young car buyers. In 2005, the company's signature TV advertisement featured a loose-limbed girl in a Babe Ruth hat sitting in the passenger seat of a turbocharged coupe called the Eclipse. In dreamy slow motion she grooved to a robotic techno-ditty. There's no doubt the ads were cool, and they succeeded in attracting the adenoidal set. There was one problem—to actually sell cars to its teenybopper target market, Mitsubishi had to offer easy credit: nothing down, no interest, and no payments until, well, whenever. It seems that Mitsubishi didn't ask if the rave crowd—once it had covered the monthly nut for Ecstasy and glow sticks—would have much left over for car payments.

In just six months, Mitsubishi lost a half-billion dollars in loans gone bad. The firm tried to retool its sales pitch to a more mature buyer, but it struggled to sell soccer moms on the advantages of bright-yellow pocket rockets straight off the set of *The Fast and the Furious*. Mitsubishi was crippled in the United States, and has yet to recover. And yet the myth of 18-to-34 persists, undimmed by corporate tears.

Advertisers have their reasons for targeting teens and twenty-somethings. First among them is the belief that long-term brand loyalties are set when people are young and impressionable. The problem is that the belief is based on market research that is forty years out of date. "It's a cliché and a fallacy to think you can build a customer for life," says Al Ries, a longtime New York ad exec turned marketing consultant. "As people grow up, they change brands." Or as British adman Andrew Cracknell put it: "The belief that once you get a customer they're yours for life is complete bollocks."

People don't just drift from brand to brand. As they get older they go out of their way to reject brands they once embraced, brands they now associate with their less sophisticated, former selves. When a young woman heads off for college, chances are she isn't going to plaster her dorm room with the boy-band posters that used to decorate her walls at home. Just because the Jonas Brothers have a robust teen following doesn't mean that the Jonas Brothers brand has built customers for life.

Over the course of her college career that same young woman may well drink countless kegs of Milwaukee's Best at frat parties. But once she has a job in the big city, she isn't likely to fill her fridge with cheap beer. And while our friend is paying off her student loans, she might gladly buy a Chevrolet Aveo. But that hardly means GM has a lock on her. "When a guy gets promoted, he doesn't get a more expensive Chevy," says Ries. "He buys a BMW."

As much as businesses may angle to get customers for life, skewing their advertising strategies, companies don't necessarily want loyal consumers. Being a company's most loyal customer is not the same as being its most valuable customer. Business-loyalty consultant Timothy Keiningham argues that companies need "to determine which loyal customers are profitable and which are not." Lots of loyalists have been around with a company long enough to know when and how to get its products on sale; they demand "an excessive amount of service that they are not willing to pay fairly to receive."[5] Loyal people are often thought of as "anchors." But if you're trying to swim in deep water, you may not want an anchor chained to your leg.

Then there are those customers who, instead of just shaping their identities according to the brands they buy, end up affecting the identity of the brand by their patronage. A few years ago, Frédéric Rouzaud took over as the managing director of Champagne Louis Roederer, the firm that makes Cristal. In an interview with *The Economist*, Rouzaud expressed discomfort with hip-hop's long-standing love of Cristal. Here you have customers who are not only loyal, but celebrities at that. But if you are trying to emphasize that one's champagne is the drink of choice for oenophiles, it can be a problem having your product treated as liquid bling, stuff to be sloshed and sprayed around.

Rapper Jay-Z accused Rouzaud of racism, but it is perfectly conceivable that the Roederer firm was free from racial animus, and simply thinking long-term. If the brand is synonymous with rap, then when rap has become passé—whether that's five years from now or twenty—so will the company's champagne. Companies don't get to be more than two hundred years old by betting the store on a given fashion in popular music.

THE WORLD OF music provides a microcosm of the problems that companies have in maintaining long-term relationships with their employees. Think of the music that might have been made if the fellows in the Beatles had had more loyalty to the firm, that particularly profitable partnership they all enjoyed. But that partnership made them all superstars, making each perfectly capable of going out on his own. It took only one defector to destroy the company.

When vibraphonist Terry Gibbs was with the Woody Herman band in the late 1940s, he contributed a comic, scat-sung vocal to a tune called "Lemon Drop." The recording became something of a surprise hit, as the band soon discovered by the number of requests they would get for it in an evening. After a week of playing "Lemon Drop" three or four times a night, Gibbs went to Woody and threatened to quit if he didn't get a raise. Soon they were playing the song "seventeen times a night," and Gibbs went to his boss for another boost in pay.

Herman was in a jam—he had a hit on his hands, but needed a key employee to deliver the goods.

That's why Dizzy Gillespie, for one, didn't always populate his bands with the cream of the bebop crop. Though Diz "was a vocal admirer of Bud Powell's fire and Thelonious Monk's originality," jazz historian Scott Knowles DeVeaux writes, he "preferred support personnel who were more loyal, reliable, and tractable."[6]

Many management mavens have made the case that loyal employees are to be valued as effective, committed, capable workers. But I doubt Dizzy was the only employer to look for loyalty for reasons beyond a favorable assessment of the worker's abilities. The best and the brightest are rarely the most loyal of staff, if for no better reason than that they are the ones who are regularly lured with better deals by competing organizations. When it comes time to hire, a company doesn't always want a highflier. Sometimes a firm is more interested in finding a hire who will stick around a while (thus avoiding the hassle and expense of searching for candidates all over again in a year), in which case the company may well choose the man with a penchant for loyalty. But that isn't because the business values loyalty per se, or thinks that loyalty translates into superior skills. No, it generally means that the company is happy to have a journeyman who can not only do the job, but who will be grateful to have it.

Then again, as cynical as it may seem to apply the precepts of loyalty to a business enterprise, that doesn't mean it can't happen. For all the bands that fell apart in the twentieth century's orgy of popular music, one band that cleaved together, neither spinning off all its stars to maximize individual payoffs in the good times, nor collapsing from minimized payoffs in the bad times was Duke Ellington's Famous Orchestra. Ellington had a knack for management that few bandleaders enjoyed, and perhaps even more important, his success as a songwriter gave him the financial wherewithal to float the enterprise even in the bleak days around 1950 when the big bands were faltering. But far and away, the most important thing about the Ellington orchestra was Ellington—the respect the musicians had for him and his compositions, and the love he inspired in them. That love was expressed by Harry Carney, the spectacular baritone saxophonist who joined Ellington in 1927. When he heard, in 1974, that Duke had died, Carney wept. "This is the worst day of my life. Now I have nothing to live for." Without Ellington to live for, Carney lived just four months more. *The New Yorker*'s jazz portraitist Whitney Balliett concluded, "Harry Carney died of bereavement."

But of course, Carney's commitment to Ellington was more an expression of friendship than a business relationship. Carney wasn't devoted to the enterprise that was Duke's orchestra, but to Duke. And this is the core problem with the idea that we, as customers or employees, might have a committed relationship with a commercial entity—the question: With what (note, not with *whom*) does one have the relationship? A corporation is considered a person for certain legal purposes, but that is a transactional fiction. What is a business? If it is a sole proprietorship or a partnership it may be tied closely to an individual, and the commitments that particular individual feels binding may well affect what the business does. But when those individuals die, though sometimes the firm associated with them collapses and dies off as well, more often than not the business goes on under new ownership. Will those new owners feel bound—beyond the terms of specific contractual obligation—to a loyal relationship with the company's old customers and employees?

Consider the employees of an old family business that passes on to a group of heirs who have never had much involvement with the company and have little interest in running it. The heirs sell the firm and new ownership arrives. What obligation do the new bosses have to the old employees? None, unless some specific and specified treatment of the old staff was part of the terms of sale. And in practice, the new employers are going to look at the "lifers" as a liability rather than an asset. Corporate lifers are workers who settle in for the long haul in one job and expect it to be their last. If a business needs to be nimble to survive, these may not be the employees a company really wants. "Lifers are loyal, but they are risk-averse," according to organizational psychologist Adrian Furnham. The old-timers are "liable to be alienated as performance management systems replace seniority-based or service ideologies."[7]

I know an editor who was recently hired to take over a magazine full of writers who had seen the publication as their second home. He didn't perceive a stable masthead as a wonderful testament to loyal commitment or a resource of institutional memory; instead he took the longevity of the employees as an indication that many weren't valuable enough to have been lured away. One of the first acts of his tenure was to work up an early retirement buyout deal to make room for new blood.

Our instinct might be to decry such management choices. And no doubt, as has been argued by writers such as sociologist Richard Sennett, loyal long-term employees are often repositories of crucial institutional memory, and they likely have built relationships of trust with one another, an esprit de corps that can be tremendously valuable in getting important things done. But we don't really expect that loyalty to advance the workers' careers. Consider the manager who has to choose between two candidates for a big promotion. One is the loyal long-term employee who will stick with the company even if his hopes for advancement are disappointed; the other is a young hotshot who will hop to the competition if he isn't rewarded, and fast, with a raise and a corner office. All else being equal, who do you think gets the job?

How terribly unfair, we're inclined to think. But it's easier to argue that loyalty should be honored and rewarded when you don't have a stake in the success of the enterprise. Imagine you've been in a crippling car crash that has shattered the bones in your legs. As you're wheeled into the operating theater, would you prefer that the surgeon, whose skill will determine whether you walk again, was hired because he was the most doggedly loyal of residents? Or would you want your femur reconstructed by the hotshot, mercenary free agent who enjoys that status on the basis of the results he gets?

Employees are no paragons of loyalty either. Offered a new and lucrative job with our employer's hated rival, are we likely to consider, as part of our career calculations, that we have any obligation to stay with our current employer—who has, after all, given us a livelihood for however many years? Gone are the days when an employee would even think of being loyal to his employer—at least where loyalty might be defined as forgoing a more lucrative salary being offered by a competing company. We are, in effect, taking the advice of Harvard Business School professor and management guru John Kotter, who argues that a long-term job is a snare and an entanglement when an economy is changing quickly. Michael Lewis, in his book *Liar's Poker*, writes about a head trader in bonds at Salomon Brothers who announced he was quitting to take a new gig with a heftier salary at Goldman Sachs. Salomon execs begged him to stay and asked if he didn't feel any loyalty to the firm. The trader's reply? "You want loyalty, hire a cocker spaniel." What kind of trader would he have been if he let his decision be colored by a sense of loyalty?

We don't find that sort of assertion the least bit shocking. We've become more comfortable with the sentiment expressed by pitcher Don Sutton—who played for five different teams in his last seven seasons: "I'm the most loyal player money can buy."

—

IN LOVE, FAMILY, and friendship, we make commitments, but usually not contracts. Yes, marriage may be a contract of sorts, but not the specific sort that we see in commerce. Think of the tens of thousands of tiny words that we sign off on when we download a single piece of software. Compare that with the short, simple declarations that make up the vows of marriage—an agreement of rather greater import in our lives than the terms of service for Adobe Acrobat. And when marriages do start to have the contractual specificity of a commercial enterprise, as with a tycoon's well-lawyered prenuptial agreement, we feel that such a contract chafes against the spirit of marriage. Loyalty figures so prominently in friendship because it is a relationship that can't be contractually ordered. Indeed, if a pair of friends governed their interactions with binding contractual terms, we would say they weren't friends at all.

By contrast, nothing could be more appropriate than to govern buying and selling with specific, clearly stated commitments, agreements made binding by our signatures on the bottom line. Loyalty is the stuff that lets us tie ourselves to others in an open-ended way that recognizes we can't predict the problems we might face. But contracts do away with the need for loyalty by making concrete carefully delineated and enforceable obligations. If a company wishes to have long-term employees, it needs to engage them with contracts that guarantee attractive rewards for extended service. If a company wants repeat customers over the long haul, it needs to deliver great products and services every time.

Which is not how everyone sees it. The most compelling argument for valuing loyalty in corporations has been made by Albert O. Hirschman in his classic study *Exit, Voice, and Loyalty: Responses to Decline in Firms, Organizations, and States*. Loyalty plays a key role in the survival of organizations by giving people a reason to speak up and speak out. When "the most quality-conscious customers or members [are] the first to exit," they deprive "the faltering firm or organization of those who could best help it fight its shortcomings and its difficulties." But if they are tethered to the company by loyalty, "these potentially most influential customers and members will stay on longer than they would ordinarily, in the hope or, rather, reasoned expectation that improvement or reform can be achieved 'from within.'" Hirschman concludes that loyalty makes us improve our organizations rather than abandon them.[8]

I'm not convinced. Though it can help a struggling business if aggrieved customers make themselves heard, I have not found it particularly rewarding to stick with enterprises that have lost their way. I had a favorite restaurant in Washington, a place where I ate two or three times a week for the better part of two decades. A couple of years ago the quality started to slip. The little extras that had always been part of the meal were now annoyingly priced add-ons. The most interesting dishes disappeared as the menu was streamlined and simplified to cut costs. Prices went up. Unwilling to head for the exit, I gave it my best Hirschman-certified voice: I complained to the managers; I wrote an impassioned letter detailing the problems. Soon I learned what was going on. The restaurant's original owner had quietly sold it to an investment group that was determined to squeeze every penny out of its investment. And of course, as the old patrons disappeared over the following months, the new owners turned to a fashionable marketing technique—they started a loyalty program. Which begged the question: Who's going to eat ten bad meals in order to get an eleventh bad meal free?

We've found that loyalty, though powerful and valuable, is also rife with conflicts. Why add more objects of loyalty—why multiply the opportunities for conflict—when it isn't necessary? Contracts are the way to bind ourselves in business. And just as contracts are an awkward fit for managing relationships of love and friendship, loyalty is the wrong way to chain our commercial selves together.

7

Tell Me It Smells Like Roses

When the nuttier ravings of Rev. Jeremiah Wright first surfaced, Barack Obama said that, though he disagreed with some of his pastor's remarks, he would not toss him under the bus. "I can no more disown him than I can disown my white grandmother," he declared in March 2008. It was seen as an astonishing act of personal loyalty. "I would think much, much less of him if he disowned a spiritual guide because of that man's explicable if inexcusable resort to paranoia," Andrew Sullivan blogged, adding later, "I do not believe his refusal to disown Wright is a function of politics, but a function of human loyalty and love."

We aren't used to displays of loyalty in politics, and especially rare is when it is exhibited by a leader. Followers are expected to fall on their swords for the boss, not the other way around. Thus the kudos that first greeted Obama's assertion of unbreakable fidelity to his old friend and mentor. *What a different sort of politician! How refreshing!* But it didn't last long. Soon Wright was at the National Press Club playing to the cameras and needling his prominent parishioner. Andrew Sullivan was done with praising the virtues of loyalty, and instead urged Obama "to publicly and clearly and irrevocably disown him and say in words that are clear and bright that Wright is now anathema."

But what was it that made Wright anathema? Was it his crude race-baiting remarks? Hardly. If anything, at the Press Club the old minister toned down the rowdy "God damn America" rhetoric. No, Wright's new and unforgivable offense was his bold and unmistakable disloyalty to Obama—who had, days before, secretly met with the pastor to beg him not to put on a media circus. Wright went on with the show. He declared that his preaching had been within the tradition of the black church, which embraced "radical change" and the social transformation promised by "liberation theology." In other words, Wright proclaimed that his was a gospel of left-wing, race-based politics. This, just as Obama was casting himself as a candidate of the political middle, a man who would transcend the old politics of race. He made his gesture of loyalty to Wright, and the pastor responded by kneecapping his protégé. And if there were any doubt that Wright was acting with disregard for how his comments would affect the candidate's hopes, he sneered that Obama was "a politician."

The candidate definitively disowned Jeremiah Wright. "How could someone I knew, someone I trusted, do this to me?" Obama complained to his aides. "He scarcely hesitated to cut his former friend loose," according to campaign biographer Richard Wolffe. And by so doing, he proved he was "cold-blooded enough to win."[1]

LEADERS LOOK FOR loyalty from their followers, and there's a reason they may not reciprocate. Leaders have duties and responsibilities that may override personal loyalties. Subordinate your political life to your friendships, and you make it possible for those friends to end your public career. Which is why, if you place a high personal value on loyal friendship, politics may not be your best life choice. Or, if you want to succeed in politics while still enjoying the pleasures and benefits of loyal friendship, the old Washington adage has been to "get a dog."

"Friendship's the privilege of private men, for wretched greatness knows no blessing so substantial,"[2] wrote seventeenth-century poet and dramatist Nahum Tate. And he's right about that (even if Tate's judgment is brought into question by having rewritten *King Lear* with a happy ending). Heavy hangs the head, don't you know. Friendship, as we've seen, is facilitated by a rough equality in status. That makes it hard for kings or presidents or CEOs to find fellows sufficiently elevated.

Beyond disparate fortune there is a further question. A ruler can't afford to let sentimental attachments or conflicting obligations take primacy over his commitment to the public interest. At least that's the most positive way to put it. The realpolitik version is to note that leaders don't last very long if they don't do what it takes to maintain, expand, and defend their power. When Prince Hal becomes King Henry he gives Falstaff the heave-ho, not because he's a jerk, but because kings can't afford to be loyal to their old drinking buddies. Still, we feel for poor, discarded Falstaff, and we dislike the new, ruthless Henry, described by W. H. Auden as a "Machiavellian character, master of himself and the situation." Shakespeare's Henry V who rouses his troops to the challenge of St. Crispin's Day is a great, inspiring leader; sad as it is true, such leadership isn't achieved by worrying about old friends' hurt feelings. It's only a few scenes before the St. Crispin's speech that Henry has Bardolph, one of the disreputable pals of his youth, hanged for looting.

Auden derided Hal as a sort of template for personal disloyalty in leaders. "Hal is the type who becomes a college president, a government head, etc., and one hates their guts."[3] One hates their guts because they are either not capable of or not at liberty to indulge in friendship and the loyalties that makes friendship possible. Before the Battle of Shrewsbury, Falstaff asks Hal, on "a point of friendship," to watch his back in the fighting and stand astride him protectively should he fall. Hal makes a crack about how it would take a colossus to stand astride such obesity, but he does give Falstaff a straight answer about whether he can expect the prince's loyal protection: "Say thy prayers and farewell."[4]

Auden may well be right that we hate the guts of such a

Machiavel, but Hal would never have defeated the likes of Harry Hotspur if he had been busy watching out for Falstaff—or any old friend, worthy or not. Savvy leaders have followed Hal's example in putting friendship aside. King George II did not much like Robert Walpole—they were most certainly not friends—but Queen Caroline had confidence in the courtier and made the case to her husband that he should choose his advisers without regard to personal feelings. "She told His Majesty that wise princes always made their resentment yield to their prudence, and their passion to their interest; and that enmity as well as friendship in royal breasts should always give way to policy," Lord Hervey recounted in his memoirs. A king has to stifle enmity and subjugate love, and instead, "whatever would strengthen his hands, confirm his power, and establish his government, should be consulted preferably to any other views whatever."[5]

It's a ruthless approach, but arguably a sound one, because when leaders give personal loyalties pride of place, they very often end up with bad policy. Take the Brownie fiasco. On September 2, 2005, as New Orleans drowned in the wake of Hurricane Katrina, President George W. Bush finally flew to the area. He touched down at the Mobile Regional Airport to meet with emergency officials and local politicians. Soon he had his arm around the shoulder of FEMA director Michael Brown, and—in what is now widely regarded as the moment America turned on the Bush administration—W. proclaimed, "Brownie, you're doing a heck of a job." What was Bush doing other than loyally supporting a subordinate—someone he knew well enough to have christened with a nickname? Clearly, there are limits to the efficacy (and advisability) of loyalty. As Jacob Weisberg, editor of the online magazine *Slate*, puts it, loyalty is "the most overrated virtue in politics."

In this view, loyalty isn't just an overrated virtue, but a vice. "Presidents who fixated on personal allegiance, such as Lyndon Johnson, Richard Nixon, and George W. Bush, tended to perform far worse in office," Weisberg argues. Such leaders become insular and paranoid, devolving "toward a mafia view of politics that lends itself to abuse of power."[6]

But it is an indication of loyalty's tug that even Weisberg can't help but sneak back in an appreciation of it. In an article in January 2010, Weisberg tried to explain why Obama's appeal and approval was slipping. He suspected that the electorate was feeling distanced and disaffected by the president's "cool, detached temperament." The problem, according to Weisberg, was not that people didn't admire Obama but that they didn't "come away from any encounter feeling closer to him." Why ever not? Because Obama "is not warm," nor is he "deeply involved with others." And perhaps most problematic: "he is not loyal."[7]

Just eight months before, Weisberg had praised Obama for his "healthy disdain for the overrated virtue of political loyalty." And yet he couldn't help but note it was "slightly chilling to watch" how ruthless Obama was in discarding anyone who became inconvenient: "If you're useful, you can hang around with him," Weisberg observed. "If you start to look like a liability, enjoy your time with the wolves."[8] It didn't take Obama long—notwithstanding all his admirers' talk of "human loyalty and love"—to learn what to do with his Falstaffs and Bardolphs. And though it may be right and it may be effective, it isn't attractive. Which shows just how tricky a virtue loyalty is for leaders. They can't afford to be sentimental, nor can they afford to be unattractive. They can't afford to be ruled by personal attachments, nor can they afford to be seen as callous or cruel.

THERE MAY NOT be much room for loyalty *from* leaders, but what about loyalty *to* leaders? What sort of leaders demand loyalty—and what sort of loyalty do they demand? Lyndon Johnson once explained what he looked for in an assistant: "I don't want loyalty. I want *loyalty.* I want him to kiss my ass in Macy's window at high noon and tell me it smells like roses. I want his pecker in my pocket."[9] Johnson was less interested in the quality of advice he was getting from his aides than he was in their loyalty. Secretary of Defense Robert McNamara came in for special praise: "If you asked those boys in the Cabinet to run through a buzz saw for their President, Bob McNamara would be the first to go through it," Johnson said.[10] Could it be that buzz-saw-braving loyalty was the very quality that made McNamara such a disastrous steward of Vietnam policy? McNamara was part of the group-thinking Johnson advisers who, as James Reston put it, "gave to the President the loyalty they owed to the country."[11]

Loyalty may well be overrated in politics, but that's not to say it is rated very highly. The virtue has never quite recovered from the damage of back-to-back administrations that put personal allegiance over the public interest. As if Johnson's demands for atrocious epistemic conduct weren't bad enough, next up was Nixon, whose obsession with loyalty set the stage for Watergate.

Well before the break-in, Nixon and his enablers established that loyalty would be the measure of success for executive-branch staff, and failure would not be tolerated. Early in Nixon's first term, Pentagon procurement bureaucrat A. Ernest Fitzgerald made the mistake of telling Congress there were $2 billion in cost overruns on C-5A planes. The White House promptly had Fitzgerald sacked. An aide to H. R. Haldeman explained the firing in an internal memo: "Fitzgerald is no doubt a top-notch cost expert, but he must be given very low marks in loyalty; and after all, loyalty is the name of the game."

Come the summer of 1971, Nixon's obsession with loyalty had blossomed into full-blown, paranoid us-versus-them-ism. When a small drop in unemployment didn't get the big media play the president wanted, he became convinced that the Bureau of Labor Statistics was trying to hobble him by shrugging off good news as a mere statistical anomaly. He even had a reason why the staff of the BLS was supposedly spinning against him: disloyalty born of being Jewish. "The government is full of Jews," Nixon told Haldeman (who can be heard throughout offering a steady stream of loyal assent worthy of Ed "You-are-*correct*" McMahon). "Most Jews are disloyal," Nixon observed; "generally speaking, you can't trust the bastards. They turn on you."[12]

"That's right," says Haldeman, agreeable as ever.

You can't help but conclude that the president would have been better served by advisers willing to shoot straight, willing to tell him the truth even if that meant contradicting him. It's clear that Nixon had enjoyed obsequious yes-men for too long when he could so comfortably launch into noxious judeophobic rants. But truth-telling was seen as dissent, and contradicting the president meant risking being pegged as disloyal. "Dissent and disloyalty were concepts that were never sufficiently differentiated in their minds," said Dr. Jerome H. Jaffe, a psychiatrist who was Nixon's drug czar. He described an organization in which concern for anything other than the president's druthers was seen as a betrayal. "That really was the tragic part," he told a reporter. "To dissent was to be disloyal. That is the theme that recurred again and again." So thoroughly did the theme define the organizational culture that it wasn't good enough merely to withhold dissent. One had to be willing to kneecap anyone who dared to dissent. The president expected his capos to deal with anyone who presented a problem, and there was no tolerance for such niceties as concern over how someone's career might be damaged: "Such a concern was viewed as a fatal flaw," Jaffe said.[13]

But of course, once Watergate had taken its toll and all the president's men were headed for the hoosegow, the very presidential advisers whose blinkered allegiance had contributed so much to the national calamity asked for leniency on the grounds that they were simply being loyal. John Mitchell's lawyer argued that loyalty was a noble thing, to be praised and rewarded, regardless of the outcome: "It does not matter if that loyalty was misguided, misplaced, unreciprocated or anything else," William Hundley said in his closing argument in federal court. "Loyalty per se you will agree is not a crime."[14] Perhaps. But loyalty may aid and abet crime. And leaders looking for loyalists, whether in politics or business, may be interested in lackeys willing to cut corners or worse. Watergate special counsel Archibald Cox (who was fired by the president when he wouldn't circumscribe his investigation) would recall that the president's downfall "serves as a reminder that there are limits to the kind of loyalty that is owed and should be given."[15]

So, what kind of loyalty is appropriate? What is it for an employee or an aide to be loyal? Cynical answers abound. Take Jack Lemmon as the poor schnook with an apartment in Billy Wilder's film *The Apartment*. He's been letting his superiors use his flat for their extramarital assignations. The top boss, Fred MacMurray, gets wind of the deal and, with trysts of his own to arrange, calls Lemmon into his office. "I've been hearing nice things about you," MacMurray begins, and then he reads from a report by Lemmon's supervisor: "Loyal, cooperative, and resourceful." *Loyal* is the dead giveaway—the keyword identifying Lemmon as someone willing to organize a shabby little conspiracy. Soon Lemmon has given MacMurray the key to the apartment, and he is rewarded with a promotion.

Presidential candidate John Edwards made MacMurray look like the soul of propriety. When one of his aides confronted him, urging him to end his affair with Rielle Hunter, Edwards saw it as a betrayal: "You work for me," he screamed at the man. "I trusted you like a son, but you broke my trust."[16] After the Edwards campaign slouched into oblivion, there were plenty of observers who concluded that the candidate's aides had broken a trust more important than any they owed their well-coiffed boss. What of their obligation to their party? And what of their obligation to the nation, which didn't need another dime-store lothario at the helm, imposing his vulnerabilities on the country?

This is the whistleblower's dilemma. Do you keep faith with the person you work for? With the company? Or are those parochial loyalties impediments to doing the right thing? We can't say that following some moral principle is always and ever the right choice—as we've seen, plenty are the traitors who are able to justify immensely damaging treason on the grounds that they were simply following their own consciences. One man's principled whistleblower is another's self-righteous backstabber. There may be no clear way to determine which is which. But given the disintegration of groups, organizations, and societies where loyalty ceases to matter, I'm inclined to make loyalty the default setting that requires a preponderance of damaging evidence before it can be overridden. And so we might approach our leaders in the same way Aristotle suggested regarding friends whose morals may have slipped into error—don't abandon them unless they exhibit an excess of wickedness.

Still, it's always a worrying thing when a leader resorts to demands of loyalty, because that is often a clue that some of that wickedness is afoot and, with the force of loyalty to overcome qualms, the right thing doesn't stand a chance. Second, appeals to loyalty are cause for worry because they all too often come from those whose overweening concern for self makes them fine ones to talk about loyalty at all. "We learn from history," wrote British military historian and theorist Basil Liddell Hart, "that those who are disloyal to their own superiors are most prone to preach loyalty to their subordinates."[17] Is it any surprise that Edwards, preaching loyal, trusting relationships to his staff, did so as a way to cover up his betrayal of his wife's trust?

The loyalty Edwards expected in his team was a fidelity to him and him alone. He sought Lemmon-like servility and would find it in staffer Andrew Young, an aide whose notion of employee devotion ultimately included not only pretending to be the baby-daddy of Edwards's love child, but enlisting his own wife in the conspiracy. Young was willing to endure humiliation, ridicule, and personal ruin for Edwards—*the very definition of loyalty!* But that doesn't mean he was actually expecting to suffer. Young was counting on being well rewarded. And then, instead, when all the skulking was over, all Edwards proposed to give him for his troubles was a job reference. (The text of such a reference would write itself: "Loyal, cooperative, and resourceful . . .")

Young was not happy. He confronted his old boss: "I then

explained that I had the sex video," the video Edwards's very pregnant mistress had made of one of her romps with him. And as if that weren't enough, Young also threatened to make public "a small library of pertinent text messages, [and] voice-mail recordings by the score."[18] Edwards gave him the brush, which led Young to conclude his old boss "was a remorseless and predatory creature." Harsh words coming from a conspirator with an extortionate streak—and one who would ultimately cash in with a tell-all book deal—but quite the fitting end to a relationship defined by demands for debased and degrading loyalty.

As DANGEROUS AS loyalty can be, legitimate loyalty is essential to getting anything done in an organization, whether a business or a government bureaucracy. Colin Powell made loyalty one of the cornerstones of his military career, arguing that success came from "hard work, learning from failure, loyalty to those for whom you work, and persistence." He would later explain his idea of what loyalty to a leader meant:

> When we are debating an issue, loyalty means giving me your honest opinion, whether you think I'll like it or not. Disagreement, at this stage, stimulates me. But once a decision has been made, the debate ends. From that point on, loyalty means executing the decision as if it were your own.[19]

This is not the blinkered *tell-me-what-I-want-to-hear* kind of fidelity. It leaves plenty of room for—indeed demands—uncomfortable truth-telling. At least the truth as each participant in the discussion sees it. Not everyone is going to agree on what facts are salient; not everyone is going to agree on the best course of action. But if an organization is to have any sort of coherent course of action, there has to be a unanimity of purpose once the course has finally been set. Loyalty in this context boils down to a commitment to respect a legitimate process. It's not unlike the basic deal made by candidates in primary elections. If I'm running for my party's nomination for some office, I may think—and I might even vociferously make the case—that my opponent is a louse, an idiot, dangerous or worse. But if he gets a few more votes than I do, I'm duty bound not only to recognize him as the winner, but to support him and campaign for him in the general election. Similarly, working in an organization, I may put forward my own ideas for the direction the business or bureaucracy should go, but if my ideas are not the ones to win the day, I should be ready to support the decision that is made.

Or shouldn't I? Is it right to throw yourself into a policy that you believe to be wrong? Doesn't that smack of the "epistemic bad conduct" that so riles philosophers? Not necessarily. By participating in the process of an organization we make a promise to support the outcome of the process. And when members of an organization aren't willing to let the decision of the organization overrule their own opinions, the organization falls apart. We all have a stake in our own views, even if for no better reason than that they are our own. You could say there is some small measure of suffering whenever we have to abandon our pet projects, championing opinions we regard as stepchildren. A willingness to bear that minor displeasure is not incorrectly considered a type of loyalty, and can be seen either as loyalty to a leader or to the organization that he leads. Either way, loyalty helps get things done. And so movie mogul Samuel Goldwyn may have had good reason for saying of his employees, "I'll take fifty percent efficiency to get one hundred percent loyalty."[20] Efficient men all going off efficiently in their own directions don't get nearly as much done as a group of less capable men reliably rowing in unison.

Still, if loyalty gets the credit for holding organizations together and keeping fractious groups focused on achieving some policy goal, when the policy in question proves problematic, loyalty takes the blame. All of a sudden it's transformed into that unfortunate stuff that makes men acquiesce in dubious decisions against their better judgment. How fragile a virtue to be at the mercy of such vagaries, but so it is. Many have argued that the loyalty that served Colin Powell so well through his military career was ultimately his undoing. Having argued with President George W. Bush against the plan to invade Iraq in 2003, Secretary of State Powell fell in line behind the president when he decided that Saddam had to go. It was Powell who was dispatched to the United Nations to make the case that Iraq was bristling with chemical and biological weapons. When those claims proved to be wrong, Powell's prestige was profoundly diminished. Though he would later insist that he was truly convinced Saddam's arsenal was stuffed with WMDs, it's hard to believe the dovish Powell would have done the official saber rattling had it not been for his loyal commitment to execute the decision as if it were his own.

Smart leaders are the ones who find ways to ease the demands put on loyalty, who are able to keep their crews sailing on course without excessive appeals to duty. Gen. Douglas MacArthur, instead of simply demanding that his subordinates fall into line behind his decisions, went to elaborate lengths to make his junior officers think that every decision went their way. "MacArthur has a wonderful knack of leading a discussion up to the point of a decision that each member present believes he himself originated," according to Gen. George Kenney, who was on MacArthur's staff in the Pacific. "I have heard officers say many times, 'The Old Man bought my idea,' when it was something that weeks before I had heard MacArthur decide to do." Kenney recognized that, "As a salesman, MacArthur has no superior and few equals."[21] It was a skill that banked loyalty rather than drawing it down. If only MacArthur had thought to lavish some of that loyalty-building salesmanship on his ultimate superior, Harry Truman might not have handed him his gold-braided hat.

When a leader inspires loyalty, it is usually a marker that he's done his job of persuading his subordinates that decisions are being made well. Richard Neustadt argues in his classic text on executive authority, *Presidential Power*, that a leader's primary asset is his power of persuasion. According to Neustadt, a successful president never stops persuading—whether the people, the Congress, the bureaucracy, or even his own staff—that what he wants done is what is in their own best interest. Like MacArthur with his junior officers, an effective president encourages cooperation by convincing people that his decisions are really their decisions. There's a lot to be said for this take on power politics, but Neustadt also misses something—that a president who has to persuade everyone of everything all the time is a president who can't help but be hobbled and exhausted. Yes, on the particularly big things, a president may need to make the case to his administration so that they are on board and enthusiastic. But as a day-to-day matter, a president has to be able to count on his people to do what he wants done, relying on a combination of respect for the authority of his office (which is itself a loyalty to the constitutional powers he commands) as well as the more direct sort of loyalty to him.

If failing to convince a given staffer meant only that the aide would be unenthusiastic and inefficient, presidents might not care so much about making sure everyone was on board. All it takes is a single member of the staff to scuttle a president's agenda or drive him into a decision he would rather not make. Anyone with access to confidential discussions is in a position to hijack policy-making. Without loyalty to constrain them, it's all too easy for aides to get their way by means of leaking. No leader can succeed if those working for him are in the habit of surreptitiously undoing his decisions.

No wonder presidents are always trying to plug leaks.

Nixon had his ill-fated plumbers and, even after their efforts demonstrated the catastrophic risks of going on leak hunts, presidents have continued to get riled by what they see as acts of disloyalty by their staff. During Obama's extended period of deliberation over which policy to pursue in Afghanistan, someone leaked Gen. Stanley McChrystal's presidential briefing report to Bob Woodward. Obama was not happy: "For people to be releasing information during the course of deliberations, where we haven't made final decisions yet, I think is not appropriate." He called the leak a firing offense.

It's easy to see how the staffer justified slipping the document to Woodward—he no doubt thought the president was dithering, leaving soldiers hanging in harm's way. The leaker likely thought he was acting in the best interests of the troops and the country by forcing the president's wavering hand. But what the leaker was actually doing, as is so often the case with leakers, was attempting to impose his will on the president. And what right did he have to do so? No one elected the leaker; he isn't the one ultimately responsible for the policy.

Disloyalty has become the norm for political professionals. Once upon a time, aides felt duty-bound to keep their bosses' private conversations private. No more. We live in the age of the dishy memoir, a disloyal idiom as destructive of political relationships as it is of love and marriage. Former senator Bob Kerrey lamented that political loyalty has been crushed by an avalanche of cash available to ambitious advisers and aides eager to make themselves look good by making their old bosses look bad: "there's money in being disloyal," whether it's in the form of a blabbing book deal or a retainer for TV punditry.

Given the well-documented hazards of political loyalty, shouldn't the trend to abandon it prove to be a public good? Yes, too much loyalty (or at least too much loyalty of the wrong sort) ends up stifling the dissent necessary for a thorough discussion and consideration of the issues. A president surrounded by yes-men is one who hears only the echo of his own views and misses the information and analysis he needs to make good decisions. But too little loyalty is just as damaging to healthy debate. Who can be open and honest when he's worried about how his every word will be parsed in the newspaper or online? If you've ever known a compulsive blogger or Twitter tweeter, you have a sense of the candor-crushing nature of total disclosure. You wouldn't speak freely to a friend who posts your unguarded comments online (or if you did, you would learn quickly not to do so again). And the same goes quadruple for politicians. "We already don't write things down for fear of having the documents subpoenaed," Kerrey told *The New York Times*. "Now, in a meeting, you'll have people staring at each other afraid to say anything—for fear that it'll end up in a book." Kerrey is right about the problem, though maybe it isn't as new a phenomenon as it might seem. Oscar Wilde observed more than a century before, "Every great man nowadays has his disciples, and it is always Judas who writes the biography."[22]

Is it any wonder that politicians are now requiring staff to sign the sort of nondisclosure agreements that celebrities have long used to keep staff from selling their secrets to the tabloids? Even politicians' wives have resorted to such legalisms: When Rudy Giuliani was running for president, his wife got his aides together over dinner for some strategizing one evening and began the festivities by having her assistant give each of them a nondisclosure contract to ink. It may seem paranoid or excessive, but can you really blame her? After all, even with the contracts signed by all in attendance, someone later told every detail of that evening's conversation to journalists working up a book on the campaign.[23]

Nondisclosure agreements are "our new loyalty oaths," writes journalist Christine Rosen, necessary, she laments, because "we trade our professional loyalties for a mess of published pottage."[24] What was once governed by a code of personal decency and loyalty now has to be governed by crass contractual obligation. There is no room left for anything quite so quaint as reticence.

BUT WHAT OF those dilemmas when a leader expects his subordinates to subordinate their consciences? Where there are two objects of loyalty—1) a person, and 2) the Constitution—there are bound to be irreconcilable conflicts between competing obligations. Take Jiggs Casey, the colonel played by Kirk Douglas in the political thriller *Seven Days in May*. He's a loyal right-hand man to his mentor, Burt Lancaster's Gen. James Mattoon Scott. Lancaster counts on Douglas to back him in a military coup. When Douglas refuses—and exposes the plot—Lancaster is infuriated by the personal betrayal: "Do you know who Judas was?"

"Yes, I know who Judas was," Douglas spits back. "He was a man I worked for and admired until he disgraced the four stars on his uniform."

Dramatic as it may be, this conflict isn't much of a dilemma. Unlike the hopelessly tortured position of an Agamemnon, who has contradictory obligations none of which he can escape, the conflict of competing loyalties Douglas faces is easily resolved. Douglas is right to decide that his loyalty to Lancaster is null once Lancaster has proven himself disloyal to the country. That's not because of some reverse-Forster maxim asserting that friends must always be betrayed before country. Rather, the conflict is easily resolved because there is no friendship to betray—theirs is a different sort of relationship, that of leader and subordinate. Lancaster's mistake is to think that Douglas should be loyal to him on a personal level. But their personal relationship was established and shaped by the legal structure governing the military. Theirs is a bond established through the giving and taking of orders, orders that have force because of the oath both men have taken.

Lancaster's actions are self-nullifying, not unlike the effort by Shakespeare's Richard II to seize the hereditary lands of Lord Hereford. Richard's uncle, the Duke of York, cautions him that to disregard the rules and rights of inheritance is to cast aside the very things that made him king: "Be not thyself, for how art thou a king / But by fair sequence and succession?" Richard will have none of York's sage advice, and it's his undoing. Whether with Richard II or Gen. James Mattoon Scott, if a leader is to expect loyalty, he has to remain faithful to the institutions and laws that are the basis of his authority.

Which isn't to say leaders must be deserving to deserve loyalty. In the book, and later the film, *The Caine Mutiny*, a smart, sophisticated, and disgruntled junior navy officer convinces his credulous comrades their captain is cracked. Captain Queeg helps in that endeavor by being a bit of a wreck—there's the nervous fumbling with those awful stainless-steel worry balls, the obsession with phantom strawberries, and the yellow-stained weakness under fire. We end up rooting for the men who take command of the ship in a storm. We find ourselves agreeing that Queeg didn't deserve to command, and our sentiments are with the mutineers as they stand trial. But of course we're wrong, and Herman Wouk means for us to be startled into the realization that we're wrong. In the movie's climactic scene, the mutineers are celebrating their acquittal; their lawyer, disgusted with having gotten them off, confronts them: "At one point, Queeg came to you for help, and you turned him down," the lawyer says. "He wasn't worthy of your loyalty. So you turned on him. You made up songs about him. If you'd been loyal to Queeg, do you think all this would have come up?" The lawyer hammers it home: "You don't work with the captain because of his hairstyle, but because he's got the job, or you're no good."

For all the complicated twists and convoluted turns loyalty pretzels itself up with, that simple blunt statement rings true. We have an abiding, visceral response to the disloyal—they're just no damn good. Still, we can't escape our ambivalence about loyalty. As much as we admire it, as much as we share in the damning judgment that the disloyal are no-goodniks, we don't much trust loyalists. We're leery of company men; and in the political world we deride those George Bernard Shaw called "good party people" as unimaginative hacks. We expect them to be smug and self-satisfied in their closed-mindedness. They take their loyalty to be a virtue and we dismiss them for it. We suspect that Shaw was right in saying, "In politics there should be no loyalty except to the public good."[25] But when it comes to endeavors that require some coordinated effort, having everyone act on his own stubborn convictions may not do the public much good.

Whether the endeavor is a ship or the ship of state, there can be no effective leadership without some measure of loyalty. We may not like it—the downsides and pitfalls are obvious—but there's no escaping it. "Leadership," as Judith Shklar puts it, "for better or worse involves fidelity."[26]

8

Reasons for Treason

One month after Al-Qaeda hijacked passenger jets and crashed them into the World Trade Center and the Pentagon, American University professor Akbar Ahmed traveled to Cleveland to present a lecture on Muslim-Christian understanding. He had wondered whether to call the talk off, given the tensions of the moment, but decided instead that his message of tolerance was all the more needed. The evening before the lecture, a Pakistani-American doctor hosted a dinner in Ahmed's honor. It was a private affair, with the professor and five dozen of Cleveland's more prominent Muslims—doctors, lawyers, and businessmen. When, in the course of the private dinner, Ahmed called the recent attacks "un-Islamic" and a "major setback" for their community, a number of the guests disagreed vehemently: "They called September 11 a glorious event for Islam," Ahmed recalled. "The taking of innocent lives was justified, they argued, as September 11 was the continuation of a full-scale war taking place against Israel, which is backed by the United States." Nor was this an isolated incident. Ahmed heard the same sort of claims at a dinner with the Muslim Council of Britain—it was "illustrative of the thinking wherever Muslims lived."[1]

The debate at the dinner in Cleveland was whether terrorist attacks were good or bad for Islam. Missing from the discussion—or at least from Ahmed's account of it—was any question of what was good or bad for America. The loyalties the men displayed were to the *ummah*, not to the country in which they lived.

Loyalty to country, once so boisterously demanded of one and all in America, is now seen as quaint at best and delusional or destructive at worst. Try to imagine dozens of Japanese Americans getting together over dinner in January 1942 to applaud Pearl Harbor. It's unthinkable. And yet the fear that divided loyalties would lead to subversion once ran so high that the government had the entire mainland community of Japanese Americans herded behind barbed wire. I guess we can look at it as progress of a sort that no small number of Muslim Americans in Cleveland, a mere month after 9/11, felt safe enough in their civil rights to voice their admiration for Osama bin Laden's handiwork.

AS A COUNTRY of immigrants, we have long worried about divided loyalties. World War I brought the fear that German

Americans were plotting and scheming for the Kaiser. That fear was front and center come the next war. After Hitler had conquered Europe, Franklin Roosevelt urged the United States to be prepared if the war crossed the Atlantic. In a May 26, 1940, Fireside Chat, FDR made the case for military readiness and warned that the United States could be attacked with weapons other than guns and bombs: "The Trojan Horse. The Fifth Column that betrays a nation unprepared for treachery. Spies, saboteurs, and traitors." Roosevelt argued for unity of purpose and suggested that German propaganda would try to sow division in the guise of democratic politics. "These dividing forces I do not hesitate to call undiluted poison."[2]

We've come to see such worries as a kind of paranoia, an exploitation of primal fears used by the powerful to stifle honest political dissent. But it's worth noting that, in the 1930s, the German American Bund was indeed a Nazi propaganda front. And during World War I, though the vast majority of German Americans were entirely loyal to their new home, a small network, acting on orders from the German high command, did indeed implement an ambitious campaign of sabotage. Using pencil-size incendiary sticks, they set off an explosion at Black Tom, an island in New York Harbor connected to Jersey City, NJ, by a causeway, and used as an ammunition dump. The blast was so powerful it shattered windows in Times Square, over five miles away.

And then there was Dr. Anton Dilger, whose father had immigrated to America from Germany in time to fight for the Union at Gettysburg (where he was awarded the Medal of

Honor for his heroics). Dilger was born in America but educated in Germany, eventually becoming a medical doctor with a specialty in tissue cultures—oh, and yes, sabotage. In 1915 Dr. Dilger returned from Germany to the land of his birth and set up a laboratory in the Washington suburb of Silver Spring, Maryland. There he cultured anthrax. His ring of saboteurs would take vials of the stuff to the stockyards outside Baltimore, infecting horses, mules, and cattle gathered for shipping to Britain and France.

Still, even where there is some identifiable sabotage and sedition, efforts to stamp it out have a tendency to get ugly or worse. Once the United States entered World War I, Woodrow Wilson's campaign to demand unambiguous loyalty of German Americans quickly devolved into a frenzy of anti-squarehead bigotry. German Americans made frantic and loud declarations of fidelity, but the flag-kissing wasn't enough to stop the official government assault on German-language newspapers, German music, unions made up predominantly of German-American workers, and even beer.

The Temperance Union had been trying for decades to impose a national prohibition on alcohol. Its main organized opposition was made up of the beer barons, who had used their deep pockets—and the political clout of German-American organizations around the country—to blunt the prohibitionist assault. Those barons had inconvenient names such as Pabst, Schlitz, Blatz, and Busch, and the teetotalers took aim. When the United States finally entered the war, old Adolphus Busch's widow just happened to be in Germany visiting daughters who had married Teutonic aristocrats. Pointing to her residence in enemy territory, the temperance types moved to have the assets of Anheuser-Busch seized as alien property. August Busch had his mother whisked back to the States. When she arrived by ship at Key West, she was detained by federal marshals for days, subjected to withering interrogation and a full body-cavity search upon the absurd suspicion she was carrying secret papers for the Kaiser.

Like other German Americans, August Busch felt it necessary to proclaim publicly his pledge *"to sacrifice everything except loyalty to country, and its own honor, to serve the Government in bringing this war to a victorious conclusion."* But the prohibitionists had their opportunity and pounced, denouncing the beer barons as subversives working for the enemy by stealing grain from the troops: "Every bushel of grain that is destroyed" making beer, editorialized the *American Issue*, "serves the Kaiser just as well as a bushel sunk by a submarine at sea."[3] Woodrow Wilson ordered all breweries closed. And with the beer industry effectively muzzled, the Eighteenth Amendment slipped through thirty-six state legislatures, and National Prohibition became law.[4] Such are the affronts to liberty that can happen when campaigns of enforced loyalty are afoot.

Such campaigns have proved disastrous for the concept of loyalty in America, tainting the legitimate demands of country and Constitution. Such abuses have contributed to the modern notion that, when at odds with friends or family or conscience, commitment to country comes last. Perhaps no abuse has done more to discredit the demands of love and loyalty to country than the decision by Franklin D. Roosevelt in the days after Pearl Harbor to lock up Japanese Americans in dusty desert detention camps.

Part of what made the "relocation centers" so offensive was not just that they represented an assault on the civil liberties of Americans. It was the implicit accusation that these Americans, because of their heritage, could not be trusted, the assumption that until proven otherwise, they were to be assumed disloyal. This, even though the attorney general of California reported to Washington just a couple of months after Pearl Harbor, "We have had no sabotage and no fifth column activity since the beginning of the war."[5]

What was the worst thing suffered by Japanese Americans in World War II? Was it the loss of their property, as their abandoned farms and businesses were snatched up? Was it the loss of their freedom, as they were herded into the stark confines of the internment camps? Or was it the loss of a very basic sort of dignity, the degradation of being suspected of disloyalty? When the roundup began, the Japanese-American Citizens League told its members that going along with the relocation was the patriotic thing to do. "You are not being accused of any crime. You are being removed only to protect you and because there might be one of you who might be dangerous to the United States," the league told the Nisei and Issei at the behest of the federal government. "It is your contribution to the war effort. You should be glad to make the sacrifice to prove your loyalty."[6]

The young men of Japanese descent would have been willing to make far greater sacrifices if their loyalty hadn't been questioned. In Hawaii, where the fear of fifth columnists might have been more likely—it was the site of Japan's attack on U.S. territory, and the islands had a much larger population of Japanese Americans than the mainland—there was no effort to quarantine the suspect group. One in three eligible Japanese-American men in Hawaii signed up for military service. Army recruiters got very different results when they went looking for volunteers at the internment camps—only one in fourteen young men joined up. People will risk much if given their due as good citizens and true. Treat people as disloyal, put them under suspicion, and you end up, if not destroying loyalty, at least dampening the enthusiasm for it.

THESE WERE OUTRAGEOUS and excessive reactions, and yet the prickly question of divided national loyalties remains. The Department of Defense continues to have an interest in figuring out whom it can trust not to spy and whom it should keep an eye on. Once upon a time the biggest problems were either ideological (many of the Soviet Union's most helpful spies were Americans and Brits enthralled by the Communist cause) or financial (the CIA was a bit slow to realize that agent Aldrich Ames's salary couldn't sustain his habit of buying new Jaguar sedans). But now it's the lingering extranational ties of immigrants and their children that are proving to be the biggest security risk.

Between the end of World War II and the end of the Cold War, loyalties divided by an allegiance to a home country other than the United States were the motive in fewer than 20 percent of espionage cases. But since 1990, according to a Department of Defense report, 57 percent of Americans caught committing espionage were motivated by divided loyalties of that sort. Among them was Chi Mak, a Chinese immigrant who found work as an engineer with American defense contractors. He started sending military secrets to China in 1983 and kept at it for two decades—even though he became an American citizen in 1985. He is typical of the most recent generation of traitors, of whom "More were naturalized citizens, and more had foreign attachments (relatives or close friends), foreign business connections, or foreign cultural ties."[7]

During the postwar Red Scare of the late forties, Arthur Schlesinger, Jr., argued in the pages of *The New York Times Magazine* that liberal or even socialist views did not make one un-American. "The only criterion for disloyalty," he wrote, "is superior loyalty to another country."[8]

Though, clearly, superior loyalty to another country can indeed be a problem, it isn't the only modern source of disloyalty. The father of modern radical-Islamist ideology, Sayyid Qutb, proclaimed, "A Muslim has no nationality except his belief." The scholar Fouad Ajami calls the heirs of Qutb's ideology the "Nowhere Men" of Islam. They belong to nowhere because they are bound by loyalty to no country. Indeed, they abjure love of country as an affront to the primacy of their obligations to God.[9]

There's nothing new in this sort of claim, the notion that God (or the secular equivalent, an overweening ideology) comes first. We shouldn't be surprised that men who betray their country do so in the full, if twisted, belief that they are the principled ones, the *loyal* ones (just loyal to something they consider more important than country). As Thomas Carlyle observed, "No man at bottom means injustice; it is always for some obscure distorted image of a right that he contends."[10] Such self-satisfied delusions have always worked to the advantage of spymasters. They look to recruit the alienated, those desperate to glom some meaning onto their isolated lives. Or they search out the fervent, those eager to prove that they will put their beliefs above all else. Hede Massing ran a Washington spy ring for the Soviets in the 1930s. When one prize prospect proved hesitant, saying, "What about loyalty to my country?" Massing responded, "Loyalty to humanity" has "precedence over any other kind of loyalty."

Anwar al-Awlaki—the American-born Muslim preacher who gave guidance and encouragement to Maj. Nidal Malik Hasan—made the same sort of case in calling for American Muslims to attack the United States: "How can you have loyalty to a government that is leading the war against Islam and Muslims?" he demanded from his hideout in Yemen. It's a challenge we have to take seriously. We may be hesitant to make a big issue of loyalty, what with the ugly excesses that such demands have produced in our recent history, but our self-proclaimed enemies have no such qualms.

—

IN THE YEARS just after World War II there was a national fad for "loyalty oaths," with demands that everyone from Hollywood stars to elementary school students profess their fidelity to the American way. In Indiana, you had to sign a loyalty oath to be allowed a career in professional wrestling. Hoping to out-flank Republicans getting political mileage out of anticommunism, President Harry Truman instituted by executive order a Federal Employees Loyalty and Security Program, meant to expose Commies and subversives working in the federal government. It never amounted to much, perhaps because someone willing to be disloyal to his country isn't likely to hesitate when asked to sign a loyalty oath.

This has long been recognized as a bit of a problem for the whole oath-taking business. John Lilburne, a revolutionary pamphleteer of the English Civil War, warned in 1647 that loyalty oaths "are nothing but cloaks of knavery, and breeders of strife and mischief." It's hard to argue with his observation that those who make nothing of an oath will break it whenever it suits their purpose, "whereas to him that conscientiously scruples an oath, his bare word . . . is the sincerest tie in the world."[11]

And yet loyalty oaths have often been used, with greater or lesser success (usually lesser), for centuries. Critics of the loyalty programs of the 1940s and '50s complained that requiring people to take oaths of allegiance was inconsistent with the nation's founding principles. But loyalty oaths were commonplace as the approach of the Revolutionary War prompted a frenzy of oath-taking. Nor were those proofs of loyalty voluntary. George Washington was one of the most prominent advocates for public tests of loyalty. In 1775 he wrote, "It is high time a test act was prepared and every man called upon to declare himself; that we may distinguish friends from foes."[12] Thomas Paine demanded loyalty oaths so that everyone could know, "square by square and house by house, who are in real allegiance with the United Independent States, and who are not. Let but the line be made clear and distinct, and all men will then know what they are to trust to."[13]

The oaths that Washington pushed—and he pushed them not only on the soldiers under his command but on civilians wherever his soldiers marched—were less about ensuring fidelity to the new nation than about forcing people to make a public break with any loyalty to Britain. The most common oath started off by declaring Americans "owe no allegiance or obedience to George the 3rd, King of Great Britain; and I renounce, refuse and abjure any allegiance or obedience to him." It was a wedge Washington and his generals used aggressively, with the main effect being to reinforce a public sense that people were abandoning their ties to the king and the old country. Washington—and John Adams and Thomas Jefferson—were convinced that history and experience had proved that "loyalty oaths were wonder-workers in causes sacred and profane."[14]

Loyalty oaths may have worked wonders at making Tories feel abandoned by the fellow royalists they had expected to stand fast, but they didn't do anything to restrain traitors. In the summer of 1776 a Mata Hari in a Tory brothel convinced a customer named William Hickey—who was one of Washington's bodyguards—to hand his boss over to the British. The plot failed and Hickey hanged. Like the traitor Benedict Arnold a few years later, Hickey had duly signed the Continental Army's loyalty oath.

As with the years leading to the Revolution, secessionists in the South used loyalty tests in the run-up to the Civil War as a way to force people to declare publicly that they put their state, not the Union, first. Once the war was under way, though, it was Lincoln who made the most of loyalty tests. He offered them to rebel prisoners of war as a get-out-of-jail card; Southern civilians whose towns fell to Union troops had to swear an oath if they wanted to have access to food and other supplies. Lincoln demanded loyalty tests be signed by all federal job seekers. Not surprisingly, rebel spies looking to infiltrate official Washington were more than happy to sign on the line.

The ancient Greeks were right to identify "loyalty" with "trustworthiness," and you can't expect an honest answer from someone who is untrustworthy. No less a Red hunter than Richard Nixon himself rejected the notion of loyalty oaths, arguing that they were worthless—that Alger Hiss would have signed one happily. As vice president, Nixon urged President Eisenhower to strip the word *loyalty* from all aspects of the federal government's security apparatus, to focus instead on who might be a "risk," where riskiness was not just a matter of one's foreign connections but behaviors (such as homosexuality) that might leave one open to blackmail by foreign agents. They came up with Executive Order 10450, which allowed the administration to give the boot to any federal employee whose "behavior, activities or associations . . . tend to show that the individual is not reliable or trustworthy." It was a powerful club to wield, and Nixon would brag, ahead of the 1954 mid-term election, that they had kicked thousands of "communists and fellow travelers" out of government.[15]

In practice it had the same fundamental flaws as loyalty oaths—a feebleness in the face of professional spycraft. Spooks worth their salt would simply avoid associations and entanglements that might bring suspicion on them, just as the most hard-core of subversives could be expected to be the first in line to lavish the flag with kisses.

The Supreme Court started to rein in the loyalty follies in the 1950s. Among the many loyalty-oath rules in the United States was a California law requiring, in order to claim one's tax exemptions, a promise not to advocate the violent overthrow of the government. The Supreme Court ruled the law unconstitutional. In his concurring opinion, Justice Hugo Black echoed John Lilburne's argument about the hopeless inefficacy of such efforts: "I am certain that loyalty to the United States can never be secured by the endless proliferation of 'loyalty' oaths," he wrote. "Loyalty must arise spontaneously from the hearts of people who love their country and respect their government."[16]

Such oaths have been seen as undermining loyalty by punishing honest criticism of the government policies. Which has made a very live issue out of an ancient question: Is patriotism a sustaining virtue or a destructive vice? Of all the loyalties that bind us, is commitment to country the most important (as Creon argued to Antigone) or just the most dangerous?

WHEN MARK TWAIN was twenty-year-old Samuel Clemens, he lived in a Cincinnati boarding house, where he became friends with an everyman scholar, a Scot named Macfarlane. The fellow worked in some trade Twain never was able to discover, but he had given himself a remarkable education—for one, learning the dictionary forward and backward. He was a sort of instinctive Darwinian, years before Darwin riled the world with *On the Descent of Man.* For Macfarlane, *descent* was indeed the operative term when talking about man, because he felt that the progress of evolution had stumbled and fallen when man finally was reached. According to Twain's friend, "man's heart was the only bad heart in the animal kingdom." Only man felt "malice, envy, vindictiveness, revengefulness, hatred, selfishness." But of all the vices attendant to that degraded creature, one stood out: Man is "the sole animal in whom was fully developed the base instinct called *patriotism.*"[17]

Twain reveled in tweaking the pieties of his age, and goodness knows chest-thumping and flag-waving were great late-nineteenth-century enthusiasms. So it should be no surprise that Twain was happy to adopt his old friend's contempt for the patriotic urge. And now, after a century in which criminal regimes festooned their charnel houses with blood-red flags and demanded everyone salute, Twain's disdain for patriotism has a greater resonance. Even in countries with legitimate governments, patriotism is not uncontroversial. Many have been the critics who (usually with the excesses of old Tail-Gunner Joe in mind) have seen patriotism as little more than a cudgel used to discourage debate and silence dissent.

Though the ceremonial rites of patriotism may be natural and unproblematic for most, in some sophisticated circles all that saluting and pledging and flag-worshiping smacks of a tacky yahooism at best, and a bullying jingoism at worst. The modern intellectual disdain for the trappings of patriotic observance was well expressed by *The New Yorker*'s E. B. White in 1946: "We take pains to educate our children at an early age in the rituals and mysteries of the nation," he wrote, "but lately the most conspicuous activity of nations has been the blowing of each other up, and an observant child might reasonably ask whether he is pledging allegiance to a flag or to a shroud." Reciting the Pledge of Allegiance remains rather unfashionable among those who don't know which to lament more in "The Star Spangled Banner," its bellicosity or the leaden quality of its poetry. Controversialist Nicholas Von Hoffman doesn't think much of the Pledge: "standing at attention and unthinkingly reciting words whenever one is told to do so is either ridiculous or imbecilic or an obedience drill for a people already susceptible to group think." And when it comes to the Stars and Stripes itself, Von Hoffman razzes what he called "flagolatry," a fetish employed in "bamboozling the moron masses with showy irrationalities."[18]

The sophisticate's discomfort with the flag as a symbol of loyalty to country popped up early in the 2008 presidential primary season when Barack Obama made a point of not wearing an American flag on his lapel. He called the display of flag pins "a substitute for I think true patriotism, which is speaking out on issues that are of importance." He proudly proclaimed: "You show your patriotism by being true to your values and ideals."[19] The candidate soon learned that, however well received such a sentiment would be at Harvard or the University of Chicago, it didn't go over well with heartland voters. Obama had a flag pinned to every suit in his closet.

Twain would have been bitterly amused. "Patriotism is merely a religion," he proclaimed in his crotchety old age, a "worship of country."[20] If Twain himself had been devout, this might have suggested he regarded patriotism as fundamentally impious, with the flag as the modern manifestation of the golden calf. Instead, what Twain meant was that patriotism exhibits the same faults he saw in religion, specifically, a dull-witted willingness to subjugate one's critical faculties to a mindless mob.

Twain thought that for most people patriotism is nothing more than "the safe thing, the comfortable thing." Safe and comfortable because it is unthinking: "Does the reader believe he knows three men who have actual reasons for their pattern of patriotism—and can furnish them?" Twain said people get their patriotism "at the public trough" and have "no hand in its preparation themselves."[21] He denounced the regular sort of patriotism not because it entailed devotion to country, but because those who embrace it get their instruction in what devotion requires from mountebanks and charlatans, phonies and third-raters—or as Twain more colorfully puts it, the average fellow gets his patriotism from "the windy and incoherent six-dollar sub-editor of his village newspaper."

Real patriotism, in Twain's view, demands that the citizen think for himself: "The patriot is the conscience-instructed man, the man who is true to his convictions." The right sort of patriotism is that "reasoned out in the man's own head and fire-assayed and tested and proved in his own conscience."[22] This is a criticism of loyalty that we will find familiar—the worry that in its reflexive, emotional way, devotion shoulders rationality aside. And Twain's alternative to the common sort of patriotism—simply being true to one's convictions—is not without appeal. In the full chill of the Cold War, Henry Steele Commager made the same argument Twain had forwarded half a century before, that the American loyalty of the day lacked "intellectual conviction" and asked of citizens nothing but "mere outward conformity."[23] True loyalty, he argued, meant embracing the American tradition of "the Higher Law, or of obedience to the dictates of conscience rather than of statutes."[24]

But no matter how admirable being "conscience-instructed" may be, it isn't clear that "obedience to the dictates of conscience" necessarily qualifies as something we would recognize as "patriotism." It doesn't take much to imagine a man who consults his conscience and reasons that he is morally bound to betray his country—and such a man might even be right, if his country is evil enough. That doesn't mean he is a patriot. He might just be a self-righteous traitor.

Typical of the type is U.S. State Department intelligence analyst Walter Kendall Myers, who, along with his wife, slipped damaging secrets to Cuba for three decades. He did so "out of conscience and personal commitment." Such was the gloss his lawyer tried to put on it when Myers pleaded guilty in November 2009. The fact that Myers passed secrets for thirty-some years with complete confidence in his own moral judgment hardly earns him the honorific *patriot*. When it comes to doing right by your country, a supercilious conscience may be just as problematic as a supine one.

Myers had nurtured a bitter contempt for the United States and a love of Cuba, and his affection for Castro's little island tyranny shows us why conscience alone is not enough to provide us with the stuff of patriotism. We have to ask: Do we have the best interests of our country at heart? Which gets to the heart of the matter: To be loyal to one's country begins with loving one's country. The patriot can be disappointed in his country, frustrated with his country, even angry with his country—just as he can feel those emotions toward his family. The patriot can express those emotions, can dissent, without calling into question his commitment to the well-being of his country—just as the family member can express unhappiness with those closest to him without there ever being a question of his commitment to his kin.

Just as loyalty is the crucial element in love, love—and an exclusive sort of love at that—is essential in defining certain kinds of loyalty, patriotism among them. "The man who loves other countries as much as his own stands on a level with the man who loves other women as much as he loves his own wife," Teddy Roosevelt said in a 1918 speech. "One is as worthless a creature as the other."[25]

LOVING ONE'S COUNTRY is the prerequisite for patriotism. But such love is not without its risks, as patriotism's detractors are quick to point out. The same philosophers who worry that friendship leads us into "bad epistemic conduct" (because our affections lead us to think unrealistically well of pals) are alarmed at the prospects for "bad faith" among patriots, what with their tendency to think the best about their own country, the evidence be damned. "Patriotic attitudes are such that the patriot is likely to have biased, poorly supported beliefs," writes Simon Keller; he assumes the patriot suffers from "an inflated view of her own country's value and importance."[26] Keller is convinced that such thinking isn't just faulty but naughty, and thus grounds enough to write off patriotism as a hopeless vice. George Bernard Shaw (who despised patriotism as "a pernicious, psychopathic form of idiocy") made the same point with a blunt eloquence: "Patriotism is your conviction that this country is superior to all other countries because you were born in it."

It isn't hard to find empirical evidence that patriotic conviction can lead to biased beliefs. Comedians Penn and Teller devoted an episode of their cable television show *Bullshit!* to lampooning mindless devotion to country. In the guise of a phony and cartoonishly patriotic organization called the America Is #1 Foundation, producers for the show asked passersby to sign a petition. The document they presented called on the United Nations to pass a resolution recognizing that "amongst all nations in the world, America is clearly the best," enjoying a landscape "more majestic than any other landscape" and with people who "are better citizens than any other citizens." With cameras in their faces (and plenty of pressure not to look unpatriotic) there was no shortage of people willing to sign.

The most vigorous and succinct statement of this concern comes from Leo Tolstoy, who saw in the German anthem, "Deutschland über alles," a claim of objective superiority. "What," he asked, "if all patriots think their respective countries are the best?" It is "very stupid," Tolstoy declared. "Stupid, because if every state will consider itself better than any other, it is obvious that they will all be in the wrong."[27] (Nor is "Deutschlandlied" the only such offender—think of the patriotic song "This Is My Country," with its bold assertion that, among all the nations of the world, America is "grandest on earth.")

It's hard to argue with Tolstoy's logic, but I suspect that he, Keller, and Penn and Teller are all overstating the extent to which patriotism is rooted in unjustifiable beliefs about one's country's superiority. Isn't it possible that love of country is like love of family? Being devoted to one's family doesn't require a belief that it is the best family in the world. Rather, what makes my family an object of loyal commitment is that it is *my* family. I don't love my mother because she is the best mother in the world (though, I should hasten to add, she is). It is because she is *my* mother, who together with my father made my life possible, gave me every opportunity they could, and supported me at every turn. Gratitude, affection, and a good dose of sentimental attachment to those with whom my life has been shared—all these things go into the love and loyal commitment I have to my family. Why can't these same factors provide me, unobjectionably, with a love and loyal commitment to my country?

G. K. Chesterton was on to something when he wrote that saying "My country, right or wrong" was rather like saying "My mother, drunk or sober." C. S. Lewis thought that Chesterton's analogy captured the heart of the best sort of patriotism: Just as a man who loves his mother will persevere in his affections, whatever becomes of her, "A man who truly loves his country will love her in her ruin and degeneration."[28] Which doesn't mean a man should glibly cooperate in his loved one's self-destruction. If his mother is a drunk, he might well express his devotion to her not by running to the liquor store for her, but by shuttling her off to the ministrations of the Betty Ford people. So too, the man who loves his country will try to save his country, not only from assault, but also from its own worst instincts. "No doubt if a decent man's mother took to drink he would share her troubles to the last," Chesterton argued, which is not the same thing as being "in a state of gay indifference as to whether his mother took to drink or not."[29] A man who loves his country doesn't boast of his indifference to whether its wars are just. Loyalty means not only being proud of your country, but being ashamed of it as well when one's country does something regrettable. We don't feel ashamed of something that is not ours, or to which we have no connection.[30] Shame can be an expression of loyalty in that it is an affirmation of the committed relationships we have, whether with family or country.

There is another reason, one that Lewis identifies, for hewing to a notion of patriotism that doesn't require one to believe in the superiority of one's homeland. If commitment to country is based on a belief in its unmatched greatness, any disappointment of that unrealistic predicate is likely to lead to disillusionment. When one's country proves not to be perfect or is found to be no longer the grandest on earth, when it falls short of being the most worthy or the most virtuous, well, then the reason for loving her is gone. An arrogant patriotism isn't just an offense against good epistemic conduct, it's a rickety, fragile sort of devotion.

How much better if the patriot celebrates the distinctive characteristics of his country, not because those characteristics are superior to all others, but because they help define and identify the community of which he is a part. To use family as an analogy once again, I have a soft spot for a Saturday-evening supper of burgers off the Weber grill and baked beans out of the oven. This is not because I think this is the best possible meal for a Saturday night, but because, growing up, it was a family staple, a small tradition. As far as family characteristics go, it was a trivial and unoriginal one. But I have an emotional attachment to it. Embracing it is just one way to embrace my family. So too, affection for my country's particularities, however trivial they may be, gives me a way to express my love of country, a way to embrace my nation. This is a problem?

We want, as Justice Hugo Black put it, love of country to arise spontaneously. But that doesn't mean that such affection will flourish without being nurtured. The husband and wife who would keep their marriage together learn to tell each other "I love you" on a regular basis. There is a reason that religions universally involve rituals of devotion. We might want love of God to "arise spontaneously from the hearts of people," and there may even be some who experience such a wholesome and direct epiphany. Many have been the detractors who dismiss liturgy as rote repetition, who sneer at creeds as the recitation of so many archaic words. But weekly worship has its reasons (and reasons beyond the standard jokes about passing the offering plate). Most of us need to express gratitude and adoration to feel it, and before we can do it, we need to learn how to express ourselves. It isn't hard to say "I love you" to family, standing as they are right in front of us.

We need symbols to stand in for God and country, to make our devotion to them as tangible as is our love for the people we see. A nation isn't just the territory it occupies, nor simply the people who live there, nor even just the principles enshrined in its constitution (if it has one). It's a complex of all these things, and it's hard to say "I love you" to a complex. That's where the flag comes in. It provides an object to which we can address our love of country. It's easy to scoff at the foolishness of "flagolatry"—after all, what's the big deal with a scrap of cloth? But the flag is just a symbol, as is all language—words and images are not the things they represent (*Ceci n'est pas une pipe*). Oaths and pledges and the other rituals of patriotism may strike us as contrived. Henry Steele Commager insisted that true loyalty was "not the indulgence in ceremony—a flag salute, an oath of allegiance, a fervid verbal declaration." And he's quite right: Ceremony is no substitute for loyalty. But that doesn't mean it isn't important in making loyalty to country flourish. Ceremonial affirmations keep our affections primed, just as the rote repetition of "Love you, honey," said as the lights go out, helps keep the commitments of a marriage from withering. There will be those who say the words without meaning them, without feeling them, but for many, or most, the expression is an essential part of making the emotion endure.

Such arguments are compelling, of course, only if you think commitment to country is a sentiment worth shoring up. Those who think patriotism is a vice aren't likely to have changed their minds yet. In fact, when it comes to denouncing patriotism, they're just getting warmed up.

TOLSTOY DIDN'T JUST think patriotism was stupid, he thought it was downright immoral: "Immoral, because it inevitably leads every man who experiences the feeling to try to obtain advantages for his own state and nation, at the expense of other states and nations." This tendency, Tolstoy wrote, "is directly opposed to the fundamental moral law recognized by all men: not to do unto another what we do not wish to have done to ourselves."[31]

Does doing right by one's own country mean doing wrong by others? A common analogy for the loyalty of patriots has been to liken it to the loyalty of sports fans. It's a fine and illuminating analogy—but only so far as it goes. The fan favors his team because it is *his* team, a part of his community; the true fan sticks with his team, whether it's winning or losing; the true fan loves his team. The patriot does all these things and properly so. But if patriotic loyalty is like sports loyalty, it can't help but be marred by belligerence. Sportsmanship, by its very nature, is competitive. Sport requires winners and losers. If rooting for the USA is like rooting for the Yankees (and, goodness knows, both franchises are hated by those who have repeatedly lost contests to them), then supporting the USA means wishing the defeat of every other nation. The Yankees don't succeed unless every other team is beaten— and the more convincingly and humiliatingly the opponents are crushed, the better.

That's the desire Martha Nussbaum sees in the popular chant "U-S-*A*! U-S-*A*!" Hearing it at a ball game not long after 9/11, she felt the chanting "seemed to express a wish for America to defeat, abase, humiliate its enemies."[32] She found this to be troubling.

Social theorist Thorstein Veblen would have made the same observation. He was convinced the sports metaphor captured what was wrong with patriotism, an emotion he derided as "a patent imbecility." Patriotism never rises "to the consummate pitch of enthusiastic abandon except when bent on some work of concerted malevolence," Veblen wrote. Its "highest and final appeal is for the death, damage, discomfort and destruction of the party of the second part."[33]

That may be a pretty good description of the relationship between the Yankees and the Red Sox, but I'm not sure it captures the true nature of patriotism. Sports are the very definition of zero-sum games. In most contests, someone has to win and someone has to lose. Yes, in times of war, nations do end up in such win-or-lose contests. But as frequent as wars unfortunately are, most nations are usually at peace with one another. Under those commonplace circumstances, nations are not in zero-sum struggles (at least as long as you don't count the Olympics). The surest way to promote the success of my own country may well be to promote a broadly enjoyed prosperity around the world. The best hope for my own freedoms may well be to encourage similar freedoms for those who are oppressed. I can wish America well without wishing France ill, just as I can wish my own family well without needing my neighbor to suffer.

Still, Tolstoy had an even deeper and more profound complaint about patriotism. How can we call it any sort of virtue when it runs contrary to the fundamental moral principle of respecting the "equality and brotherhood of all men"? Patriotism means preferring in some basic way one's countrymen over other people, a sentiment, according to Tolstoy, that is "not only not a virtue, but unquestionably a vice."[34] This is the cosmopolitan critique, a rebuke to patriotism that is both ancient and enduring. Diogenes the Cynic, and the Stoics who followed his lead, extolled the virtues of world citizenship. The philosopher Theodorus said, "a wise man's country was the World."[35] When Anaxagoras was chided for having no affection for his country, he responded, "Be silent," and pointing to heaven, said, "I have the greatest affection for my country."[36]

As is only appropriate for a moral doctrine that abjures borders, the cosmopolitan cause is common to many cultures and ethical traditions. For example, in the *Panchatantra*, a Hindu collection of stories providing guidance on how to live a wise life, we're told, "To consider 'is this man one of ourselves, or an alien?' is the thought of little-minded persons."[37]

Stoic philosopher Marcus Aurelius (whose day gig was emperor of Rome) proclaimed we are all equal members of the only political community that matters, the great state made up of all rational beings. Christianity, with its message of universal brotherhood, has often been at odds with the rather less-than-universal nature of patriotic devotion. A seventeenth-century Jesuit described the tension between the demands of Christianity and the claims of country by calling patriotism "a plague and the most certain death of Christian love."[38] The early Christians weren't exactly the most patriotic citizens of Rome—which is why Marcus Aurelius did his part to oppress them (no one ever said cosmopolitans were better at living up to their principles than the rest of us).

Cosmopolitanism is *au courant*, enjoying many modern champions. It is a natural fit with the mainstream secular ethics of the last century, whether Kantian or utilitarian, which call for treating all people the same. Treating people differently based on something so trivial as where they live is an affront to their status as rational beings worthy of respect. The cosmopolitan asks how something so morally arbitrary as an international border can have any principled role in our moral deliberations. Why, the cosmopolitan wonders, do we feel responsibilities toward our countrymen that we don't feel toward foreigners? Think of how the nightly news reports a plane crash on the other side of the world—yes, we're given a figure of the total number killed, but the main information is how many unlucky Americans died. The jet that plows into a forest without a single American aboard isn't likely to get much coverage in the United States.

Shouldn't we be moved by any and all suffering, without regard to passports? At least that's the cosmopolitan argument, one that isn't easily dismissed. But even so, it isn't clear to me why an international boundary is "morally arbitrary." At least in a democracy, my fellow citizens share with me the rights and burdens of governing, whether through choosing representatives or passing referenda. The laws we live under are the product of our shared endeavor. Why shouldn't I give some greater regard to my fellow citizen-legislators than I give to those who have no hand in creating the rules that shape my life? Beyond that, there is the simple matter of reciprocity in defense—my fellow citizens pay the taxes that provide for police and firemen and a standing army, resources essential for my safety and that of my family. How is it morally arbitrary to have some measure of commitment to those who contribute to my security?

ONCE BENEDICT ARNOLD loomed large in the American imagination. Children were schooled in his betrayal, and didn't have to be taught to see his actions with contempt and dismay. They were told the story of how an English major, John André, sneaked through American lines to conspire with Arnold. They arrived at a deal whereby the traitor agreed to hand over the fort at West Point in exchange for seven thousand pounds and the rank of brigadier-general in the king's army. Arnold gave André papers detailing American defenses and outlining General Washington's overall strategy, and a passport to get back through the lines. After two days of back-road sneaking, André was nearly home free when he was stopped along a country lane by three men in mufti—John Paulding, David Williams, and Isaac Van Wart. He mistook them for British irregulars (a bit of confusion they encouraged by way of testing him). André rashly proclaimed himself a British officer. "We are Americans," Paulding replied, "and you are our prisoner."

The men searched the major, and in his boots found the

damning papers from Arnold. "By God," shouted Paulding, "he is a spy!"

In the popular telling, André was not yet alarmed. After all, he had just seduced a famed major-general in the Continental Army, buying him with a handsome pile of cash. How little, by contrast, it would take to pay off the lowly bumpkins who had pounced on him in the woods like a band of highwaymen. "If you will release me, I will give you a hundred guineas," said the spy, throwing in his horse, saddle, and gold watch for good measure. The men refused, and André upped the offer: "I will give you a thousand guineas, and you can hold me hostage till one of your number returns with the money."

"No" was Paulding's conclusive response. "If you should give us ten thousand guineas you should not stir one step."

Arnold got word of André's capture in time to make his own mad dash of an escape over to the British. They gave him his commission and his cash, but they despised him. (Samuel Pepys had, more than a century before, captured the universal contempt felt by those aided by others' treachery: "I love the treason, I hate the traitor.")[39]

André was duly convicted of being a spy, and was, in due course, hanged. But by contrast with how the British hated the traitor who had helped them, the Americans admired the British spy and hated to have to hang him. He may have been dangerously sneaky, but since he was acting as an agent loyal to his own country, he was not considered a villain.

And as for Paulding, Williams, and Van Wart, the Continental Congress passed a resolution praising the men for "nobly disdaining to sacrifice their country for the sake of gold." Congress created a medal with which to pin them, the Fidelity Medallion, struck with the motto *Amor patriae vincit*, or "Love of country conquers."

That claim may be an overstatement. But the negative formulation of the same sentiment is no doubt true—lack of love of country brings defeat. Could the invasion of Normandy have succeeded if an aide to Ike had been a secret Nazi sympathizer? Or, consider that World War II might have gone on for years more if it hadn't been for the success of mathematicians at England's Bletchley Park who broke Germany's code machine, Enigma. But that success would have been for nothing if a single person had passed information of the decryption to the Wehrmacht. This is the great danger that treason presents: the actions of one person—whether born of greed, or some festering gripe, or even a self-satisfied notion of the good—can undo an entire nation.

Consider the sad fate of Eretria, an ancient Greek city on the island of Euboea. When a mighty Persian invasion force arrived outside the walls of Eretria in 490 B.C., the people of the city were able to hold out against the fierce assault for a week. They might have held out longer—even long enough for the Athenians to come to their rescue—but on the seventh day of the siege, two Eretrian aristocrats, Euphorbos and Philagros, decided to secure their own personal safety (and a tidy reward) by betraying their countrymen. In the wee hours they opened the gates to the invaders. The Persians burned the city, enslaved the people, and turned toward Athens, fortified and emboldened.

The ancient writer Pausanias blames the great danger Athens then faced on "the most ungodly of all crimes, and one by which in the whole course of history Greece has never ceased to be afflicted: treachery to a man's country and people for the sake of his personal profit."[40] It wasn't just Eretria that succumbed to betrayal. A generation later, the Persians would take Thessaly and then Thebes, thanks in each case to the disloyalty of one or two of those cities' most prominent citizens. Pausanias offers an exhaustive catalogue of the traitor's art and the grim consequences that followed for those betrayed.

Who knows what would have happened to the American cause if Benedict Arnold had succeeded in playing Euphorbos? And are we now so safe and secure that we don't have to worry about the Philagroses in our midst? It's worth remembering Shakespeare's description of what treason means in practice. Before he sails with his army for France, King Henry V discovers that three of his noblemen have sold him out. In exchange for French gold they have promised to stab him in the back. He confronts them with the crime of joining "an enemy proclaim'd":

Wherein you would have sold your king to slaughter
His princes and his peers to servitude,
His subjects to oppression and contempt,
And his whole kingdom into desolation.[41]

Desolation is the price paid by those who are betrayed. If loyalty and love of country can counteract the lures and enticements of treason, we need to encourage it. We remember Benedict Arnold's name (infamy being more enduring than fame), but the names Paulding, Williams, and Van Wart have been obscured by time. It's worth remembering them.

Saying no to treachery is the most basic sort of loyalty to country. And that's a good place to start, a necessary minimum sort of fidelity that societies need to foster if they would survive. But we could also stand to embrace a more robust set of patriotic loyalties. We've been so discouraged by abusive demands of allegiance that we've come to see loyalty as a threat to freedom and self-government. In truth, it is just the opposite. For self-government to succeed, we have to be able to trust our countrymen. We have to believe that our disagreements are family squabbles, that even our most vigorous disputes are nothing but differences about what is best for the nation.

"Republics, and liberal democracies especially, rely on mutual trust between governments and citizens to an unusual degree," Judith Shklar observed. "Threats to the established constitution, even when no foreign state is involved in the enterprise, are therefore perceived as attacks on every established political relationship and every social agreement."[42] For self-government to succeed, we have to know we can rely on one another. Which is where patriotism comes in. It is a promise, both outward and inward, that we can be counted on when it counts. Sneering at the rituals of patriotic observance may be one's right, but it does little to build trust. Those who would challenge the orthodoxies of their countries are likely to have more luck the more they are trusted, the more they make it clear their recommendations are expressions of tough love—with the emphasis on love. If dissent devolves into hatred of one's country or countrymen (as it did for State Department spy Walter Kendall Myers, who told an FBI agent posing as a Cuban spymaster, "The trouble with this country, there's just too many North Americans . . . believe me, those North Americans, you don't want them."), democracy is undermined. "An enemy is not recognizable as a social critic; he lacks standing," observes political philosopher Michael Walzer. "We expect and simultaneously discount criticism from our enemies."[43]

The man who loves his country will care enough to speak out when his country is in the wrong. But just because a true patriotism entails a willingness to criticize one's country doesn't mean that all criticism is an expression of loyal commitment. Criticism grounded in love of country is the criticism that counts. The opposition worth engaging is the loyal opposition.

If we prize liberal democracy, then we need to embrace patriotic love of country. It isn't just the reactions of the reactionaries that crush dissent in troubled times, it is the disloyalty of those who use the freedoms of a free society as a stalking horse for their particular hobbyhorse, be it the interests of another country, the ambitions of an expansive ideol ogy, or the demands of a religion that makes no room for rendering unto Caesar.

Love of country, like all types of love, can be dangerous, volatile, and irrational. We need to be vigilant in restraining the ugly impulses that can flow from an unreflective and untethered jingoism. But we need loyalty to country if we are to hold our communities together, especially if those communities are self-governing. Rousseau was right to argue for schooling men to be "patriots by inclination, by passion, by necessity."[44]

9

The Lifeboat Ethic

A Night to Remember and *Titanic* are very different films, but both take note, in their depictions of the ship's chaotic sinking, of an elderly couple who refuse to be separated.

"Please," says the husband to his wife in *A Night to Remember*, the 1958 film, "get into the boat." Others urge her to climb down into the lifeboat, but she'll have none of it.

"I've always stayed with my husband," she calmly tells them. "So why should I leave him now?"

Her husband pleads with her to be sensible.

"We have been living together for many years," she tells him, settling the matter with words from the book of Ruth: "Where you go, I go."

In James Cameron's 1997 version we see them cuddled together in their cabin, calm and resolved, as the *Titanic* sinks, their bed floating on the rising water.

It is as moving an example of loyalty as we're ever likely to see and it would be hopelessly corny if it weren't true.

Isidor Straus, co-owner of Macy's department store, would not take a place in the boats while there were still women and children on the doomed ship, but he had pleaded with his wife, Ida, to save herself. The dialogue was heard by all the ladies in lifeboat number 8, and was recounted with astonishment when they made it to New York. The story was told in newspapers big and small. *The New York Times* quoted one survivor who saw the couple on deck: "Mr. Straus was urging his wife toward the boat. She was insisting on remaining with him."[1] The *Turtle Mountain Star* of Rolla, North Dakota, described how an "officer strove to help her to a seat of safety, but she brushed away his arm and clung to her husband, crying 'I will not go without you.'"

But as far and wide as the story was repeated, nothing impressed it quite on the minds of Americans as did the telling of it by Elbert Hubbard, a prominent writer and publisher, and a character who himself could not have been invented. A philosophical impresario with a knack for capturing the popular imagination, Hubbard was one of the most uplifting preachers of turn-of-the-century uplift. Which made him the perfect man to expound on the Strauses' loyalty to one another.

Born in 1856, Hubbard jobbed around as a newspaperman before becoming marketing maven for a soap company. But inspired by the great nineteenth-century English advocates of artisanal handicrafts, William Morris and John Ruskin, Hubbard devoted himself to leading a similar movement in America. First he instituted the Roycroft Press to print beautiful editions of inspirational works (primarily his own humorous homilies—the writing of which he was remarkably prolific). The effort soon blossomed into a small community of skilled carpenters and potters making Arts and Crafts furniture and ceramics and other goods, all under the banner of the Roycroft Shops. As part of the enterprise, Hubbard published several magazines, including a literary monthly called *The Philistine* and a monthly devoted to artful living, *The Fra.* It was in that strangely named journal that Hubbard took up the story of Ida and Isidor.

"Mr. and Mrs. Straus, I envy you that legacy of love and loyalty left to your children and grandchildren," Hubbard wrote. "You knew how to do three great things—you knew how to live, how to love and how to die." He extolled the virtues of cashing in one's chips in a grand accident as opposed to getting sick. "All disease is indecent." By contrast, "to pass out as did Mr. and Mrs. Isidor Straus is glorious. Few have such a privilege. Happy lovers, both. In life they were never separated and in death they are not divided."[2]

The Strauses' story was a natural for Hubbard, who was a great advocate of loyalty as a linchpin of morality. In his own business dealings, he rated loyalty even more highly than Sam Goldwyn would: "An ounce of loyalty," he wrote, "is worth a pound of cleverness." And well he may have thought, especially given that it was in praising loyalty that Hubbard made his name.

In 1899 he penned an essay about a U.S. Army lieutenant, Andrew S. Rowan, who had been sent to reconnoiter in the Cuban jungle with rebel general Calixto Garcia e Iñiguez. Hubbard's article, "A Message to Garcia," became a sensation. Originally published in *The Philistine*, it was reprinted in newspapers and as a pamphlet distributed by the New York Central Railroad; it was handed out by employers to inspire their workers; it was included in U.S. Army training manuals; it was an essential text in a generation of junior high school "readers." Hubbard would later estimate there were some 40 million copies of the piece in print. "A Message to Garcia" became so ingrained in the culture that, as one wag put it, "for decades . . . it was possible to raise a chuckle with the graffito 'Garcia—call your wife.'"[3]

The loyalty espoused by Hubbard was of a particularly energetic, can-do sort. Without much embellishment (nor any particular narrative-squelching concern for factual accuracy) he details how Lieutenant Rowan was given a letter from President McKinley to be taken to General Garcia; how, a few nights later, he approached the Cuban coast by dinghy and slipped ashore; and how Rowan "disappeared into the jungle, and in three weeks came out on the other side of the island, having traversed a hostile country on foot, and delivered his letter to Garcia." But the details of this most minor of military missions are of no particular interest to Hubbard. What fills him with enthusiastic admiration is the virtue Rowan displays simply by doing his job:

McKinley gave Rowan a letter to be delivered to Garcia; Rowan took the letter and did not ask, "Where is he at?" By the Eternal! there is a man whose form should be cast in deathless bronze and the statue placed in every college of the land. It is not book-learning young men need, nor instruction about this and that, but a stiffening of the vertebrae which will cause them to be loyal to a trust, to act promptly, concentrate their energies: do the thing—"Carry a message to Garcia."[4]

Hubbard's notion of loyalty is the sort that has attracted the virtue no small measure of scorn. Loyalty so conceived has often been lamented as unthinking or obsequious, the *Yes, sir, whatever you say, sir* sort of loyalty so prone to abuse by tyrants and Mafiosi and mid-level managers. And no doubt the businessmen who eagerly saw to it that every one of their employees had a copy of Hubbard's essay a century ago were moved, in part, by the thrilling notion that their workers might stop asking pesky questions. Such loyalty is easily lampooned as doltish, credulous, and an open invitation to manipulation by the clever (whatever one might say about the pound-for-pound value of cleverness).

And yet the loyalty Hubbard celebrates isn't quite so much at odds with smarts as it first appears. He admires Rowan because the man doesn't have to be given specific directions how to accomplish the task before him—he has the active intelligence to figure out how to do what needs to be done. He has initiative. He is capable. And what brings his active intelligence to bear on solving the problem he's been given is loyalty, a virtue that, yes, inspires acts of great heroism, but even more so motivates the little everyday actions that make and reveal one's character.

This is one of the great appeals of loyalty: It isn't just a set of rules or a list of obligations; it isn't the dour sense of duty that we think of as standing opposed to our desires and inclinations. Loyalty is a spur to action, a personal, emotional stake that we have in being worthy of a trust. The loyal aren't simply committed to fulfilling a trust, they're sustained by an ungrudging willingness to do so. "Civilization," Hubbard wrote, "is one long, anxious search for just such individuals."

We might find this as inspiring as millions of readers did a century ago. Or perhaps, moderns that we are, well schooled in the unimportance of being earnest, we might be inclined to shrug off Hubbard's encomium as a laughable bit of Rotarian hokum, some self-improvement bunkum employed by rapacious employers to keep the rubes from asking for a raise.

But before indulging that conceit, it's worth noting that Hubbard himself was no humbug. When the moment came that put the virtue he celebrated to its ultimate test, he didn't fail.

Three years after he had lauded the loyal love of Isidor and Ida Straus aboard the *Titanic,* Hubbard sailed with his wife, Alice, from New York to Liverpool. Or at least they were headed for Liverpool: Off the coast of Ireland their ship, the *Lusitania*, took a torpedo from a German U-boat. As people raced for life jackets and clambered into the few lifeboats able to get clear, Elbert and Alice stood calmly on the pitched deck, arm-in-arm. "He did one of the most dramatic things I ever saw done," a survivor would later write to Hubbard's son. "He simply turned with Mrs. Hubbard and entered a room on the top deck, the door of which was open, and closed it behind him. It was apparent," said this last person to see them alive, "that his idea was that they should die together, and not risk being parted on going into the water."[5]

Ida and Isidor would have been proud.

WE DON'T MUCH expect that sort of loyalty these days. In fact, we don't expect much loyalty at all. The virtue has been in decline, if not eclipse, for decades. True, the virtue has ever been in decline. Generation after generation regrets its passing, imagining it to have been the standard of behavior in some recent golden past. But we hardly even lament loyalty nowadays. We're inclined to look at it with suspicion, leery that loyalty is an excuse for nepotism and other varieties of corrupt favoritism. We're all too aware that it can be the glue that holds together tawdry little schemes or grand conspiracies. We worry that the strident demands of those shouting for loyalty are nothing but a way to silence critics and crush dissent.

We're inclined to view loyalty as a sucker's bet. "Be disloyal," Graham Greene whispers to us. "It's your duty to the human race. The human race needs to survive and it's the loyal man who dies first from anxiety or a bullet or overwork."[6] Loyalty's for chumps, he counsels. And beyond the question of mere survival, Greene touts disloyalty as the key to creativity and sympathy both, encouraging us "to roam experimentally through any human mind."

Should we be surprised that loyalty's reputation has sunk so low, what with the many beatings it's taken of late? The Cold War hunt for domestic Communists may have done little to blunt Soviet ambitions, but it did succeed in tainting the very idea of loyalty, casting it as nothing but a reactionary cudgel. And when it comes to loyalty oaths, the ones most often and most publicly taken—marriage vows—have become something of a joke. We've come to accept them as little more than gestures of hope in the face of experience, and we aren't surprised by the infidelities that now seem a matter of course. If we can't maintain loyalty when we swear it in front of God and everybody, what use is it?

And yet, though loyalty isn't the fashionable virtue it once was, we all feel its tug, at the very least in negative terms: No one, not even the most hardened cynic, accepts betrayal without bitterness. And so, unless we are willing to abjure love and friendship altogether, we find ourselves longing to find those who will be loyal to us, and to whom we can be loyal.

Loyalty is a virtue that sustains long-term relationships, whether of lovers, friends, or even the members of a community. But as our society has fragmented into perpetually migrating, atomistic selves, the ideal of long, loyal relationships has faded, replaced with such ephemera as computerized social networking. It's all very modern—or even postmodern. But is it what we're looking for in our relationships?

Is it the sort of personal bond we crave? Just ask yourself how many of your Facebook "friends" would face up to adversity for you, would be there for you when you find yourself in a Jobian jam. Say you are accused of some heinous crime—is there anyone you could count on to put his own reputation at risk standing by your side?

The same questions apply with the little quotidian questions. Can you trust your co-workers, or do you find yourself getting blindsided in meetings by colleagues who know they are your competitors, not your friends? Can you trust your fiancée, or do you need a prenuptial agreement? Can you trust that the friend who asks you to make an investment in his company won't find a loophole in the incorporation papers allowing him to dilute the value of your stock? These are all questions of loyalty. Without some reasonable expectation of loyalty where loyalty is due, there can be no trust, no friendship, no love.

Being loyal brings frustrations and challenges. But frustrating as they may be, we have to at least strive to meet those challenges even if there are times when the intractable conflict of contradictory loyalties trips us up. We also have to wonder how to know when a given loyalty is right, how to know who deserves our loyalties and who is exploiting them. Loyalty's flaws are inescapable, irreducible. It is a virtue no less afflicted by human frailty than any other. But if we give up on it as a moral touchstone, love, trust, and commitment go with it.

Is it possible to head off the calamities of contradictory

loyalties? Edmund Burke suggested that our loyalties could be built one upon the other, in an orderly fashion, with the fidelity to family we learn as children shaping the bonds we have to friends, to community, to country, and to all people. It's a notion of loyalty that is informed by Alexander Pope, who suggested in his "Essay on Man" that our capacity for love develops in the same way.

Self-love but serves the virtuous mind to wake,
As the small pebble stirs the peaceful lake;
The centre mov'd, a circle strait succeeds,
Another still, and still another spreads,
Friend, parent, neighbour, first it will embrace,
His country next, and next all human race.

It's an image as old as the Stoic philosopher Hierocles, who imagined our affections radiating in concentric circles. And if only it were so neatly possible, loyalty would not be so nearly fraught with moral peril. Alas, the rings don't stay so nicely ordered with our attachments fitting one inside the other. However much we may try to keep our loyalties from running afoul of one another, the various rings of our obligations are like so many unruly oblongs jumbled together. We've come to expect, with modern systems of morality, that we should always be able to find a win-win solution to any ethical predicament. It is one of the least attractive features of loyalty that it can present us with lose-lose scenarios, situations in which either of two bad options will leave us culpable.

But such intractable moral conflict isn't the only downside to the vexing virtue. When totalitarian mass-murderers make a concept central to their organizational scheme—as Hitler and Stalin both did with loyalty—one hesitates to call it a virtue at all. Even if we recognize the good loyalty can do, we find ourselves ever wary that it will soon devolve into a deadly vice.

Even in the normal day to day, it is suspect. "Loyalty is a noble quality, so long as it is not blind and does not exclude the higher loyalty to truth and decency," wrote Basil Liddell Hart. "But the word is much abused. For 'loyalty,' analyzed, is too often a polite word for what would be more accurately described as 'a conspiracy for mutual inefficiency.'" But as we've seen, trying to fix the problems of "lesser" loyalties by trumping them with "higher" loyalties is no sure path to virtue. The traitor who fancies he's serving humanity sleeps well at night. And Hart ultimately understands that a hierarchy of values is not the answer. Loyalty "is not a quality we can isolate," he observed. "So far as it is real, and of intrinsic value, it is implicit in the possession of other virtues."[7]

Loyalty has bonds of its own. It is tethered to all of the other virtues. The person whose character is marked by generosity, courage, modesty, friendliness, and truthfulness is not one likely to use loyalty as a pretext for scheming, let alone evil. And even more important, the full range of virtues relies on loyalty for motivation. Loyalty gives us the emotional investment in meeting our obligations. It launches us into action. Duty is a dour voice that drones and drones, and which we find all too easy to tune out. Loyalty, by contrast, is an internal urge that launches us cheerfully to do our part. We don't ask why, we don't look for excuses, we take the letter to Garcia!

Is there room for anything so unironic in our glib, sarcastic, postmodern age? I hope so, for whatever the perils, whatever the pitfalls to which loyalty is prone, without it there is no real love or friendship. Loyalties—whether to people, to community, or to God—are essential in shaping and defining our identities. Allow loyalty to fall into disrepair and disrepute and character crumbles along with it, both in the antique notion of character as an expression of virtue, as well as the less judgmental modern sense we have of *character* as just another word for personality. We are, you could say, what we are loyal to. To identify loyalties is to sift and sort the core things we care about. Too few loyalties and our lives are shallow, thin, and unsatisfying; too many loyalties and we end up with a cacophony of claims, a dissonance that leaves our lives more muddled than meaningful. We need to take loyalty seriously enough to find the right balance.

We can make the bonds of loyalty stronger by taking seriously what it means to be a friend, expecting more of ourselves and others. We can be vigilant to avoid betraying friends, family, and country; we can do our best to sort out the potential conflicts among them long before their demands clash. And if that fails to avert catastrophe, we can recognize—as Agamemnon did not—that even a forced and unwilling act of disloyalty is a terrible harm; we should try to make amends if possible, and at the very least grieve for the damage we've done.

To be loyal is to be trustworthy. To be loyal is to keep your word. It is the simplest, most fundamental stuff of life. What good is love without loyalty? Who can be said to have lived a flourishing life who hasn't enjoyed the comforts of true friendship—which is to say *loyal* friendship? Who has faith without fidelity? Who can betray, or be betrayed, without being blighted? Who would walk the tightrope of life without the net of faithful friends and family?

Loyalty may be a forgotten, forlorn relic. But as frustrating, as vexing as the virtue may be, it's time to dust it off and give it a try.

Acknowledgments

I'm grateful to the many friends who helped me with their musings on loyalty (and in so doing also provided examples of the boundless benefits of loyal friendship), including Philip Chalk, Erich Eichman, Andrew Ferguson, Mark Pastin, Daniel Akst, Garrett Graff, Lowell Edmunds, Gerry Lynam, and William Schulz.

Many thanks to my agent, Esther Newberg, who championed this book from the start, and who was a tremendous help in focusing the concept for it.

My editor, Alice Mayhew, made this book possible, from helping to shape the broad contours of the argument to saving me from indulging in overly glib prose. There's a reason she's known as the best friend a writer can have. I am much obliged to Simon & Schuster publisher Jonathan Karp for his enthusiasm and support. Karen Thompson was also a great help.

I appreciate the encouragement (and sharp minds) of my editors at *The Wall Street Journal*, where I tried out a few of the ideas in this book: Paul Gigot, Eric Gibson, Naomi Schaefer Riley, Nancy deWolf Smith, and Barbara Phillips.

I'm also indebted to the late Judith Shklar, with whom I was fortunate to study many years ago, and whose own writings on loyalty and betrayal are essential reading.

Lastly, I wish to thank those exemplars of patient love and loyalty, my family. I'm grateful to my parents Lester and Barbara Felten; my brother David; my children Priscilla, Greta, and Thaddeus; and most of all, my wife, Jennifer.

Notes

INTRODUCTION

1. Justin McCarthy, "Queen Victoria and Her Subjects," *The Galaxy,* February 1869, p. 188.
2. William Shakespeare, *As You Like It,* Act II, scene 3.
3. Mary Lewis Shaw, *The Cambridge Introduction to French Poetry* (Cambridge, U.K.: Cambridge University Press, 2003), p. 122.
4. *A Dictionary of Select and Popular Quotations: Which Are in Daily Use* (Philadelphia: Finley, 1828), p. 27.
5. Josiah Royce, *The Philosophy of Loyalty* (New York: Macmillan, 1908), p. 284.
6. Arthur Koestler, *Janus: a Summing Up* (New York: Random House, 1978), p. 77.
7. Simon Keller, *The Limits of Loyalty* (Cambridge, U.K.: Cambridge University Press, 2007), p. 152.
8. Heinrich Himmler, *Die Schutzstaffel* (1938).
9. Bradley F. Smith, *Heinrich Himmler: A Nazi in the Making* (Stanford: Hoover Institution Press, 1971), p. 171. Also, George C. Browder, *Foundations of the Nazi Police State* (Lexington, Ky.: University Press of Kentucky, 2004), p. 18.
10. Isaiah Berlin, *Letters, 1928–1946* (Cambridge, U.K.: Cambridge University Press, 2004), p. 170.

11. Cyril Connolly, *Enemies of Promise* (Boston: Little, Brown, 1939), p. 153.

1. THE POWER OF LOYALTY

1. Frank J. Grady, *Surviving the Day* (Annapolis: Naval Institute Press, 1997), p. 67.

2. Ibid., p. 71.

3. Dora Costa and Matthew Kahn, *Heroes & Cowards: The Social Face of War* (Princeton, N.J.: Princeton University Press, 2008), p. 123.

4. Grady, *Surviving the Day,* p. 67.

5. Ibid., p. 71.

6. Jon Krakauer, *Into Thin Air: A Personal Account of the Mt. Everest Disaster* (New York: Villard Books, 1997), p. 207.

7. Charles Houston and Robert Bates, *K2, the Savage Mountain* (New York: McGraw-Hill, 1954), p. 269.

8. Costa and Kahn, *Heroes & Cowards,* p. 119.

9. Alan Soble, ed. *Sex from Plato to Paglia: A Philosophical Encyclopedia,* 2 vols. (Westport, Conn.: Greenwood Press, 2006), p. 685.

10. Charles Ardant du Picq, *Battle Studies* (*Etudes sur le combat: Combat antique et moderne*) (Paris, 1942), p. 121.

11. Samuel P. Huntington, *The Soldier and The State: The Theory and Politics of Civil-Military Relations* (Cambridge, Mass.: Harvard University Press, 1957), p. 304.

12. Roy R. Grinker and John P. Spiegel, *Men Under Stress* (Philadelphia: Blakiston, 1945), p. 45.

13. S.L.A. Marshall, *Men Against Fire* (New York: William Morrow, 1947), p. 42.

14. Ibid., p. 161.

15. Leonard Wong, "Why Professionals Fight: Combat Motivation in the Iraq War" in *The Future of the Army Profession,* 2nd edition, eds. Don M. Snider and Lloyd J. Matthews (New York: McGraw Hill, 2005), p. 498.

16. Stephen Ambrose, *Band of Brothers: E Company, 506th Regiment,*

101st Airborne from Normandy to Hitler's Eagle's Nest (New York: Touchstone, 1992), p. 122.

17. Ibid.

18. Ibid., p. 156.

19. A concept that Huntington would use as the title for his best-known work, on the enduring conflict between Islam and the West.

20. Huntington, *The Soldier and The State,* p. 465.

21. Ibid., pp. 304–5.

22. Alexis de Tocqueville, *Democracy in America,* trans. Gerald Bevan (London: Penguin Classics, 2003), p. 610.

23. Ibid., p. 611.

24. Jean-Jacques Rousseau, *The Social Contract & Discourses,* trans. G.D.H. Cole (New York: Everyman's Library, 1920), p. 210.

25. Robert Axelrod, *The Evolution of Cooperation* (New York: Basic Books, 1984), pp. 27–54.

26. S. M. Amadae, *Rationalizing Capitalist Democracy: The Cold War Origins of Rational Choice Liberalism* (Chicago: University of Chicago Press, 2003), p. 296.

27. Robert W. Rieber, *Manufacturing Social Distress: Psychopathy in Everyday Life* (New York: Plenum Press, 1997), p. 41.

28. Theodore Millon et al., eds., *Psychopathy: Antisocial, Criminal, and Violent Behavior* (New York: Guilford Publications, 1998), p. 162.

29. H. J. Paton, *The Categorical Imperative: A Study in Kant's Moral Philosophy* (Philadelphia: University of Pennsylvania Press, 1971), p. 20.

30. Judith N. Shklar, "Obligation, Loyalty, Exile" in *Political Thought & Political Thinkers* (Chicago: University of Chicago Press, 1998), p. 39.

31. Joseph Alexander Leighton, *Man and the Cosmos: An Introduction to Metaphysics* (New York: D. Appleton and Co., 1922), p. 445.

32. Robert Frank, *Passions Within Reason* (New York: W. W. Norton, 1988), p. 53.

2. LOYALTIES AT LOGGERHEADS

1. Graham Greene, *A Sort of Life* (Harmondsworth: Penguin, 1974), pp. 18–19.

2. Henry J. Donaghy, ed., *Conversations with Graham Greene* (Jackson, Miss.: University Press of Mississippi, 1992), p. 53. (Vidkun Quisling, of course, lent his name to traitors everywhere by facilitating the Nazi conquest of his own country, Norway, a betrayal for which he was rewarded with command of the collaborationist government—and for which he was executed after the war.)

3. Marie-Françoise Allain, *The Other Man: Conversations with Graham Greene* (New York: Simon and Schuster, 1983), p. 27.

4. Donaghy, ed. *Conversations with Graham Greene,* p. 53.

5. Allain, *The Other Man,* p. 27.

6. Ibid.

7. Shklar, "Obligation, Loyalty, Exile" in *Political Thought & Political Thinkers* (Chicago: University of Chicago Press, 1998), p. 43.

8. Sophocles, *Antigone,* trans. Robert Whitelaw (Oxford: Clarendon Press, 1906), lines 205–6.

9. Ibid., lines 189–90.

10. Martha Nussbaum, *The Fragility of Goodness* (Cambridge, U.K.: Cambridge University Press, 1986), p. 34.

11. Aeschylus, *Agamemnon,* trans. W. W. Goodwin (Cambridge, Mass.: Harvard University Press, 1906), p. 16, lines 208–12.

12. Ibid., p. 14, line 180.

13. Plato, "Euthyphro," *Dialogues of Plato,* vol. I, trans. B. Jowett (New York: Scribner, 1874), p. 292.

14. Willard Sperry, "The Double Loyalty of the Christian Ministry," *Harvard Theological Review,* April 1920.

15. Ambrose Bierce, *The Cynic's Word Book* (New York: Doubleday, Page & Co., 1906), p. 113.

16. Josiah Royce, *The Philosophy of Loyalty* (New York: Macmillan, 1908), p. 63.

17. Todd A. Forney, *The Midshipman Culture and Educational Reform* (Newark, Del.: University of Delaware Press, 2004), p. 105.

18. "Armed Forces: What Price Honor?" *Time,* June 7, 1976.

19. Richard C. U'Ren, "West Point: Cadets, Codes and Careers," *Society,* vol. 12 (May/June 1975), pp. 23–29.

20. "Armed Forces: What Price Honor?"

21. Evan H. Offstein, *Stand Your Ground: Building Honorable Leaders the West Point Way* (Westport, Conn.: Praeger, 2006), p. 84.

22. David Lipsky, *Absolutely American: Four Years at West Point* (Boston: Houghton Mifflin, 2003), p. 224.

23. Mental Health Advisory Team (MHAT) V (Operation Iraqi Freedom 06–08: Iraq, Operation Enduring Freedom 8: Afghanistan), February 14, 2008, pp. 54–55.

24. Ibid., p. 55.

25. Public Law 96-303, 94 Stat. 855 (July 3, 1980).

26. Morton Grodzins, *The Loyal and the Disloyal: Social Boundaries of Patriotism and Treason* (Chicago: University of Chicago Press, 1956), p. 135.

27. Crane Brinton, *The Anatomy of Revolution* (New York: Vintage Books, 1952), pp. 121–22.

28. Mike Pincombe and Cathy Shrank, *The Oxford Handbook of Tudor Literature* (New York: Oxford University Press, 2009), p. 319.

29. John H. Schaar, *Loyalty in America* (Berkeley: University of California Press, 1957), p. 38.

30. Thomas à Kempis, *The Imitation of Christ,* book II, chapter 7.

31. Plutarch, *Plutarch's Themistocles and Aristides,* trans. Bernadotte Perrin (New York: Scribner's, 1901), p. 126.

32. William James, *The Principles of Psychology,* vol. I (New York: Holt & Co., 1890), p. 294.

33. Louis D. Brandeis, "The Jewish Problem" 1915, in *Brandeis on Zionism* (Washington, D.C.: Zionist Organization of America, 1942), pp. 28–29.

34. Marion Elizabeth Rodgers, *Mencken: The American Iconoclast* (New York: Oxford University Press, 2005), p. 176.

35. Immanuel Kant, *Introduction to the Metaphysic of Morals* in *Kant's Critique of Practical Reason and Other Works on the Theory of Ethics,* trans. Thomas Kingsmill Abbott (London: Longmans, Green, and Co., 1909), p. 280.

36. Ibid.

37. Immanuel Kant, "On a Supposed Right to Lie Because of Philanthrop-

ic Concerns" (1797), in *Practical Philosophy,* trans. Mary J. Gregor (Cambridge, U.K.: Cambridge University Press, 1996), pp. 605–16.

3. THE EVER READY ACCOMPLICES

1. Sheri Fink, "Strained by Katrina, a Hospital Faced Deadly Choices," *The New York Times,* August 30, 2009; "Reports Raise Concerns About Patient Euthanasia After Hurricane Katrina," *The NewsHour with Jim Lehrer,* August 21, 2006.

2. National Research Council Disaster Research Group, *Disaster Study,* Issue 14, p. 47; W. H. Form and S. Nosow, *Community in Disaster* (New York: Harper, 1958), p. 162.

3. National Research Council Disaster Research Group, *Disaster Study,* Issue 14, p. 46; Lewis Killian, "The Significance of Multiple-Group Membership in Disaster," *American Journal of Sociology* 57 (January 1952), p. 312.

4. David Alexander, *Natural Disasters* (New York: Routledge, 2001), p. 555.

5. District Attorney Leon Cannizzaro declined to prosecute Dr. Cook after the Orleans Parish coroner, Frank Minyard, ruled that, despite all the morphine injections given with the intention of hastening Jannie Burgess's demise, he couldn't determine that the morphine was the specific cause of her death. "Dr. Cook thinks that he knocked her off," Minyard said, "but we can't prove that. He might have, he might not have. Because it's not 100 percent proved, we have to call it unclassified." Sheri Fink, "New Orleans Coroner Rules Post-Katrina Death 'Unclassified.'" *ProPublica,* March 11, 2010.

6. Josiah Royce, *The Philosophy of Loyalty* (New York: The Macmillan Company, 1908), pp. 220–24.

7. I Timothy 5:8.

8. Simon Keller, *The Limits of Loyalty* (Cambridge, U.K.: Cambridge University Press, 2007), pp. ix–x.

9. J. Sabini and M. Silver, *Emotion, Character, and Responsibility* (New York: Oxford University Press, 1998), p. 5.

10. Mario Puzo, *The Godfather* (New York: New American Library, 2002), p. 14.

11. Edward Banfield, *The Moral Basis of a Backward Society* (New York: The Free Press, 1958), p. 10.

12. Paul Ginsburg, *A History of Contemporary Italy* (New York: Palgrave Macmillan, 2003), p. 2.

13. Plato, *Republic,* Book V, 460b.

14. Edmund Burke, *Reflections on the Revolution in France* (London: J. Dodsley, 1790), p. 57.

15. Max Horkheimer, "Authoritarianism and the Family Today," in *The Family: Its Function and Destiny,* ed. Ruth Nanda Anshen (New York: Harper & Bros., 1949), p. 374.

16. Michael Burleigh, *The Third Reich: A New History* (New York: Macmillan, 2001), p. 237.

17. Earl of Halifax, "The Nature of the Struggle" 1941, in *The American Speeches of the Earl of Halifax* (Oxford, U.K.: Oxford University Press, 1947), p. 48.

18. John James McGregor, *History of the French Revolution, and of the Wars Resulting From That Memorable Event,* vol. III (Waterford: John Bull, 1817), p. 371.

19. John Adolphus, *Biographical Memoirs of the French Revolution,* vol. 2 (London: T. Cadell, 1799), p. 424.

20. Communist Party organs dictated that "Pioneers who failed to inform on their families should be treated with suspicion and, if found to be lacking vigilance, should be denounced themselves." Orlando Figes, *The Whisperers: Private Life in Stalin's Russia* (New York: Picador, 2007), p. 129.

21. Wolfram Eberhard, *A History of China* (Berkeley: University of California Press, 1969), p. 333.

22. Isaiah Berlin, "The Pursuit of the Ideal," in *The Proper Study of Mankind* (New York: Farrar, Straus and Giroux, 2000), p. 15.

23. Geoffrey Cocks, *Psychotherapy in the Third Reich: The Göring Institute* (New York: Oxford University Press, 1985), p. 184.

24. *In re A & M,* 61 AD2d 426, 403 NYS2d 375 (1978).

25. *In re Agosto,* 553 F. Supp. 1298 (D. Nev. 1983).

26. Anna Quindlen, *Loud and Clear* (New York: Ballantine, 2005), p. 22.

27. *Trammel v. United States,* 445 U.S. 40.
28. Jeremy Bentham, "Rationale of Judicial Evidence," in *The Works of Jeremy Bentham,* vol. 7 (Edinburgh: Wm. Tait, 1843), p. 483.
29. Ibid., p. 484.
30. David Kaczynski, "Growing Up with the Unabomber," *The Week,* May 8, 2009, p. 45.

4. FOR BETTER OR FOR WORSE

1. George P. Fletcher, *Loyalty: An Essay on the Morality of Relationships* (New York: Oxford University Press, 1993), p. 76.
2. Linda P. Rouse, *Marital and Sexual Lifestyles in the United States* (Binghamton, N.Y.: Haworth Clinical Practice Press, 2002), p. 125.
3. Wilt Chamberlain, *A View From Above* (New York: Penguin, 1992), p. 253.
4. Bertrand Russell, *Marriage and Morals* (London: George Allen & Unwin, 1929), p. 141.
5. Naomi Schaefer Riley, "The Young and the Restless: Why Infidelity Is Rising Among 20-Somethings," *The Wall Street Journal,* November 27, 2008.
6. Arthur Schopenhauer, "Aphorisms on the Wisdom of Life," in *Philosophical Writings,* ed. Wolfgang Schirmacher (New York: Continuum, 2003), p. 282.
7. Cindy Meston and David Buss, *Why Women Have Sex* (New York: Times Books, 2009), p. 109.
8. Katherine Hertlein, Gerald Weeks, and Nancy Gambescia, *Systemic Sex Therapy* (New York: Routledge, 2009), p. 299.
9. John O'Hara, *Appointment in Samarra* (New York: Modern Library, 1953), p. 222.
10. Raphael Lyne, "Love and Exile After Ovid," in *The Cambridge Companion to Ovid,* ed. Philip R. Hardie (Cambridge, U.K.: Cambridge University Press, 2002), p. 292.
11. Jeremy Dimmick, "Ovid in the Middle Ages: Authority and Poetry," in *The Cambridge Companion to Ovid,* p. 264.
12. Ovid, *The Art of Love,* II, 153–55; III, 585–86.

13. C. S. Lewis, *The Allegory of Love* (New York: Galaxy, 1958), pp. 13–18.

14. Andreas Capellanus, *The Art of Courtly Love.*

15. Denis de Rougemont, *Love in the Western World,* trans. Montgomery Belgion (New York: Pantheon, 1956), p. 285.

16. Emily Yoffe, "Dear Prudence," web chat at WashingtonPost.com, January 25, 2010.

17. Ovid, *Metamorphoses,* trans. Arthur Golding (1567), Book IV, lines 189–90.

18. Milan Kundera, *The Unbearable Lightness of Being* (New York: Harper Perennial, 1999), pp. 90–91.

19. Thomas Hardy, *The Return of the Native* (New York: Scribner's, 1917), p. 69.

20. Esther Perel, *Mating in Captivity: Unlocking Erotic Intelligence* (New York: HarperCollins, 2006), p. 128.

21. Oscar Wilde, *The Picture of Dorian Gray* (Oxford, U.K.: Oxford World Classics, 2006), p. 14.

22. Ibid., p. 44.

23. Tom Wolfe, "The Me Decade," in *The Purple Decades* (New York: Farrar, Straus and Giroux, 1982), p. 284.

24. Empedocles, Fragment 17, in *Greek Philosophy: Thales to Aristotle,* ed. Reginald E. Allen (New York: Free Press, 1985), p. 49.

25. Robert Frost, poem fragment. See William Logan, "Frost's Notebooks: A Disaster Revisited," *The New Criterion,* February 2010, p. 25.

26. Hesiod, *Theogony,* trans. Hugh Gerard Evelyn-White, in *Hesiod: the Homeric Hymns and Homerica* (New York: Macmillan, 1914), p. 87.

27. William Blake, "Love to Faults," ca. 1791–92.

28. Edmund Spenser, *The Faerie Queene,* Book III, C. xii, 7–52.

29. Garth Fletcher and Jeffry Simpson, "Ideal Standards in Close Relationships," in *The Social Mind,* eds. Joseph Forgas, Kipling Williams, and Ladd Wheeler (Cambridge, U.K.: Cambridge University Press, 2001), p. 265.

30. Wolfram von Eschenbach, *Parzival,* trans. A. T. Hatto (London: Penguin, 1980), p. 270.

31. Edmund Spenser, *An Hymn in Honour of Love,* lines 250–69.

32. Roger Scruton, *Sexual Desire: A Moral Philosophy of the Erotic* (New York: Free Press, 1986), p. 339.

33. François, duc de La Rochefoucauld, *Sentences et Maximes Morales,* no. 324 [1678].

34. John Updike, *Couples* (New York: Knopf, 1968), p. 456.

35. Russell, *Marriage and Morals,* p. 144.

36. "Five Bullets for Monsieur," *Life,* November 24, 1952, pp. 49–52.

37. G. Johannes Botterweck, Helmer Ringgren, and Heinz-Josef Fabry, *Theological Dictionary of the Old Testament,* trans. David E. Green, vol. 13 (Grand Rapids: Eerdmans, 2004), pp. 53–55.

38. Terry D. Hargrave and Franz Pfitzer, *The New Contextual Therapy: Guiding the Power of Give and Take* (New York: Brunner-Routledge, 2003), p. 81.

39. Mark 10:7–9.

40. Perel, *Mating in Captivity,* pp. 128–29, 134.

41. O'Hara, *Appointment in Samarra,* p. 256.

42. Leonard Michaels, *Time Out of Mind: The Diaries of Leonard Michaels* (New York: Riverhead Books, 1999), p. 124.

43. Philip Blumstein and Pepper Schwartz, *American Couples* (New York: William Morrow, 1983), p. 298. Also Rouse, *Marital and Sexual Lifestyles in the United States,* p. 124.

44. Barbara Taylor Bradford, *Barbara Taylor Bradford's Living Romantically Every Day* (Kansas City, Mo.: McMeel, 2002), p. 102.

45. Thomas Schelling, *Choice and Consequence* (Cambridge, Mass.: Harvard University Press, 1984), p. 113.

46. C. S. Lewis, *Mere Christianity* (New York: HarperCollins, 2001), p. 109.

47. De Rougemont, *Love in the Western World,* p. 292.

48. David Popenoe and Barbara Dafoe Whitehead, "The Top Ten Myths of Marriage," National Marriage Project, Rutgers University.

49. Plutarch, "On Love."

50. Shakespeare, Sonnet 116.

5. THE THOUSANDTH MAN

1. Jane Austen, *Northanger Abbey* (Boston: Little, Brown & Co., 1903), p. 39.
2. Ovid, *Tristia,* Book 1, trans. S. G. Owen (Oxford: Clarendon Press, 1885), p. 61.
3. Ting-Yi Oei, "My Students. My Cellphone. My Ordeal," *The Washington Post,* April 19, 2009.
4. John Dryden, "The Hind and the Panther," lines 46–47.
5. David Konstan, *Friendship in the Classical World* (Cambridge, U.K.: Cambridge University Press, 1997), p. 33.
6. Lucan, *Pharsalia,* trans. Jane Wilson Joyce (Ithaca: Cornell University Press, 1993), lines 534–35.
7. Marcus Tullius Cicero, *De Senectute; De Amicitia; De Divinatione,* trans. W. A. Falconer (Cambridge, Mass.: Harvard University Press, 1979), p. 135.
8. L.I.C. Pearson, *Popular Ethics in Ancient Greece* (Palo Alto: Stanford University Press, 1962), p. 136.
9. Stephen Baker, "Learning, and Profiting, from Online Friendships," *BusinessWeek,* May 21, 2009.
10. Juvenal, *The Sixteen Satires,* trans. Peter Green (London: Penguin, 1998), p. 92.
11. Henry Fielding, *The History of Amelia* (New York: Harper & Bros., 1837), p. 169.
12. Judith Shklar, *Ordinary Vices* (Cambridge, Mass.: Harvard University Press, 1984), p. 138.
13. Benjamin Franklin, *Poor Richard's Almanac,* 1740, 2.249.
14. Isaiah 36:6.
15. Eliza Cook, "The Life-Boat Is a Gallant Bark," *Eliza Cook's Journal,* vol. 9 (London: Charles Cook, 1853), p. 416.
16. Mark Twain, *Pudd'nhead Wilson,* chapter 8.
17. Aaron Lazare, *On Apology* (New York: Oxford University Press, 2004), p. 3.
18. Dean Cocking and Jeanette Kennett, "Friendship and Moral Danger," *The Journal of Philosophy,* vol. 97, no. 5 (May 2000), p. 278.

19. Sir Walter Scott, *The Letters of Sir Walter Scott* (London: Constable & Co., 1938), vol. 7, p. 28.

20. Cocking and Kennett, "Friendship and Moral Danger," p. 289.

21. Mahatma Gandhi, *An Autobiography: The Story of My Experiments with Truth* (Boston: Beacon Press, 1993), p. 19.

22. Ibid., pp. 98–99.

23. George Orwell, "Reflections on Gandhi," *Collected Essays* (London: Mercury, 1961), pp. 455–56.

24. Sarah Stroud, "Epistemic Partiality in Friendship," *Ethics* 116 (April 2006), p. 499.

25. Thomas Paine, *The Age of Reason,* in *Collected Writings* (New York: Library of America, 1955), p. 666.

26. Simon Keller, *The Limits of Loyalty* (Cambridge, U.K.: Cambridge University Press, 2007), p. 41.

27. Ibid., p. 35.

28. Jane Austen, *Pride and Prejudice* (New York: Scribner's, 1918), p. 50.

29. Kingsley Amis, *The Russian Girl* (New York: Viking, 1992), pp. 107, 112, 293.

6. BONDING AND BRANDING

1. Sam Schulman, "Frequent Buyers," *In Character,* Fall 2005.

2. Scott McCartney, "Plunging Value of Fliers' Miles Saps Loyalty," *The Wall Street Journal,* December 8, 2008.

3. Joanne Kaufman, "Buyer Be Wary: My Loyalty Was Betrayed," *The Wall Street Journal,* February 19, 2010.

4. Jeremy Clarkson, "Alfa Romeo MiTo," *The Sunday Times,* March 22, 2009.

5. Timothy Keiningham and Lerzan Aksoy, "When Customer Loyalty Is a Bad Thing," *Harvard Business Online,* May 8, 2009.

6. Scott Knowles DeVeaux, *The Birth of Bebop* (Berkeley: University of California Press, 1997), p. 414.

7. Adrian Furnham, *The Psychology of Behaviour at Work: the Individual in the Organization* (Hove, U.K.: Psychology Press, 2005), p. 111.

8. Albert O. Hirschman, *Exit, Voice, and Loyalty: Responses to Decline in*

Firms, Organizations, and State (Cambridge, Mass.: Harvard University Press, 1970), p. 79.

7. TELL ME IT SMELLS LIKE ROSES

1. Richard Wolffe, *Renegade: The Making of a President* (New York: Crown, 2009), pp. 184–85.
2. Nahum Tate, "The Loyal General," in *The Laureates of England,* ed. Kenyon West (New York: Stokes, 1895), p. 68.
3. W. H. Auden, *Lectures on Shakespeare* (Princeton: Princeton University Press, 2000), p. 110.
4. Shakespeare, *1 Henry IV,* Act IV, scene 1, lines 121–24.
5. Baron John Hervey, *Memoirs of the Reign of George the Second,* vol. I (London: John Murray, 1855), p. 64.
6. Jacob Weisberg, "Loyalty: It's the Most Overrated Virtue in Politics," *Slate,* November 29, 2008.
7. Jacob Weisberg, "Only Connect!" *Slate,* January 23, 2010.
8. Jacob Weisberg, "Notes Toward a Theory of Obama," *Slate,* May 16, 2009.
9. David Halberstam, *The Best and the Brightest* (New York: Random House, 1972), p. 434.
10. Ibid.
11. James Reston, "The Doubts and Regrets of the Johnson Dissenters," *The New York Times,* March 9, 1969.
12. Richard Nixon and H. R. Haldeman, Oval Office Tape 536-016, July 3, 1971.
13. United Press International, "Portrait of Nixon Aides: Misguided 'Loyalty,'" January 12, 1976.
14. Associated Press, "Attorney Claims Mitchell a 'Fall Guy,'" December 24, 1974.
15. Justin Hughes, "Cox Reflects on Watergate Era," *Harvard Law Record,* vol. 77, no. 7, November 18, 1983, p. 12.
16. John Heilemann and Mark Halperin, *Game Change* (New York: Harper, 2010), p. 134.
17. Sir Basil Liddell Hart, *Through the Fog of War* (New York: Random House, 1938), p. 357.

18. Andrew Young, *The Politician* (New York: St. Martin's Press, 2010), p. 293.

19. Colin Powell, *My American Journey* (New York: Ballantine, 1995), p. 309.

20. Arthur Marx, *Goldwyn: A Biography of the Man Behind the Myth* (New York: Ballantine, 1977), p. 452.

21. George Churchill Kenney, *The MacArthur I Know* (New York: Duell, Sloan and Pearce, 1951), pp. 64, 69.

22. Oscar Wilde, "The Critic as Artist," *The Writings of Oscar Wilde,* vol. 10 (London: Keller-Farmer, 1907), p. 110.

23. Heilemann and Halperin, *Game Change,* p. 290.

24. Christine Rosen, "To Thine Own Self Be True: What Tell-All Memoirs Tell Us About Ourselves," *In Character,* Fall 2005.

25. Bernard Shaw, *The Intelligent Woman's Guide to Socialism and Capitalism* (London: Constable, 1928), p. 382.

26. Judith Shklar, "Obligation, Loyalty, Exile," *Political Thought & Political Thinkers* (Chicago: University of Chicago Press, 1998), p. 42.

8. REASONS FOR TREASON

1. Akbar S. Ahmed, *Islam Under Siege* (Cambridge, U.K.: Polity Press, 2003), pp. 149–50.

2. Franklin Roosevelt, *FDR's Fireside Chats,* eds. Russell Buhite and David Levy (Norman: University of Oklahoma Press, 1992), p. 161.

3. Maureen Ogle, *Ambitious Brew: The Story of American Beer* (New York: Harcourt, 2006), p. 173.

4. Ibid., pp. 168–82.

5. Edward Spicer et al., *Impounded People: Japanese-Americans in the Relocation Centers* (Tucson: University of Arizona Press, 1969), p. 34.

6. Ibid., p. 60.

7. Katherine Herbig, "Changes in Espionage by Americans: 1947–2007," Technical Report 08-05, March 2008 (Department of Defense), pp. vii–viii, xi, 19–20.

8. Arthur M. Schlesinger, Jr., "What Is Loyalty? A Difficult Question," *The New York Times Magazine,* November 2, 1947.

9. Fouad Ajami, "Islam's Nowhere Men," *The Wall Street Journal,* May 10, 2010, p. A17.

10. Thomas Carlyle, *The Works of Thomas Carlyle: Critical and Miscellaneous Essays,* vol. 16 (New York: Collier, 1897), p. 208.

11. John Lilburne, *Rash Oaths Unwarrantable: and the Breaking of Them as Inexcusable* (1647).

12. George Washington, *The Writings of George Washington from the Original Manuscript Sources, 1749–1799,* vol. 4 (Washington, D.C.: Government Printing Office, 1944), p. 201.

13. Thomas Paine, "The American Crisis III," in *Collected Writings* (New York: Library of America, 1955), p. 145.

14. H. M. Hyman, *To Try Men's Souls: Loyalty Tests in American History* (Berkeley: University of California Press, 1959), p. 86.

15. Geoffrey R. Stone, *Perilous Times: Free Speech in Wartime from the Sedition Act of 1798 to the War on Terrorism* (New York: W. W. Norton, 2004), p. 351.

16. Hugo L. Black, *Speiser v. Randall,* 357 U.S. 513, 532 (1958).

17. Mark Twain, *The Autobiography of Mark Twain* (New York: Harper Perennial, 2000), p. 127.

18. Nicholas Von Hoffman, *Hoax: Why Americans Are Suckered by White House Lies* (New York: Nation Books, 2004), pp. 36–37.

19. "Obama Dropped Flag Pin in War Statement," ABC News, October 4, 2007.

20. Mark Twain, "As Regards Patriotism," in *The Complete Essays of Mark Twain,* ed. Charles Neider (Cambridge, Mass.: Da Capo Press, 2000), p. 567.

21. Ibid.

22. Ibid.

23. Henry Steele Commager, *Freedom, Loyalty, Dissent* (New York: Oxford University Press, 1954), p. 142.

24. Ibid., p. 155.

25. Theodore Roosevelt, *The Great Adventure* (New York: Charles Scribner's Sons, 1918), p. 193.

26. Simon Keller, *The Limits of Loyalty* (Cambridge, U.K.: Cambridge University Press, 2007), p. 83.

27. Leo Tolstoy, "Christianity and Patriotism," in *The Complete Works of Count Tolstoy,* trans. Leo Wiener (Boston: Dana Estes & Co., 1905), p. 431.

28. C. S. Lewis, *The Four Loves* (New York: Harcourt, Brace, 1960), p. 28.

29. G. K. Chesterton, *The Defendant* (New York: Dodd, Mead & Co., 1902), p. 125.

30. Andrew Oldenquist, "Loyalties," *Journal of Philosophy* 79, no. 4 (1982).

31. Tolstoy, "Christianity and Patriotism," p. 432.

32. Martha Nussbaum, *For Love of Country?* (Boston: Beacon Press, 2002), p. xi.

33. Thorstein Veblen, *An Inquiry into the Nature of Peace and the Terms of Its Perpetuation* (1917), p. 33.

34. Tolstoy, "Christianity and Patriotism," p. 432.

35. Diogenes Laertius, *The Lives and Opinions of Eminent Philosophers,* trans. C. D. Yonge (London: George Bell and Sons, 1901), p. 93.

36. Ibid., p. 59.

37. John Muir, *Religious and Moral Sentiments Metrically Rendered from Sanskrit Writers* (Edinburgh: Williams & Norgate, 1875), p. 109.

38. Edward Westermarck, *The Origin and Development of the Moral Ideas,* vol. 2. (London: Macmillan, 1908), pp. 177–79.

39. Samuel Pepys, *The Diary of Samuel Pepys,* vol. 6 (London: George Bell, 1904), p. 211.

40. Pausanias, *Guide to Greece,* vol. 1, trans. Peter Levi (London: Penguin, 1971), p. 253.

41. Shakespeare, *King Henry V,* Act II, scene 2, lines 170–73.

42. Judith Shklar, *Ordinary Vices* (Cambridge, Mass.: Belknap Press, 1984), p. 145.

43. Michael Walzer, *Interpretation and Social Criticism* (Cambridge, Mass.: Harvard University Press, 1987), p. 59.

44. Jean-Jacques Rousseau, *The Plan for Perpetual Peace, On the Government of Poland, and Other Writings on History and Politics,* trans. Christopher Kelly and Judith Bush (Lebanon, N.H.: Dartmouth College Press, 2005), p. 179.

9. THE LIFEBOAT ETHIC

1. "Made Women Leave Against Their Will," *The New York Times,* April 19, 1912, p. 6.
2. Elbert Hubbard, *Selected Writings of Elbert Hubbard,* ed. Elbert Hubbard II (New York: Wise & Co., 1922), pp. 20–22.
3. Robert McHenry, "About That Message to Garcia . . ." *The American,* November 26, 2008.
4. Elbert Hubbard, *A Message to Garcia: Being a Preachment* (East Aurora, N.Y.: The Roycroft Press, 1913), p. 8.
5. Ernest C. Cowper, letter to Elbert Hubbard II, March 12, 1916, in *The Book of War Letters: 100 Years of Private Canadian Correspondence,* eds. Audrey Grescoe and Paul Grescoe (Toronto: McClelland & Stewart, 2003), p. 92.
6. Graham Greene, "Under the Garden," in *Collected Short Stories* (New York: Penguin, 1986), p. 202.
7. Sir Basil Liddell Hart, *Through the Fog of War* (New York: Random House, 1938), p. 357.

Index

About the Author

Eric Felten writes *The Wall Street Journal*'s well-regarded culture column "Postmodern Times." For four years, he wrote the *Journal*'s celebrated cocktail column "How's Your Drink?," which won a James Beard Foundation award for Best Newspaper Writing on Wine, Spirits, or Beer. He is a jazz singer and trombonist, and his TV concert special has been seen on PBS stations nationwide. He lives in Washington, D.C., with his wife and three children.